The economy of the earth

Cambridge Studies in Philosophy and Public Policy

GENERAL EDITOR: Douglas MacLean

The purpose of this new series is to publish the most innovative and up-to-date research into the values and concepts that underlie major aspects of public policy. Hitherto most research in this field has been empirical. This series will be primarily conceptual and normative; that is, it will investigate the structure of arguments and the nature of values relevant to the formation, justification, and criticism of public policy. At the same time it will be informed by empirical considerations, addressing specific issues, general policy concerns, and the methods of policy analysis and their applications.

The books in the series will be inherently interdisciplinary and will include anthologies as well as monographs. They will be of particular interest to philosophers, political and social scientists, economists, policy analysts, and those involved in public administration and environmental policy.

The economy of the earth

Philosophy, law, and the environment

MARK SAGOFF

CENTER FOR PHILOSOPHY AND PUBLIC POLICY
UNIVERSITY OF MARYLAND

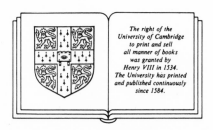

The right of the
University of Cambridge
to print and sell
all manner of books
was granted by
Henry VIII in 1534.
The University has printed
and published continuously
since 1584.

CAMBRIDGE UNIVERSITY PRESS

CAMBRIDGE

NEW YORK   PORT CHESTER   MELBOURNE   SYDNEY

Published by the Press Syndicate of the University of Cambridge
The Pitt Building, Trumpington Street, Cambridge CB2 1RP
40 West 20th Street, New York, NY 10011-4211, USA
10 Stamford Road, Oakleigh, Victoria 3166, Australia

First published 1988
Reprinted 1989
First paperback edition 1990
Reprinted 1991

Printed in Canada

Library of Congress Cataloging-in-Publication Data
Sagoff, Mark.
The economy of the earth: philosophy, law, and the environment /
Mark Sagoff.
p.   cm. – (Cambridge studies in philosophy and public policy)
Bibliography: p.
Includes index.
ISBN 0-521-34113-2 (hb)
1. Environmental policy – United States.   2. United States
– Economic policy.   3. United States – Social policy.
4. Environmental law – United States.   5. Social legislation – United
States.   I. Title   II. Series.
HC110.E5S34   1988
363.7′056′0973 – DC19   87-16091

British Library Cataloging in Publication applied for

ISBN 0-521-34113-2 hardback
ISBN 0-521-39566-6 paperback

For my father
who gave me my first copy of Thoreau's *Walden*

Contents

Acknowledgments

I wrote almost all of this book while a research associate at the Center for Philosophy and Public Policy at the University of Maryland. There is little in this essay that did not arise out of discussion with my colleagues at the Center, or from some thought suggested by their work, or in response to their sympathetic criticism, or to the ideas they offered me. No institute other than the Center for Philosophy and Public Policy, as far as I know, provides a similar opportunity for philosophers to pursue politically informed conceptual analysis on a sustained basis. Each page of this book acknowledges implicitly, as I do explicitly here, the help I received from my colleagues at the Center, Robert Fullinwider, Judith Lichtenberg, David Luban, Douglas MacLean, Claudia Mills, and Henry Shue. I should also like to thank Carroll Linkins, who dealt cheerfully and patiently with the secretarial problems I created in writing and revising this manuscript.

I am deeply grateful to good friends outside the Center who have encouraged my efforts and guided my thoughts, especially Max Black, Philip Bobbitt, Peter Jutro, and Sheldon Novick. Colleagues in philosophy and in other fields, moreover, reviewed earlier versions of this book and sent me extensive and penetrating written criticisms. I am grateful to C. Edwin Baker, Robert Goodin, Toby Page, and Clifford Russell, who, along with several anonymous reviewers, have helped make the book better, although some of them may disagree with much that it contains.

The National Science Foundation, especially the Ethics and Values Studies program, headed by Rachelle Hollander, over the years has supported my research. Working within a tiny budget, Dr. Hollander has helped to create the field of ethical analysis of science and technology; she is in large measure responsible for its development. All of us who work in this interdisciplinary area know how important her energetic advice and guidance have been; the EVS program exemplifies the very best way the government may support scholarship. I should also like gratefully to acknowledge additional support I have received from the National Endowment for the Humanities, the Maryland Sea Grant Program, and the Environmental Protection Agency. The views expressed in the book are those of the author only, however, not necessarily those of any governmental agency.

I wish to thank my wife, Kendra, and children, Jared and Amelia, for giving me the energy I needed to complete this book. They provide the reason and the reward for writing; they teach me "not from the positions of philosophers but from the fabric of nature."

In writing this book I have borrowed, built on, revised, or otherwise worked from several essays published previously. Chapter 2 borrows from the *Arizona Law Review* 23(1982): 1281–98; Chapter 3 draws upon "We Have Met the Enemy and He Is Us *or* Conflict and Contradiction in Environmental Law," *Environmental Law* 12(1982): 283–315; Chapter 4 takes passages from "Economic Theory and Environmental Law," *Michigan Law Review* 79(1981): 1393–1419; a version of Chapter 5 appeared in *Ethics* 96(1986): 301–16; Chapter 6 relies on material that appeared in "On Preserving the Natural Environment," *Yale Law Journal* 84(1974): 205–67; Chapter 7 is a revision of an essay published in *Environmental Law* 16(1986): 775–96; Chapter 8 borrows passages from "Do We Need a Land Use Ethic?" *Environmental Ethics* 4(1981): 293–308; and Chapter 9 contains material from the *Ecology Law Quarterly* 14(1987): 201–59; the *Minnesota Law Review* 71(1986): 19–95; and the *Law of Environmental Protection*, Sheldon Novick, Donald Stever, and Margaret Mellon, eds. (New York: Clark Boardman Co. & Environmental Law Institute, 1987), chapters 5 and 9. I wish to thank these editors and journals for permission to revise and to reprint copyrighted and previously published material.

Chapter 1

Introduction

This is a book about social regulation. By "social regulation," I refer to governmental programs, many of which were initiated in the United States in the 1960s and 1970s to protect the quality of the environment, reduce risks and hazards in the workplace, ensure the reliability and safety of consumer products, and provide equality of opportunity in housing and employment. These efforts at societal self-improvement reflect a consensus that a safer, cleaner, healthier, more equitable society is to that extent a better society, one more in keeping with long-recognized national ideals and aspirations.

This book argues for an ethical, aesthetic, and cultural interpretation of the goals and purposes that underlie social legislation, and it explains how such an interpretation can help us adjust those goals to the economic, technical, and other constraints that might otherwise prevent us from achieving them. It contends that the conceptual vocabulary of resource and welfare economics, on the other hand, which once served to justify social, especially environmental, policy, has largely outlived its usefulness and has become a distraction and an important obstacle to progress. This book presents a philosophical defense of one conception of social policy, then, and a philosophical critique (I should say, an autopsy) of another.

In this Introduction, I describe the argument of the book, identify the view I have come to praise and the view I have come to bury, discuss briefly the conceptual distinctions on

1

which I rely, and sketch the historical context of the views I propose to criticize and to defend.

SOCIAL AND ECONOMIC REGULATION

Let me begin by invoking the useful, if rough, distinction between economic and social regulation. By "economic regulation," I refer to federal programs that set prices, performance standards, entry requirements, schedules, and so on, in the railroad, trucking, securities, telecommunications, and other industries thought to be "affected with a public interest."[1] Congress generally limits the jurisdiction of agencies that administer economic regulations – for example, the Federal Communications Commission – to specific industries. Congress also tends to make these agencies "independent," which is to say, it insulates them in various ways from direct control and oversight by the president.

Agencies that administer social regulations – for example, the Environmental Protection Agency (EPA) and the Occupational Safety and Health Administration (OSHA) – in contrast, generally have jurisdiction over a large range of industries and are located in the executive branch of the government, where the president can exercise more control over what they do.[2] Congress created these agencies not primarily to address the problems of competition in specific industries but to pursue broad ethical and social objectives, such as an unpolluted environment and a safer workplace, that cut across the entire economy. Sometimes the president may take a less than enthusiastic view of these objectives, and he may direct the agencies, against the will of Congress, to pursue a different policy agenda. In recent years, conflicts of this sort have spilled into the courts.[3]

Many economists, policy analysts, and experts in public administration suggest that two principal values underlie and justify all regulation: first, efficiency in the allocation of the resources necessary to produce wanted goods and services, and, second, equity in the distribution of the wealth necessary to purchase those goods and services.[4] The government,

2

on this view, may legitimately intervene to "correct" markets when they would otherwise fail, because of certain standard flaws, to allocate resources to those willing to pay the most for them, and thus fail to make the social "pie" (the total amount of goods and services of the kinds that people want to buy) as big as possible. According to this view, the government may also legitimately act to redistribute buying power, so that everyone might have a decent "slice" of that social pie.[5]

This "efficiency and equity" approach allows for a difference in emphasis between the goals of economic and of social regulation. The main concern of economic regulation, according to this approach, is to make industry competitive, for instance, by dealing with the problems of market failure associated with cartels, price fixing, and monopoly. In the past decade, economic deregulation has encouraged greater competition in several industries, for example, the airlines. And the steel and automotive industries find themselves beset by competition – the Koreans and the Japanese see to that.

Social regulation, on this general view, in contrast, not only serves redistributive purposes but also attempts to ensure that all the things industry uses or produces (including the bad things, like pollution) receive prices that reflect their positive or negative worth. The government, for example, might charge firms for the use of "unowned" or "common" resources by taxing emissions and effluents, so that the prices industry asks for its products will reflect the true social costs of making them, including "spillover" costs to unconsenting third parties. This would make production more efficient from a social point of view.

While testifying before a congressional committee in 1970, Allen Kneese, a respected resource economist, explained some of the reasons that lead many economists to believe that environmental and natural resource policy ought to be based on the goal or the criterion of economic efficiency, that is to say, on the idea that the government may intervene in markets to allocate resources to those who will pay the most for them and, in that sense, to those who value them most.[6] (Kneese recognizes, of course, that the government may also intervene in markets for redistributive reasons, but this presumably would be a function more of tax or welfare than of environmental and natural resource policy.) Because Kneese's remarks succinctly state the view I intend to criticize, I shall quote some of them here.

Kneese began his prepared testimony by identifying the philosophical approach that opposes his, roughly, the idea "that what we need is a new morality or a new ethic if we are to avoid despoiling the earth. This is really a call for a new set of values which lays more emphasis on the natural, the tranquil, the beautiful, and the very long run."[7] This ethical approach – which I shall defend – emphasizes the normative goals of, and constraints upon, social policy. These goals and constraints are founded on political deliberation rather than on academic theory. They concern the natural, the tranquil, the beautiful, the very long run, and other public values that have a strong constituency outside departments of economics and that are found in legislation.

Kneese argued that "the frequent calls for morality with respect to the environment"[8] illustrate a "lack of understanding of what some of the central problems are."[9] In introducing what he considers a better approach to environmental and social regulation, Dr. Kneese offered the committee a lesson in civics. The framers of the Constitution, Kneese said, created a social system

> ...built largely on the concepts of private property and in-
> dividual freedom within the framework of laws to keep the
> channels of commerce open. This reflected the conviction that
> private ownership, freedom of individual choice, and the profit
> motive would direct resources to those uses where they were
> most productive, given individual preferences for various
> goods and services and the incomes of the population. This
> conviction, plus the fear of losing personal freedom, have un-
> derlain our national assumption that the role of collective ac-
> tion through government should be minimized and have been
> used to justify our traditional antipathy toward planning.[10]

Here Kneese presents the familiar view that the primary business of government is to enforce rights to person and property so that individuals may bargain with one another to satisfy the interests they have as individuals. Markets that meet certain conditions will then transfer resources, goods, and services to those who are willing to pay the most for their consumption or use. If one defines "social welfare" in terms of the satisfaction of preferences ranked by willingness to pay, moreover, one might argue that efficient markets vindicate personal freedoms, honor property rights, and (tautologously) maximize welfare as well.

Within this conception of the legitimate business of government, Dr. Kneese outlined a leading theory of the cause and cure of environmental problems. These problems generally arise, he argued, because various resources such as air and water are unowned or are owned in common; they are "common property." Dr. Kneese testified:

> Our usual method for limiting the use of resources and leading them to their highest productivity employments is the prices which are established in markets through exchanges between buyers and sellers. For common property resources this mechanism does not function. . . . This idea has been well developed in the economics literature.[11]

In the literature to which Kneese refers,[12] and which I shall criticize in later chapters, economists suggest ways the government may help to bring common or unowned assets and market "externalities," for example, spillovers like pollution, into the pricing mechanism, and so narrow the gap between the "private" and the "social" costs of production. These economists argue that the government can make up for the failure of markets in various ways, for example, by taxing effluents and by setting "shadow" or hypothetical market prices for otherwise unowned or unpriced resources. These resources will then go to those willing to pay the most to use or consume them, and in that sense they will contribute as much as possible to overall social productivity, welfare, or wealth.

According to many economists, including Kneese, social regulation, particularly public policy concerning natural resources and the environment, should create or simulate (through questionnaires and other methods of data-gathering) markets for unowned and unpriced resources so that markets – or if that is impossible, the government – can charge for these resources prices that reflect their value to society. "As far as economists are concerned," George Eads and Michael Fix observe, "the problems of environmental pollution, excessive levels of workplace hazards, or unsafe consumer products exist largely because 'commodities' like environmental pollution, workplace safety, and product safety do not trade in markets."[13]

In this book, I shall argue against the use of the efficiency criterion in social regulation, and against the idea that workplace, consumer-product, and environmental problems exist largely because "commodities" like environmental pollution, workplace safety, and product safety are not traded in markets. I shall argue, in contrast, that these problems are primarily moral, aesthetic, cultural, and political and that they must be addressed in those terms. The notion of allocatory efficiency and related concepts in the literature of resource economics, as I shall show, have become academic abstractions and serve today primarily to distract attention from the moral, cultural, aesthetic, and political purposes on which social regulation is appropriately based.

This is not to say that I oppose markets or that I am insensitive to the many virtues of a free market economy. I do not deny that competition is an important value – it is surely one that Americans cherish – or that economic regulation and deregulation, insofar as they enhance competition, are prima facie good things. Like Dr. Kneese, moreover, I respect private property ownership and the freedom of individual choice.

I shall argue, however, that although many important virtues may underlie a free market – freedom, autonomy, competitiveness, respect for property rights, and so on – efficiency is not one of them. Free markets are rarely if ever

6

efficient. Efficiency, I shall contend, functions not as a vindication of personal or property rights but primarily as a pretext for centralized governmental planning. A planner rarely has to look far for an "externality" or "free rider" problem with which to justify a favorite regulation.

There are important shared values, for example, health, well-being, safety, cleanliness, and respect and reverence for nature, however, that unlike the goal of efficiency, justify governmental intervention in markets, whether or not these markets are efficient. These values, I shall argue, provide a sound basis for social regulation.

FOUR DISTINCTIONS

The argument I shall give relies on four distinctions, which I should like to identify here. These distinctions are drawn between: (1) the citizen and the consumer, (2) values and preferences, (3) public and private interests, and (4) virtues and methods. After I present these distinctions, I shall state the positive and negative theses of this book.

The citizen and the consumer

In *The Presentation of Self in Everyday Life*, Erving Goffman describes a variety of roles each individual plays and a variety of attitudes, values, beliefs, and expectations each person brings to those roles. This variety is familiar to us all: Each of us recognizes that he or she acts in different ways and expresses different thoughts in different roles and situations – with strangers or with close friends, with family members or with fellow professionals, and so on. The desires and purposes a person pursues in one role often conflict with those appropriate to another, for example, when as a professional one might want to go to the office on a weekend, but as a parent one knows one should help with the children. When what we want to do in one role conflicts with what we want to do in another, we are sometimes unsure about the priority to give to each.

In this book, I shall be concerned with two rather abstract social roles we all play, namely, the role of citizen and the role of consumer. As a *citizen*, I am concerned with the public interest, rather than my own interest; with the good of the community, rather than simply the well-being of my family. Thus, as a citizen, I might oppose a foreign adventure, like the Vietnam War, because I think it is tragic from the point of view of the nation as a whole. As a consumer or producer of goods and services, however, I might at the same time look at the war as a good thing for me if, for example, neither I nor my children must serve and I have a lot of investments in war-related industries.

In my role as a *consumer*, in other words, I concern myself with personal or self-regarding wants and interests; I pursue the goals I have as an individual. I put aside the community-regarding values I take seriously as a citizen, and I look out for Number One instead. I act upon those preferences on which my personal welfare depends; I may ignore the values that are mine only insofar as I consider myself a member of the community, that is, as *one of us*.

In subsequent chapters, I shall contend that social regulation should reflect the community-regarding values we express through the political process and not simply or primarily the self-regarding preferences we seek to satisfy in markets. I shall argue that the interests, goals, or preferences we entertain as citizens with respect to social regulation, moreover, differ *logically* from those we seek to satisfy as individuals.

When an individual states his or her personal preference, he or she may say, "*I* want (desire, prefer . . . .) *x*." When the individual states a view of what is right or best for the community – what the government should do – he or she may say, "*We* want (prefer, desire) *x*." Sentences that express the interest or preference of the community make a claim to intersubjective agreement – they are correct or mistaken – since they take the community ("we" rather than "I") as their logical subject. This is the logical difference between consumer and citizen preferences.

Values and motives

In an important essay on the nature of human freedom, Gary Watson distinguishes between the valuational and motivational systems of a person.[15] "*The valuational system* of an agent," Watson writes, "is that set of considerations which, when combined with his factual beliefs . . . , yields judgments of the form: the thing for me to do in these circumstances, all things considered, is *a*. . . . The motivational system of an agent is that set of considerations which move[s] him to action."[16]

We may use this distinction to divide among preferences, desires, or wants in the following way. All preferences, however well or ill considered, however autonomous or heteronomous, however altruistic, self-regarding, or malevolent, may lead a person to action. Real and hypothetical markets, at least in principle, can measure the strength or intensity of these preferences in terms of willingness to pay, and thus, at least in theory, markets can rank these preferences in a quantitative way.

Some of these preferences – we shall call them "values" – reflect a considered judgment the individual makes about what is right or good or appropriate in the circumstances. We can measure the intensity of these values, but we may also inquire about their justification; that is, we can ask the individual why he or she holds these values or views. Thus, officials might respond to these "preferences" by inquiring how much citizens are willing to pay to satisfy them. Alternatively, officials might respond to the reasons and arguments citizens offer to justify their opinions.

To see this difference, imagine a public hearing like the one at which Dr. Kneese testified. Representatives of environmental and other public interest groups testified as well. How should the views of groups such as these enter into the policymaking process? Should officials determine the intensity of the preferences involved, for instance, by asking how much public interest groups collect in dues? (Should the committee have asked Dr. Kneese how much analysts such as he are willing to pay to vindicate their theories? Would this constitute a "breakthrough" in quantifying the importance of these beliefs?) When should public officials balance interests? When should they deliberate about ideas?

It is plausible to think that public officials ought to consider citizen values – the judgments citizens defend and the reasons they give – on the merits rather than to try to price them, as it were, at the margin. In a later chapter, I shall argue that economic analysts who seek to find quasi-market prices for citizen values (which they sometimes call "intangibles" or "fragile values") commit what philosophers call a "category mistake." They ask of objective convictions and beliefs a question that is appropriate only for subjective wants and desires.

In making this criticism, I rely, of course, on the idea that the political process involves deliberation or judgment going to the merits of proposals; government does not act, then, mechanically as an extension of, or as a prophylactic on, markets. This brings me to the last two distinctions I need to introduce here.

Public and private interests

In an essay on democracy in America, Cass Sunstein contrasts republican and pluralist conceptions of government. The republican vision, which Sunstein attributes to James Madison and the Federalists, emphasizes the distinction between the personal or private interests individuals pursue as individuals and the public or objective opinions they would defend as citizens. On this Madisonian view:

> Politics consisted of self-rule by the people; but it was not a scheme in which people impressed their private preferences on the government. It was instead a system in which the selection of preferences was the object of the government process. Preferences were not to be taken as exogenous, but to be developed and shaped through the political process.[17]

"Distinct from the republican understanding of government," Sunstein writes, "is a competing conception that might be called pluralist." Under the pluralist view, "politics mediates the struggle among self-interested groups for scarce social resources. . . . Preferences are not shaped through governance, but enter into the process as exogenous variables."[18]

The view Sunstein attributes to the framers of the American Constitution draws, of course, from Rousseau, who argued that the business of the political process is to pursue the *common* or *public* interest of the community, which is determined by vote after suitable public deliberation. This general interest is logically separate from the aggregate *private* interest of individuals, which we might define today in terms of a social calculus or an efficient market.[19]

Since citizens cannot deliberate and vote on every policy issue, they delegate this responsibility, in part, to their political representatives, who enact statutes setting forth general goals, values, and policy decisions. These laws also authorize regulatory agencies to deliberate over and to decide specific questions in ways consistent with these larger values and purposes. Sunstein explains:

> The underlying idea is that the administrator must attempt to identify and implement the public values that underlie the statute, and that, in the absence of statutory guidance, must be found through a process of deliberation. To say this is hardly to deny that the promotion of (particular) private interests is often a legitimate function of regulation; but it is to say that the administrator must deliberate about those interests, rather than responding mechanically to constituent pressures.[20]

We are led, then, to a distinction between deliberation, on the one hand, and a mechanical or mathematical balancing of interests, on the other. Let us turn to this last distinction.

Virtues and methodologies

Richard Rorty, in a paper on the philosophy of science, distinguishes between two senses of the word "rational." In the first sense,

> ...the word means something like "sane" or "reasonable" rather than "methodical." It names a set of moral virtues: tolerance, respect for the opinions of others, willingness to listen, reliance on persuasion rather than force.... In this sense of "rational," the word means something more like "civilized" than "methodical."[21]

A lively debate in the philosophy of science today centers on whether scientific inquiry depends primarily on the intellectual virtues Rorty mentions – such as honesty, attention to detail, and unforced agreement – or whether it depends primarily on adherence to a method or on criteria of success – such as "correspondence with reality in itself" – that can be laid down in advance. In his essay, Rorty argues that philosophical attempts to identify the "scientific method" as something other than a list of virtues, or to unpack metaphors like "correspondence with reality," are bound to fail; he draws on the work of such pragmatists as Quine, Davidson, and Kuhn to show why this is so. Rorty contends that science – and, indeed, every form of cooperative human inquiry – has an ethical basis in intellectual and social virtues; no metaphysical or epistemological basis for scientific inquiry need or can be found.

I shall argue that public deliberation, like scientific reasoning, might be rational as long as it adheres to the virtues of inquiry. "On this construction, to be rational is simply to discuss any topic – religious, literary, or scientific – in a way that eschews dogmatism, defensiveness, and righteous indignation."[22] A scientific and rational approach to social policymaking, then, need not depend on methods, theoretical underpinnings, or criteria laid down in advance.[23] Rather, a rational approach emphasizes the virtues of clarity and open-mindedness in describing problems and finding ways to solve them.

Although pragmatism in the philosophy of science is a popular position, it has many critics who seek to establish a second, "stronger" conception of "rational" inquiry: "a sense which is associated with objective truth, correspondence to reality, method and criteria." When the word "rational" is used in this second sense, "to be rational is to be methodical: that is, to have criteria of success laid down in advance."[24]

Many academic economists and social choice theorists in recent years have developed, in great mathematical detail, theories and criteria for collective choice. They have also elaborated, often with mathematical brilliance, problems in, and criticisms of, their models and theories. These analysts sometimes become impatient with those who fail to see the point of such abstract and theoretical exercises – or who fail to understand how they help us make progress, for instance, in protecting the ozone layer or in reducing acid rain. These analysts, T. C. Schelling writes, complain "that they have failed to get their message across, or that their audience is perversely or irrationally predisposed against their ideas."[25] Economists like Kneese point out that criticisms of their methodology "are all manifestations of this lack of understanding of what some of the central problems are."[26]

The quest for certainty – the vision of science as revealing Truth rather than as solving problems – tempts analysts to try to develop theories, models, and mathematical criteria as ways to resolve practical and political problems on a rational basis. Once policy analysts have identified the rational with the methodical and theoretical, indeed, they may concentrate their abilities on working out methodological problems or on ironing out wrinkles in theories of collective choice. This vision of science remains so powerful, in spite of the pragmatist critique, that policy analysts ostensibly concerned with policy problems often dedicate their research to problems of methodology instead. I understand that academic careers are built in this way, but this kind of research, as I shall argue, has little to offer public policy.

At a recent conference, for example, I sat in with a panel of experts who were to discuss how to improve the water supply in Third World nations. Their papers dealt, in fact, with theoretical issues involved in assigning "shadow" prices to "external" and "status" preferences such as the preferences of husbands concerning how their wives spend their time. How should we measure the utility the husband gains from the status conferred by an indoor tap versus the utility he loses when his wife no longer goes to the well? At the conference, grown-up people seriously discussed abstract questions like this – and debated the stimulating theoretical insights to which these questions led.

This book will argue that to solve policy problems we need to develop the ordinary virtues of inquiry and deliberation in the agencies, even at the expense of developing stimulating theoretical insights in journals of policy and economics. This does not mean that we need to replace the absolutes of welfare economics with other absolutes such as those associated with a "no risk" society. Rather, it means that we have to get along without certainty; we have to solve practical, not theoretical, problems; and we must adjust the ends we pursue to the means available to accomplish them. Otherwise, method becomes an obstacle to morality, dogma the foe of deliberation, and the ideal society we aspire to in theory will become a formidable enemy of the good society we can achieve in fact.

WHAT THIS BOOK ARGUES

This book defends a positive and a negative thesis. The negative thesis can be stated simply: Market failure is not the basis of social regulation. This thesis should not be surprising. The statutes that give authority to agencies like EPA and OSHA generally instruct them to achieve stated ethical, aesthetic, and cultural objectives such as a cleaner environment and a safer workplace. These laws do not, as a rule, instruct these agencies to improve, ensure, simulate, or attend to the efficiency of markets. Although we may construe some environmental, public health, and public safety problems to a limited extent in terms of market failures, to do so consistently requires a willing suspension of disbelief. Attempts to explain or justify popular social policies – for example, the protection of endangered species – as necessary to "correct" market failures are often so implausible that they must bring into disrepute either the policy or the explanation.

Consider worker and consumer safety and health. These "commodities" *are* traded in markets. At the turn of the century, for example, workers voluntarily took jobs, knowing the risks, in sweatshops and on railroads, where an egregious number were injured or killed. Almost a million young children labored under cruel conditions; thousands "hurried" coal in mines. Mining companies saved money by digging narrow shafts to accommodate small children and by paying the children lower wages. Thus, private ownership, freedom, and the profit motive, as Kneese testified, directed resources to those uses where they were the most productive, given individual preferences for goods and services and the incomes of the population.

The transactions that led to child labor, the sixteen-hour workday, and hideous workplace conditions were largely voluntary and informed; no centralized bureaucracy in Washington told workers how old they had to be or what minimum they had to be paid; labor markets were efficient. The resulting levels of death, misery, and disease, even if "optimal" or "efficient" from an economic point of view, cannot be tolerated in any civilized nation.

Similarly, the food and drug industries a century ago could fairly be described as murderous; not just the conditions, such as the availability of product information, but the consequences of market transactions, such as death and injury, have been the appropriate concern of the government. Today the government licenses physicians, inspects meat, sets standards for tires, and so on; regulation of this sort prevents mayhem by constraining free market transactions.[27]

Social regulation of safety in consumer products, the workplace, and the environment historically responds to a need to make markets more humane, not necessarily to make them more efficient. These laws – whether statutory or judge-made – strive primarily to prevent injury, grief, misery, and death, not to correct market failures or to compensate for unequal bargaining power.[28] Although I approve paternalistic regulations of this sort on utilitarian grounds, I wish to mention two arguments that may be offered against them.

First, many libertarians believe that when the government engages in humanitarian regulation, it overrides freedoms and rights (e.g., freedom of contract and choice) that are even more important than the lives it saves or the mayhem it prevents. Libertarians generally understand that a free market system can lead to very nasty results, as it did in the United States before the era of regulation. Libertarians defend the free market, however, because of the rights and liberties it comprises, not because of the kind of allocation in which it results. I have no argument to make for or against libertarianism in this book. I merely wish to observe that libertarians take rights, especially property rights, very seriously. Like me, they reject the use of the efficiency criterion as a justification or as a pretext for governmental intervention in markets.[29]

Second, one may reject paternalistic or humanitarian legislation, no matter how many lives it saves or injuries it prevents, if it inhibits markets from reaching a certain outcome, namely, an efficient allocation of resources. One might make this argument if one believed, for example, that an efficient allocation of resources maximizes social welfare. One may then contend that humanitarian policies, because they impede efficiency, reduce welfare. This conception of "welfare," however, is a highly academic and theoretical notion, with no basis in utilitarian goods like health and happiness. This book will discuss how concepts like "welfare" and "well-being," when they occur within the confines of a theory, lose the meanings they have in ordinary language and common sense.

The positive thesis of this book is that social regulation expresses what we believe, what we are, what we stand for as a nation, not simply what we wish to buy as individuals. Social regulation reflects public values we choose collectively, and these may conflict with wants and interests we pursue individually. It is essential to the liberty we cherish, of course, that individuals are free to try to satisfy their personal preferences under open and equitable conditions. It is also part of our cherished conception of liberty that we are free to choose societal ideals together and free to accomplish these ideas in ways consistent with personal and political rights through the rule of law.

Social regulation most fundamentally has to do with the identity of a nation – a nation committed historically, for example, to appreciate and preserve a fabulous natural heritage and to pass it on reasonably undisturbed to future generations. This is not a question of what we *want*; it is not exactly a question of what we *believe in*; it is a question of what we *are*. There is no theoretical way to answer such a question; the answer has to do with our history, our destiny, and our self-perception as a people. And there is no methodology for making "hard decisions" and "trade-offs." We have to rely on the virtues of deliberation – open-mindedness, attention to detail, humor, and good sense.

I shall conclude this Introduction by sketching briefly the historical background of the views I propose to explore.

THE DEMISE OF UTOPIAN CAPITALISM

By the turn of the twentieth century, a particular view of capitalism had become established in the United States. This ideology entrenched itself not only in American universities but also in American folklore. It was assimilated to basic American values like democracy and the conquest of the frontier. The historian Ellis Hawley writes:

> Individualistic competition, according to the tenets of the faith, would bring the best possible society. It would call resources into use and allocate them to maximize productivity. It would

adjust all claims upon the joint product equitably, insure fair prices and high quality, and make for progress and experimentation, new blood and new ideas.[30]

Adam Smith, to whom this vision of utopian capitalism is sometimes attributed, observed at the end of the eighteenth century that prices provide private producers in free markets with the information and incentives they need to turn resources into products in ways that most adequately meet consumer demand. Accordingly, when economic activities are unplanned and decentralized – when individuals decide for themselves what to produce, trade, buy, and sell – an order and a rationality may result that could hardly be achieved by planning.

The principle that markets under certain conditions allocate resources efficiently, when coupled with a conception of fairness in the distribution of wealth, provides a theoretical basis for the belief that capitalism, when it functions properly, will bring about as utopian a social order as we may achieve. This differs from the libertarian justification of capitalism, which as I said earlier, emphasizes the freedoms and rights capitalism embodies, rather than the allocation of resources and the distribution of wealth it may achieve.

When the horrors of the industrial revolution challenged the faith in the utopian promise of capitalism, many people in America, Great Britain, and elsewhere demanded more governmental intervention in the economy. The "Progressives," as the American reformers were called, advocated three different kinds of regulation. These reformers did not abandon the basic faith in utopian capitalism. They argued, rather, that the government must work together with the private economy to keep that faith.

First, Progressives supported humanitarian laws, for example, to eliminate child labor and to set a maximum workday and a minimum wage. They also called for laws establishing safety standards for foods, drugs, and cosmetics. Laws of this kind, to be sure, constrain the kinds of trades individuals can make in markets. Progressives justified hampering voluntary exchange in this way to direct capitalism more toward humanitarian, utilitarian, or utopian ends.

Second, Americans who associated themselves with Woodrow Wilson's New Freedom believed that the concentration of economic power in industrial and financial monopolies or trusts had perverted competition and betrayed the American Dream. Louis Brandeis and many others called for laws like the Clayton Antitrust Act that sought to abolish the unfair practices that allowed monopolies to subvert competition and to control industry and trade.

Third, Americans who, as Herbert Croly did, supported the New Nationalism of Theodore Roosevelt saw the concentration of economic power as an inevitable result of mass production and technological development. They argued that the government should not try to restore the anachronistic ideal of Jeffersonian individualism but should follow the Hamiltonian course of managing big business efficiently in the public interest. "Whether the objective was to regulate monopoly or competition," Arthur M. Schlesinger, Jr., writes, "the method was to meet the power of business by expanding the power of government. The New Nationalism and the New Freedom alike affirmed the necessity of active intervention in economic life by the state."[31]

After the Depression, a consensus developed that free markets would not on their own show us the utopian side of capitalism. The government would have to intervene to exploit the strengths of capitalism while correcting or compensating for its weaknesses. The three approaches to regulation that preceded the New Deal continued and collided within it. "Under the circumstances," Ellis Hawley concludes, "it was not surprising that policy decisions rarely followed any consistent pattern. Only one thing seemed certain: Laissez-faire as a respectable policy was dead."[32]

Reformers of the 1930s and 1940s, having lived through the Depression, naturally saw the major national problems as economic – problems in regulating markets to retrieve the utopian promise of capitalism. The reformers of the 1960s and 1970s, to whom we owe a tide of social regulation, lived, on the contrary, in prosperous times. The problems they addressed were social and political, having to do with segregation, racism, education, technology, armaments, the Vietnam War, and the environment. Early in the 1960s, protesters pressed for civil rights and environmental legislation to stop moral and social abuses. The environmental movement did not base its arguments on a theory of markets or on a vision of utopian capitalism. It tried to build a better society by emphasizing the tranquil, the natural, the beautiful, and the very long run.

The generation of the New Frontier and the Great Society differed in outlook and experience from the generation of the New Deal; their political agenda differed as well. Whereas the New Deal had tried to salvage the ideal of utopian capitalism, the later generation largely ignored it. In the 1960s and 1970s, Congress set goals for society and the government to achieve by reforming themselves rather than by correcting markets. This generation assumed the existence of capitalism as a background condition but not as the cause or the cure of social and political problems.

Insofar as economic, as distinct from ethical and social, goals appeared in the political agenda of the 1960s and 1970s, they formed the basis of economic, not social, regulation. Economists like George Stigler argued persuasively that agencies that administered economic regulations after the New Deal often constrained competition in order to serve the interests of the industries they regulated.[33] Newspapers carried stories about "revolving door" employment and other forms of agency "capture" and collusion. As a result, a political and scholarly consensus formed to cut back on economic regulations and to eliminate some of the agencies that administered them. The emphasis Brandeis had placed on restoring competition reasserted itself in the program of economic deregulation that the Ford and Carter administrations pursued actively and successfully and that continued during the Reagan administration.

When Ronald Reagan took office in 1981, the speedy and successful pursuit of economic deregulation under his predecessors created high expectations among his supporters that similar results could be achieved in the area of social deregulation.[34] To meet these expectations, the Reagan administration provided little or no leadership in accomplishing the social and environmental agenda of the 1960s and 1970s. On the contrary, it followed David Stockman's calls, in his 1980 "Dunkirk" memo, for a "dramatic, substantial *recision* of the regulatory burden" and for a major "regulatory ventilation."[35]

This is not to say that Reagan turned the nation back to laissez-faire economics. His advisers, on the contrary, attempted to promote long-term economic growth by using familiar macroeconomic methods, chiefly, monetary and fiscal policies. The Reagan administration, however, would not interfere with the functioning of free markets simply to allocate resources more efficiently or to maximize benefits over costs. On the contrary, it sought to achieve a few major goals, for example, to control inflation. The idea was not to correct the failure of markets or to allocate goods efficiently; it was "to provide a stable framework, in which private individuals and business firms can plan confidently and make their own decisions."[36]

The call for regulatory recission during the Reagan years was more libertarian than utilitarian. It had more to do with limiting the role of government than with improving the efficiency of markets. President Reagan assumed the existence and superiority of capitalism; unlike Franklin Roosevelt, he did not have to assemble a brain trust to save it; he did not need to posit a utopia to be achieved by the partnership of industry and government. On the contrary, as one commentator wrote at the time, "Reagan is quietly killing the idea of utopian capitalism."[37]

This interpretation does not contradict the intent of an early executive order that required major regulations to undergo extensive cost-benefit review at the Office of Management and Budget.[38] President Carter required cost-benefit analyses in order to stall and eventually halt some pork barrel projects he opposed. Likewise, President Reagan used cost-benefit analysis as a procedural device to slow down and thus halt the flow of social regulation. The Reagan administration reasoned correctly that hundreds of economists happily whacking away at their cost-benefit analyses would constitute a layer of bureaucracy impervious to any efforts line agencies might make to fulfill their legislative mandates. This is generally how things worked out.

With the demise of utopian capitalism, those who take the goals of social regulation seriously now face a dilemma. They must ask whether a policy they favor, say, reducing the level of cotton dust in textile factories, is efficient. Can it be construed as a rational attempt to correct a market failure? If the answer is no, the policy is inadequate on cost-benefit grounds. If the answer is yes, the policy is to be rejected nonetheless. The government cannot be expected to correct every market failure, nor should it impose constraints on freedom of contract and choice simply because some bureaucrat believes that would lead to a more efficient allocation of resources.

This book is intended to show environmentalists and other advocates of social regulation the way out of this dilemma. That solution is to recognize that utopian capitalism is dead; that the concepts of resource and welfare economics, as a result, are largely obsolete and irrelevant; and that we must look to other concepts and cultural traditions to set priorities in solving environmental and social problems. To set these priorities, we need to distinguish the pure from the polluted, the natural from the artificial, the noble from the mundane, good from bad, and right from wrong. These are scientific, cultural, aesthetic, historical, and ethical – not primarily economic – distinctions.

Philosophy has an important role to play, I believe, not only because it provides conceptual and normative analysis but also because of its special responsibility to pronounce postmortems on dead theories. Philosophy is not just the midwife but also the undertaker of the sciences. The tradition and the concepts of utopian capitalism are now politically and intellectually defunct; they are merely propped up, like

Bentham's body, for academic ceremonies. Likewise, the normative theory of welfare economics, in which utopian capitalism heaves a final gasp, calls for philosophical ministrations. As Hegel said, "the Owl of Minerva takes flight only when the shades of night are falling." When philosophy paints its gray in gray, you know a form of life has died.[39]

Chapter 2

At the Shrine of Our Lady of Fatima;
or, Why political questions are
not all economic

Lewiston, New York, a well-to-do community near Buffalo, is the site of the Lake Ontario Ordinance Works, where the federal government, years ago, disposed of residues from the Manhattan Project. These radioactive wastes are buried but are not forgotten by the residents, who say that when the wind is southerly, radon gas blows through the town. Several parents at a conference I attended there described their terror on learning that cases of leukemia had been found among area children. They feared for their own lives as well. At the other side of the table, officials from New York State and from local corporations replied that these fears were unfounded. People who smoke, they said, take greater risks than people who live near waste disposal sites. One state official spoke about methodologies of rational decision making. This increased the parents' resentment and frustration.

The official told the townspeople that risks they casually accept, for example, by drinking alcohol or by crossing the street, were greater than the risks associated with the buried radioactive residues. He argued that the waste facility brought enough income and employment into the town to compensate for any hazards the residents might face. They remained unimpressed by his estimate of their "willingness to pay" for safety; his risk-benefit analysis left them cold. They did not see what economic theory had to do with the ethical questions they raised. They wanted to talk about manipulation and the distribution of power in our society. They did not care to be lectured about benefits and costs.

24

If you take the Military Highway (as I did) from Buffalo to Lewiston, you will pass through a formidable wasteland. Landfills stretch in all directions where enormous trucks – tiny in that landscape – incessantly deposit sludge, which great bulldozers, like yellow ants, then push into the ground. These machines are the only signs of life, for in the miasma that hangs in the air, no birds, not even scavengers, are seen. Along colossal power lines that crisscross this dismal land, the dynamos at Niagara push electric power south, where factories have fled, leaving their remains to decay. To drive along this road is to feel the awe and sense of mystery one experiences in the presence of so much energy and so much decadence.

Henry Adams responded in a similar way to the dynamos displayed at the Paris Exposition of 1900. To him the dynamo became a "symbol of infinity"[1] and functioned as the modern counterpart to the Virgin – that is, as the center and focus of power: "Before the end, one began to pray to it; inherited instinct taught the natural expression of man before silent and infinite force "[2]

Adams asks in his essay "The Dynamo and the Virgin" how the products of modern industrial civilization will be compared with those of the religious culture of the Middle Ages. If he could see the landfills and hazardous-waste facilities bordering the power stations and honeymoon hotels of Niagara Falls, he would know the answer. He would understand what happens when efficiency replaces infinity as the central conception of value. The dynamos at Niagara will not produce another Mont-Saint-Michel. "All the steam in the world," Adams writes, "could not, like the Virgin, build Chartres."[3]

At the Shrine of Our Lady of Fatima, on a plateau north of the Military Highway, a larger-than-life sculpture of Mary looks into the chemical air. The original of this shrine stands in central Portugal, where in May 1917 three children said they saw a lady, brighter than the sun, raised on a cloud in an evergreen tree.[4] Five months later, on a wet and cold October day, the lady again appeared, this time before a large crowd. Some in the crowd reported that "the sun appeared and seemed to tremble, rotate violently and fall, dancing over the heads of the throng."[5]

The shrine was empty when I visited it. The cult of Our Lady of Fatima, I imagine, has few devotees. The cult of allocative efficiency, however, has many. Where some people see only environmental devastation, its devotees perceive welfare, utility, and the maximization of wealth. They see the satisfaction of wants. They envision the good life.

As I looked from the shrine over the smudged and ruined terrain, I thought of all the wants and needs that are satisfied in a landscape full of honeymoon cottages, commercial strips, and dumps for hazardous waste. I hoped that Our Lady of Fatima, worker of miracles, might serve, at least for the moment, as the patroness of cost-benefit analysis. I thought of the miracle of perfect markets. The prospect, however, looked only darker in that light.

WHAT WE WANT VERSUS WHAT WE ARE

This book concerns the economic decisions we make about the environment. It also concerns our political decisions about the environment. Some people have suggested that, ideally, these should be the same – that every environmental problem should be understood as an economic one. William Baxter, for example, writes, "All our environmental problems are, in essence, specific instances of a problem of great familiarity: How can we arrange our society so as to make the most effective use of our resources?"[6] He adds:

> To assert that there is a pollution problem or an environmental problem is to assert, at least implicitly, that one or more resources is not being used so as to maximize human satisfactions. In this respect at least environmental problems are economics problems, and better insight can be gained by the application of economic analysis.[7]

On this view, there is really only one problem: the scarcity of resources. Environmental problems exist, then, only if environmental resources could be used more equitably or efficiently so that more people could have more of the things for which they are willing to pay. "To the economist," Arthur Okun writes, "efficiency means getting the most out of a given input." Okun explains: "This concept of efficiency implies that more is better, insofar as the 'more' consists of items people want to buy."[8]

Environmental economists generally define "efficiency" as the "maximum consumption of goods and services given the available amount of resources."[9] On this approach to environmental policy, it is the preferences of the consumer that are important. "The *benefit* of any good or service is simply its value to a consumer."[10] The only values that count or that can be counted, on this view, are those that a market, actual or hypothetical, can price.[11] "In principle, the ultimate measure of environmental quality," one text assures us, "is the value people place on these services . . . or their *willingness to pay*."[12]

Willingness to pay. What is wrong with that? The rub is this. Not all of us think of ourselves primarily as consumers. Many of us regard ourselves as citizens as well. As consumers, we act to acquire what we want for ourselves individually; each of us follows his or her conception of *the good life*. As citizens, however, we may deliberate over and then seek to achieve together a conception of *the good society*.

In a liberal state, we are all free to pursue our personal ideas of the good life, for example, by buying the books we want to read. In a democracy, however, we are also free to pursue our ideal of ourselves as a good society, by trying to convince one another and our political representatives of a particular idea of our national goals and aspirations.

Americans, like citizens of other countries, have national goals and aspirations – a vision of what they stand for as a nation. They believe, for example, that each person must be secure in certain basic rights if he or she is to be able to form preferences that are not merely imposed but are autonomous and express personal values and uncoerced choice. Thus, the freedoms guaranteed by the Constitution are not to be construed as preferences for which they are willing to pay. They are, on the contrary, protections needed to form and express preferences that are truly one's own and that therefore may claim societal recognition and respect.[13]

Americans' conception of their own as a good society, however, includes more than these rights, which, in any event, may be universal and would, perhaps, belong to any good society, not simply theirs. They also recognize in their legislation and, as I shall argue in a later chapter, in their culture – for example, in their literature and art – other national goals and aspirations that are more particular to them. These do not necessarily follow from (although they must be consistent with) an abstract or universal conception of justice or the rights of man. Rather, they may derive from America's history and heritage; they may have to do with the particular role Americans can play in human progress. Americans might object to policies foreign or domestic that benefit them as individuals, if those policies disgrace or depart from national ideals and ethical commitments.

Consumers who have to pay higher prices as a result, for example, nevertheless may favor safety regulations in the workplace, not as a matter of personal self-interest but as a matter of national pride and collective self-respect. I shall argue, likewise, that our environmental goals similarly derive not necessarily from self-interest – not from consumer willingness to pay in markets – but from a common recognition of national purposes and a memory even newcomers adopt of our long historical relationship to a magnificent natural environment.

Our environmental goals – cleaner air and water, the preservation of wilderness and wildlife, and the like – are not to be construed, then, simply as personal wants or preferences; they are not interests to be "priced" by markets or by cost-benefit analysis, but are views or beliefs that may find their way, as public values, into legislation. These goals stem from our character as a people, which is not something we choose, as we might choose a necktie or a cigarette, but something we recognize, something we are.

These goals presuppose the reality of public or shared values we can recognize together, values that are discussed and criticized on their merits and are not to be confused with preferences that are appropriately priced in markets. Our democratic political processes allow us to argue our beliefs on their merits – as distinct from pricing our interests at the margin. Our system of political representation and majority vote may be the best available device for deciding on these values, for "filtering the persuasive from the unpersuasive, the right from wrong, and the good from bad."[14]

WHAT IS COST-BENEFIT ANALYSIS?

In this book, I shall argue that policies for health, safety, and the environment are and ought to be grounded in what Richard Andrews calls the "philosophy of normative constraints." Andrews explains:

> In this conceptual framework, government is not simply a corrective instrument at the margins of economic markets but [a] central arena in which the members of society choose and legitimize . . . their collective values. The principal purposes of legislative action are to weigh and affirm social values and to define and enforce the rights and duties of members of the society, through representative democracy. The purpose of administrative action is to put into effect these affirmations by the legislature, not to rebalance them by the criteria of economic theory.[15]

Andrews contrasts this conception of government with one "grounded in the language, logic, and values of public investment economics."[16] Those who advocate the primacy of the language, logic, and values of public investment economics generally argue that regulatory decisions, insofar as they are rational, must be based on a conception of markets or on a theory about costs and benefits and, therefore, not necessarily on the goals or purposes set out in legislation. These analysts have mounted a strong a priori, or conceptual, argument to show that efficiency in the allocation of re-sources is the principal goal of sound regulatory policy.

The argument for the efficiency criterion, as Allen Kneese, for example, states it, begins with a definition of a perfect market, a market, in other words, that meets certain ideal conditions. "All participants in the market" first "are fully informed as to the quantitative and qualitative characteristics of goods and services and the terms of exchange among them."[17]

According to the model, moreover, all valuable assets in the economic system are fully owned, managed, and ex-changed in competitive circumstances, which is to say, no individual or firm "can influence any market price signifi-cantly by decreasing or increasing the supply of goods and services" it offers.[18] For environmental policy, two corollary conditions are especially important. First: "Individual own-ership of all assets plus competition implies that all costs of production and consumption are borne by the producers and consumers directly involved in economic exchanges." Sec-ond: "A closely related requirement is that there must be markets for all possible claims."[19]

Markets that meet these conditions will lead, voluntary exchange by voluntary exchange, to a situation, at least in theory, in which all possible gains from voluntary exchange have been exhausted. Kneese points out that theorists who accept a certain value premise have found that "the results of an ideal market are desirable or normative." The premise "is that the personal wants of the individuals in the society should guide the use of resources . . . and that those personal wants can most efficiently be met through the seeking of maximum profits by all producers."[20]

The argument for allocatory efficiency may proceed in one of two ways, depending on whether one adopts the "ideal market" (Pareto) or the "benefit-cost" (Kaldor–Hicks) defi-nition of efficiency. Those who emphasize the model of the ideal market point out that it provides a number of useful concepts to guide social regulation. This is true because ex-change in an ideal market is *not* like what happens in the actual economy. As Kneese notes, the "connection between such a market exchange and the real working economy has always been tenuous at best." The idealized model serves, then, "as a standard against which an actual economy could be judged as a resource-allocation mechanism for meeting consumer preferences."[21]

The government, on this approach, may intervene to make actual markets more perfect, for example, by charging for the use of unowned assets (such as clean air) and by requiring polluters to pay costs associated with the negative side effects, the "spillovers" or "externalities," of the production process. Markets would allocate resources much more efficiently if these "externalized" costs of production were "internalized," which is to say, made subject to the pricing mechanism. As Kneese sees it, "the main source of our environmental problems is the inability of market exchange as it is presently structured to allocate environmental resources efficiently – that is, to price their destructive use appropriately."[22] More generally, as D. W. Pearce writes, "economists have regarded environmental degradation as a particular instance of 'market failure.'"[23]

Many economists, however, see a big problem in the voluntary or "unanimous consent" processes associated with perfect competition in a free market. In a system in which everyone who is affected by a transaction must consent to it, anyone who would lose from and therefore opposes an exchange may veto it, for example, by refusing to sell a property right. This problem, as John Krutilla and Anthony Fisher note, is an old one in welfare economics. They ask, "How is a project or land use policy which results in gains to some individuals and losses to others properly evaluated? In particular, can the gains and losses be algebraically added over all affected individuals to determine the gain (from each of the alternative uses of an area's resources)?"[24]

Many economic theorists observe that we cannot make very much progress if we demand unanimous consent, that is, if we operate entirely within the criterion (associated with Vilfredo Pareto) that allocation *A* is better than allocation *B*

31

only if at least one person prefers *A* to *B* and *no one* prefers
B to *A*. Fisher and Krutilla observe that any cost-benefit policy
prescription, to avoid such a static situation, must adopt the
potential-Pareto or Kaldor–Hicks criterion, "according to
which the project is efficient, and presumably therefore desirable, if the gains exceed the losses, so that the gainers
could compensate the losers and retain a residual gain."[25]

A project or allocation *A* is more efficient than *B* in the
Kaldor–Hicks sense, then, if those who prefer *A* would out-
bid and, therefore, at least theoretically, could compensate
those who prefer *B*, and still retain a residual benefit. To
apply this criterion, a cost-benefit analyst will turn to markets, real or hypothetical, for data concerning the prices people are willing to pay for commodities and resources. The
analyst will then recommend projects and policies that allocate resources efficiently, that is, to those who would pay
the highest prices for them and, in that sense, those who
benefit from or value them most.

It is worthwhile to note here, although I shall examine this
problem more in Chapter 8, that an allocation meeting the
Kaldor–Hicks criterion is likely to differ substantially from
the outcome that a consensual market would reach. This is
true, in part, because those whom a transaction damages are
unlikely to consent to it unless compensation not only could
be but is actually paid. What is more, people may be unwilling to sell property rights, or they may be willing to sell
them only for much more than they would have paid to
acquire them in the first place. The outcome of consensual
exchange (since willingness to sell might not track with willingness to pay) will depend to a large extent, then, on the
way property rights are originally distributed.

In the sort of universal auction or bidding game envisioned
by the Kaldor–Hicks test, in contrast, the efficient allocation
of resources (as Ronald Coase has shown in a well-known
theorem) is invariant with respect to the initial distribution
of property rights.[26] Owners of resources in this sort of auction seek to maximize their profit or wealth; they would,
therefore, always sell a property right for a bit more than

they would have paid for it. I will return, in Chapter 8, to the question whether the cost-benefit criterion, in basing efficiency on willingness to pay rather than willingness to sell, remains in touch with such values as consent and respect for property rights, which are often thought to justify the market as a social institution.

In a formal cost-benefit analysis, the analyst, using market and other data, estimates, on a willing-to-pay basis, the gains and losses associated with all the major effects of a policy, program, or regulation. The analyst must go through a series of steps, which include

> ... *identification* of all nontrivial effects, *categorization* of these effects as benefits or costs, *quantitative estimation* of the extent of each benefit or cost associated with an action, translation of these into a *common metric* such as dollars, *discounting* of future costs and benefits into the terms of a given year, and a *summary* of the costs and benefits to see which is greater.[27]

The resulting sums must also be *compared across alternatives.* These tasks are Herculean. An enormous amount of highly skilled work goes into foreseeing the possible consequences of a program (which may differ considerably given other policies and decisions) and estimating the benefits and costs associated with those consequences. A good cost-benefit analysis, which may run into several volumes, can be an impressive document.

In the rest of this chapter, I shall analyze two concepts that are central to the notions of efficiency I have described. First, I shall discuss the concept of an externality as it arises in environmental policy and in economic analysis. Second, I shall investigate the conception of value or valuation on which the cost-benefit approach to social policy is based.

TWO CONCEPTIONS OF EXTERNALITIES

The concept of efficiency, when it is defined in terms of the functioning of a market free of "externalities" and other structural causes of failure, can be used in either a narrow or an expanded sense. When economists speak of "efficiency" in the narrow sense, they use the concept of an externality to refer only to physical side effects, such as pollution, that cause actual damage – the sort defined, for example, by the common law of tort – to person or property. These analysts may then measure the cost of the pollution – to individuals or to society as a whole – in terms of the health damage it causes to people and the economic losses it inflicts upon them.

During the 1950s and 1960s, economists generally worked within this narrow conception of what an externality is, and as a result they showed us how wastefully we had been using many of our environmental resources. They pointed out that publicly owned goods, such as water and air, are overexploited because no one can demand a price for their use; they argued forcefully that sound principles of conservation and management may be founded on the proper functioning of markets. During this period economists spearheaded attempts to conserve natural resources, and we cannot be too grateful for their efforts.

Resource and environmental economists during the 1950s and 1960s generally defined efficiency in the narrow sense, that is to say, in terms of a conception that tied externalities to the physical side effects of market transactions. These economists did not try to estimate on a willing-to-pay basis the "worth" of moral, aesthetic, political, or cultural concerns and convictions. On the contrary, these economists, quite reasonably, associated externalities with the failure *of* markets correctly to price commodities of the sort for which markets are appropriate and which they usually do price. These analysts did not speculate about our failure *to have* markets to cover the goals, values, and concerns that are and ought to be identified and resolved through the political process.

During the 1960s and 1970s, a series of popular statutes set out goals and programs for ending racial discrimination, improving public safety and health, controlling pollution, and enhancing the quality of life. These statutes represented

34

a considered moral judgment about our responsibilities to one another, to future generations, and to the environment. They expressed public disgust with racism, pollution, industrial blight, and other horrors; these laws set out a policy to control and, insofar as possible, eliminate these evils.

Many of the economists who developed the techniques of cost-benefit analysis – E. J. Mishan would be an example – recognized, at least implicitly, the intractability of quantifying benefits associated with the ethical and aesthetic concerns expressed in public law.[28] These economists urged analysts to list these "qualitative" benefits separately to bring them to the attention of public officials. They did not try to "price" ethical and aesthetic values but saw them as the appropriate subject of political deliberation within the legislative process.

During the 1960s and 1970s, however, owing in part to the work of Ronald Coase, which I shall not pause to describe here, economists began to argue that inefficiencies result not so much from spillover damage to unconsenting third parties, for example, damage caused by pollution, as from the inability of these third parties, because of the costs of bargaining, to organize themselves to enter into and thus influence the transactions that affect them. Accordingly, economists began to replace the notion of a *physical spillover* with the notion of a *transaction* or *bargaining cost* as the paradigm of a market failure. In evaluating the overall efficiency of a project or a policy, analysts began to ask not "What is a cause of what?" but "What is a cost of what?"[29] They widened the idea of an externality, then, to include any unpriced benefit or cost, which is to say, anything a person may be willing to pay for but which does not receive a market price that fully reflects willingness to pay.

An efficient policy was understood, at first, to be one that would result from the functioning of markets free of externalities, where externalities were conceived in the old, narrow sense, that is, in terms of physical damage or economic loss to unconsenting third parties. When the notion of an externality expanded to cover *any* unpriced benefit or cost, however, the ideas of an efficient market and an efficient policy widened as well. An efficient market then had to "internalize" or "price" not only the physical damage or property loss a transaction may inflict on unconsenting third parties, but also every belief, argument, or reason those parties might give for or against that transaction, as long as they conceivably were willing to back up those opinions with money.

Theorists who defend cost-benefit analysis as a tool for policymaking face a dilemma. In identifying the costs and benefits of an action, they must construe externalities in either the narrow or the broad sense, that is, narrowly as damage to person or property of the sort recoverable under common law or broadly as any value – economic, moral, aesthetic, or political – that markets leave unpriced. If analysts construe externalities narrowly, they must concede that many policies that appall them and almost all the rest of us for cultural, aesthetic, and ethical reasons might be perfectly efficient when externalities are understood as physical spillovers and "efficiency" is construed, therefore, in the narrow sense.

We might replace our national parks, for example, with tourist traps, we could convert every arcadia into an arcade, without lessening the market value of anyone's property or damaging anyone's lungs. More people might visit the parks, indeed, if they found casinos there. The value of surrounding property would go up. Another Shopper's World need not hurt the ecosystem terribly even if it destroys the habitat of one or more rare or endangered species. Another tract development in place of open land may not injure anyone's health.

As these and other examples suggest, many policies that are efficient in the narrow sense would conflict with and, indeed, reverse many popular environmental laws, such as the Clean Air Act, the Endangered Species Act, and various wilderness acts, the intention of which is plainly ethical and not narrowly economic. We can assume, for example, that no one would suffer any injury or loss remotely recognizable under common law as a result of the commercial development of the habitats of the Colorado squawfish and the Indiana bat, now protected as endangered species. Everyone in Tulare County, California, might benefit financially from the conversion of the little-used wilderness at Mineral King into a Disney resort in the heart of Sequoia National Park.

Many commercially exploitative policies such as these, which surely appear efficient in the narrow sense and which have no nasty spillovers that markets fail to price, are nevertheless so unpopular among the citizenry for cultural and ethical reasons that no one seriously believes Congress will permit them. Laws that protect the natural environment are intended to do just that – not necessarily to balance interests, internalize externalities, maximize benefits, or increase social wealth.

In order to make market and cost-benefit analysis applicable to public values, analysts may appeal to the wider notion of an externality, which includes not simply injury or damage of the sort that might give third parties standing to sue in common law but also any relevant attitude, opinion, argument, or belief that a person might conceivably be willing to back up with money. When analysts expand the notion of an externality in this way to embrace the opinions and beliefs of the citizenry, which are central to environmental legislation, they make a bald attempt not to inform but to replace the political process, an attempt they may not acknowledge. It is for the political process – not for economic analysis – to gather and judge these opinions and beliefs.

Policymakers need to know which beliefs about facts are credible and which arguments about values are sound. The credibility of a belief (e.g., that the earth is round) depends on evidence and expert opinion, not the amount people are willing to bet that it is true. Nor does the soundness of an ethical argument depend on willingness to pay, although economic information, of course, may be relevant. Thus, cost-benefit techniques, when they go beyond the confines of determining efficiency in the narrow sense, do not provide useful information. Rather, they confuse preference with ethical and factual judgment.

Cost-benefit analysis does not, because it cannot, judge opinions and beliefs on their merits but asks instead how much might be paid for them, as if a conflict of views could be settled in the same way as a conflict of interests. Analysts who take this approach, of course, tend to confuse views with interests. They do this by giving political, ethical, and cultural convictions technical names – "bequest values," "existence values," "intangibles," "fragile values" or "soft variables" – as if by this nomenclature they could transform beliefs that have carried the day before legislatures into the data of economic methodology.

I recognize the importance of cost-benefit analysis when it is used narrowly to inform the public and its officials about the actual market costs associated, for example, with reclaiming mined lands or increasing highway safety. To make a wise decision, society must know these costs and recognize the law of diminishing returns. Economic analysis, moreover, may also reveal less expensive ways society may reach its cultural and ethical goals, for example, by replacing "command and control" bureaucratic approaches with market incentives in order to abate pollution.

In Chapter 9 I shall discuss the usefulness of cost-effectiveness analysis and other techniques that differ from cost-benefit analysis in the following way: *Cost-benefit* analysis fixes our societal goals in advance; it presupposes that any rational policy will seek efficiency (or some mix of efficiency and equity) in the allocation and distribution of resources. *Cost-effectiveness* analysis, in contrast, helps us find the least costly means to achieve societal goals we choose through the political process and approve on moral or cultural grounds.

Although I shall defend some techniques of economic analysis in later chapters, I believe any such technique becomes invidious when used not only to help society achieve its political and ethical objectives – for example, a safer, cleaner environment – but also to determine what those goals are or ought to be. Analysts who do this may be convinced that efficiency in the wide sense is itself a goal worth pursuing, or they may construe efficiency as a meta-value in relation to which all other values may be compared or judged. In Chapters 2, 3, and 4, I shall argue against this expanded conception of efficiency and against the crazy kind of second-guessing of "consumer" preferences that is carried on in its name.

Here it suffices to say that when cost-benefit analysis attempts to do the work of ethical and political judgment, it loses whatever objectivity it might have had and becomes a tool of partisan politics. I shall argue in Chapter 3 that when cost-benefit analysis assigns "shadow" prices to "amenity," "option," "bequest," and other citizen beliefs and values, theoretical "breakthroughs" replace sound judgment and common sense. At that point, economic analysis deteriorates into storytelling and hand-waving likely to convince no one except those partisans who agree with – and possibly have paid for – its results.

EFFICIENCY AND EQUALITY

Policy analysts who favor efficiency as a social goal respect the importance of another social objective, namely, equality, equity, or justice. (Under the broad conception of efficiency, of course, they might construe justice as another "benefit" for which individuals are willing to pay.)[30] I believe that "equality," like "efficiency," may mean two different things. It may refer, first, to the way wealth is distributed: It may mean equality of income or equality of access to resources. It may refer, second, to equality before the law and within the political process. Individuals are treated as equals in this second sense only if their views receive a fair hearing on the basis of the arguments they make for them. No society can grant equality of this kind if it considers only the views of a "vanguard" party or if it dismisses all arguments but those adhering to the "correct" line.

Some commentators argue that policies favored by environmentalists – strict air-quality standards, for example – make consumer products more expensive and thus hurt the poor more than the rich.[31] Environmental protection, then,

39

may sometimes conflict with attempts to enhance social equality in the first sense. There is some evidence, for example, that the average income of Americans who visit the national parks exceeds that of Americans generally.[32] I do not know what to make of these observations. I imagine, however, that no generalizable connection holds between equality in this first sense and programs that attempt to improve the quality or maintain the authenticity of the natural environment.

Equality or justice may also refer to the right of all citizens to argue for their views or opinions *in foro publico* and to have these arguments discussed on their merits without bias or prejudice. This kind of justice may be secured, in part, when all sides to a dispute recognize that finding a solution is a shared rational enterprise in which each has an equal right to participate. This enterprise subscribes to certain virtues such as civility, respect for the opinions of others, and an unwillingness to resort to force. No one can claim a special or privileged access to the "right" decision or to the "correct" methodology. It is "equality" in this sense that is most likely to conflict with efficiency.

Those who favor efficiency as the goal of social policy tend to think of it as a grand value that takes up, incorporates, and balances all other values − because these are simply preferences for which individuals are willing to pay. These partisans, therefore, may regard views opposed to theirs not as arguable opinions deserving a fair hearing but as ideological "wants" that markets fail to price. A policy analyst, if convinced that efficiency or wealth-maximization constitutes the value of values, would not read this book to savor and answer its arguments. He or she would judge the value of the arguments by the sales of the book!

VALUES AS WANTS

Values enter political deliberation and cost-benefit analysis in very different ways. The idea behind deliberation is that the process of negotiation and discussion can be educational.

Because people must argue their views on the merits and from a public or intersubjective point of view in order to persuade each other, they may refine or even change their positions to make them plausible representations of the public interest or the general good. Disagreements are likely to turn, therefore, on scientific, technical, and legal considerations, about which both sides may then seek more evidence or better information. In the context of deliberation, in other words, positions are not construed as exogenous variables but are endogenous to the decision-making process. Participants, therefore, may redefine a problem or consider alternatives that permit an unexpected resolution.

Values enter cost-benefit analysis as exogenous variables, that is, as "given" or "arbitrary" preferences for which individuals are willing to pay. An analyst may therefore construe any policy (for example, a decision to allow air pollution in national parks) as a benefit to those who approve and as a cost to those who oppose it. Thus, analysts may construe judgments a person may back up with reasons as if they were preferences of the sort he or she would reveal in a market. The analyst supposes in all such cases that "This is right for the following reasons: . . . " and "I believe this because . . . " are equivalent to "I want this" and "This is what I prefer."

Value judgments lie beyond criticism if, indeed, they are nothing but expressions of personal preference; they are incorrigible, since every person is in the best position to know what he or she wants. All valuation, according to this approach, happens *in foro interno*; debate *in foro publico*, other than incantations in favor of efficiency or some balance of efficiency and equity, has no point.

This approach denies the educative function of political discussion; from its point of view, the political process is continuous with the kind of trading that goes on in markets. The reasons people give for their views (outside the journals of economic analysis, where *argument* apparently is to be respected) are not to be counted; what counts is how much individuals will pay to satisfy their wants. Those willing to pay the most, for all intents and purposes, have the right view; theirs is the better judgment, the deeper insight, and the more informed opinion.

The assumption that valuation is subjective, that judgments of good and evil are nothing but expressions of desire and aversion, is not unique to the economic theory on which much policy analysis is based. There are some psychotherapists – Carl Rogers is an example – who likewise deny the objectivity or cognitivity of valuation. For Rogers, there is only one criterion of worth: It lies in the "subjective world of the individual. Only he knows it fully."[33] The therapist, according to Rogers, succeeds when the client "perceives himself in such a way that no self-experience can be discriminated as more or less worthy of positive self-regard than any other."[34] The client then "tends to place the basis of standards within himself recognizing that the 'goodness' or 'badness' of any experience or perceptual object is not something inherent in that object, but is a value placed in it by himself."[35]

Rogers points out that "some clients make strenuous efforts to have the therapist exercise the valuing function, so as to provide them with guides for action."[36] The therapist, however, "consistently keeps the locus of evaluation with the client."[37] As long as the therapist refuses to "exercise the valuing function" and as long as he or she practices an "unconditional positive regard"[38] for all the affective states of the client, the therapist remains neutral among the client's values or "sensory and visceral experiences."[39] The therapist accepts all felt preferences as valid and imposes none on the client. The role of the therapist is legitimate, Rogers suggests, because of this neutrality.

Policy analysts sometimes argue that their role in policy-making is legitimate because they are neutral among competing values in the client society. The political economist, according to James Buchanan, "is or should be ethically neutral: the indicated results are influenced by his own value scale only insofar as this reflects his membership in a larger group."[40] The analyst, to maintain his or her value neutrality, might try to derive policy recommendations formally or mathematically from the preferences of all members of society. If theoretical difficulties make such a social welfare function impossible, however, the next best thing, to preserve neutrality, may be to let markets function to transform individual preference orderings into a collective ordering of social states.[41]

The analyst is able, then, to claim that the methods of cost-benefit analysis are neutral among competing preferences. The question remains, however, whether the use of cost-benefit analysis is neutral among competing conceptions of the role of regulation in a good society. The question arises whether reliance on this analytic tool is consistent with the content of current legislation or, indeed, with the idea of democracy and the rule of law.

TWO CONCEPTIONS OF NEUTRALITY

Consider, by way of contrast, what I shall call a Kantian conception of value.[42] The individual, for Kant, is a judge of values, not a mere haver of wants, and the individual judges not merely for himself or herself but as a member of a relevant community or group. The central idea in a Kantian approach to ethics is that some values are more reasonable than others and therefore have a better claim upon the assent of members of the community as such.[43] The world of obligation, like the world of mathematics or the world of empirical fact, is objective – it is public not private – so that the intersubjective virtues and standards of argument and criticism apply.

Kant recognizes that values, like beliefs, are subjective states of mind, but he points out that, like beliefs, they have objective content as well; therefore, values are either correct or mistaken. Thus, Kant discusses valuation in the context not of psychology but of cognition. He believes that a person who makes a value judgment – or a policy recommendation – claims to know what is *right* and not just what is *preferred*. A value judgment is like an empirical or theoretical judgment in that it claims to be *true* not merely to be *felt*.

43

We have, then, two approaches to social regulation before us. One approach assumes that political and economic decisions about the environment are justified in roughly the same way, that is, in relation to preferences individuals express or would express in their consumer and, possibly, their voting behavior. According to this approach, the policy that may be defended on objective grounds – as the right thing to do – is the policy of maximizing the satisfaction of these preferences; every other policy decision is an application of that one.

The Kantian approach, on the other hand, assumes that policy recommendations in general are to be judged on the basis of reasons rather than wants. This view maintains a notion of the common good as an object posited and understood by reason; this is different from thinking of the public interest as a matter to be measured in terms of subjective wants. The Kantian approach also makes individuals the ultimate sources of policy – but it submits policy to their judgment rather than deriving it from their preferences. This view treats people with respect and concern insofar as it regards them as thinking beings capable of discussing issues on their merits. This is different from regarding people as bundles of preferences capable primarily of revealing their wants.

The Kantian approach assumes that public policies may, in general, be justified or refuted on objective grounds, that is, on the basis of what can be said for or against them, not necessarily on the basis of the intensity of competing desires. The Kantian concedes, nevertheless, that many decisions are either too trivial, too personal, or too knotty to be argued *in foro publico* and thus should be left to some nonpolitical resolution, usually to a market. How many yo-yos should be produced as compared to how many Frisbees? Should pants be cuffed? These questions are so trivial or inconsequential or personal, it is plain markets should handle them. It does not follow from this, however, that we should adopt a market or quasi-market approach to every public question.

A market or quasi-market approach to arithmetic, for example, is plainly inadequate. No matter how much people are willing to pay, three will never be the square root of six. Similarly, segregation is a national curse, and if we are willing to pay for it, that does not make it better but only makes us worse. Similarly, the case for or against abortion rights must stand on the merits; it cannot be priced at the margin.[44] Similarly, the war in Vietnam was a moral debacle, and this can be determined without shadow-pricing the willingness to pay of those who demonstrated against it.[45] Similarly, we do not decide to execute murderers by asking how much bleeding hearts are willing to pay to see a person pardoned and how much hard hearts are willing to pay to see him hanged.

Our failures to make the right decisions in these matters are failures in arithmetic, failures in wisdom, failures in taste, failures in morality – but they are not market failures. There are no relevant markets to have failed.

What separates these questions from those for which markets are appropriate is this: They involve matters of knowledge, wisdom, morality, and taste that admit of better or worse, right or wrong, true or false – and these concepts differ from that of economic optimality. Surely environmental questions – the protection of wilderness, habitats, water, land, and air as well as policy toward environmental safety and health – involve moral and aesthetic principles and not just economic ones. This is consistent, of course, with cost-effective strategies for implementing our environmental goals and with a recognition of the importance of personal freedoms and economic constraints.

The neutrality of the economist, like the neutrality of Rogers's therapist, is legitimate if private preferences or subjective wants are the only values in question. A person should be left free to choose the color of his or her necktie or necklace – but we cannot justify a theory of public policy or private therapy on that basis.

What Rogers's therapist does to the patient the cost-benefit analyst does to society as a whole. The analyst is neutral among our "values" – having first assumed a view of what values are, that is, having assumed a particular theory of the good. This is a theory that fails to treat values as values and

45

therefore fails to treat the persons who have them with respect or concern. It does not treat them even as persons but only as locations at which affective states may be found. And thus we may conclude that the "neutrality" of cost-benefit analysis is no basis for its legitimacy. We recognize this neutrality as an indifference toward value – an indifference so deep, so studied, and so assured that at first one hesitates to call it by its right name.

THE CITIZEN AS CLIENT

The residents of Lewiston at the meeting I attended argued that there are crucial moral, aesthetic, and political differences between the risks they take, for example, by smoking or by driving, and the risks imposed on them, for example, by a nearby but hidden depository for nuclear wastes. There is an ethical difference between jumping and being pushed – even if the risks and benefits are the same. Many risks are acceptable because they have been accepted; they are familiar, voluntary, part of everyday life. Some risks are unacceptable because they have not been accepted: They are unknown, insidious, out of one's own hands. What is important to the residents of Lewiston is not necessarily the magnitude of the risk, about which they know experts will disagree, but its meaning, that is, what it suggests about their relationship with their government and about their ability to participate in the decisions, public and private, that affect their lives.

The officials at the other side of the table found much of this anxiety "irrational," given the trade-offs the residents were willing to make, as a rule, between safety and other goods and services. What the residents saw, fundamentally, as a political problem involving the maintenance and functioning of our democratic institutions the officials understood as a matter of making markets efficient and of balancing benefits and costs.

One official from a large chemical company dumping wastes in the area told the residents, in reply, that corporations were people and that people could talk to people about their feelings, interests, and needs. This sent a shiver through the audience. Like Joseph K. in Franz Kafka's *Trial*, the residents of Lewiston asked for an explanation, justice, and truth, and they were told that their wants would be taken care of. They demanded to know the reasons for what was continually happening to them. They were offered a personalized response instead.

This response, that corporations are "just people serving people," is consistent with a particular view of power. This is the view that identifies power with the ability to get what one wants as an individual, that is, to satisfy one's personal preferences. When people in official positions in corporations or in the government put aside their personal interests, it would follow that they put aside their power as well. Their neutrality then justifies their directing the resources of society in the ways they determine to be best. This managerial role is legitimate, they believe, because it serves their clients' interests and not their own.

Behind this managerial role, as William Simon observes of the lawyer–client relationship, lies a theory of value that tends to personalize power. "It resists understanding power as a product of class, property, or institutions and collapses power into the personal needs and dispositions of the individuals who command and obey."[46] Once economists, therapists, lawyers, or managers abjure their own interests and act wholly on behalf of client individuals, they appear to have no power of their own and thus justifiably manipulate and control everything. "From this perspective it becomes difficult to distinguish the powerful from the powerless. In every case, both the exercise of power and submission to it are portrayed as a matter of personal accommodation and adjustment."[47]

Once the affective, that is, the economic, self becomes the source of all value, the public self becomes merely "apparent" and cannot participate in the exercise of power. Power, indeed, appears to be entirely private; it is the power to satisfy one's personal preferences. It ceases to be the power to join with others in effective political action to define and pursue collective values and shared aspirations. As Philip Rieff remarks, "the public world is constituted as one vast stranger who appears at inconvenient times and makes demands viewed as purely external and therefore with no power to elicit a moral response. There is no way to distinguish tyranny from the legitimate authority that public law and public values create."[48]

The key to the emotive or interest theory of value, as one commentator has rightly said, "is the fact that emotivism entails the obliteration of the distinction between manipulative and non-manipulative social relations."[49] As soon as we accept the theory that values are subjective, that they are just "wants," we must also accept the idea that managers – whether therapists, lawyers, or cost-benefit analysts – are in the best position to handle them for us. We must also accept the idea that we all want the same thing, namely, the satisfaction of as many preferences as possible, taking their intensity into account. We consent hypothetically, counterfactually, or implicitly, therefore, to the same policies, those that promote efficiency and maximize wealth. Not socialism, but this kind of economic analysis takes us into an untenable communistic fiction about the unity of society.[50] In welfare economics, the Marxist dream is realized: the triumph of society over polity, administration over government – and thus the final withering away of the state.

"At the rate of progress since 1900," Henry Adams speculates in his *Education*, "every American who lived into the year 2000 would know how to control unlimited power."[51] Adams thought that the Dynamo would organize and release as much energy as the *Virgin*. Yet in the 1980s the citizens of Lewiston, surrounded by dynamos, high-tension lines, and nuclear wastes, are powerless. They do not know how to criticize power, resist power, or justify power – for to do so depends on making distinctions between good and evil, right and wrong, innocence and guilt, justice and injustice, truth and lies.

48

These distinctions have no significance within an emotive or psychological theory of value. To adopt such a theory is to imagine society as a market in which individuals trade to satisfy their arbitrary and subjective preferences. No individual, no belief, no faith, has authority over them. To have power to act as a nation, however, we must be able to act, at least at times, on a public philosophy, conviction, or faith. We cannot permit welfare economics to replace the moral function of public law. The antinomianism of cost-benefit analysis is not enough.

Chapter 3

The allocation and distribution
of resources

In a course I teach on environmental ethics, I ask students
to read the opinion of the Supreme Court in *Sierra Club v.
Morton.*[1] This case involves an environmentalist challenge to
a decision by the U.S. Forest Service to lease the Mineral
King Valley, a quasi-wilderness area in the middle of Sequoia
National Park, to Walt Disney Enterprises, to develop a ski
resort. But let the Court describe the facts:

> The final Disney plan, approved by the Forest Service in Jan-
> uary 1969, outlines a $35 million complex of motels, restau-
> rants, swimming pools, parking lots, and other structures
> designed to accommodate 14,000 visitors daily.... Other fa-
> cilities, including ski lifts, ski trails, a cog-assisted railway, and
> utility installations, are to be constructed on the mountain
> slopes and in other parts of the valley.... To provide access
> to the resort, the State of California proposes to construct a
> highway 20 miles in length. A section of this road would tra-
> verse Sequoia National Park, as would a proposed high-voltage
> power line.[2]

I asked how many of the students had visited Mineral King
or thought they would visit it as long as it remained undeveloped. There were about six hands. Why so few? Too many
mosquitoes, someone said. No movies, said another. Another offered to explain in scrupulous detail the difference
between chilblain and trench foot. These young people came
from Boston, New York, and Philadelphia. They were not

50

eager to subsist, for any length of time, on pemmican and rye biscuits.

Then I asked how many students would like to visit the Mineral King Valley if it were developed in the way Disney planned. A lot more hands went up. Someone wanted to know if he had to ski if he went. No; I told him if he stayed indoors, he need miss nothing. He could get snow blindness from the sour cream. He could meet Ms. Right at the après-ski sauna and at encounter sessions. The class got really excited. Two students in back of the room stood on tiptoe, bent their wrists, and leaned forward, as if to ski. I hope I have left no doubt about where the consumer interests of these young people lay.

I brought the students to order by asking if they thought the government was right in giving Disney Enterprises a lease to develop Mineral King. I asked them, in other words, whether they thought that environmental policy, at least in this instance, should be based on the principle of satisfying consumer demand. Was there a connection between what the students as individuals wanted for themselves and what they thought we should do, collectively, as a nation?

The response was nearly unanimous. The students believed that the Disney plan was loathsome and despicable, that the Forest Service had violated a public trust by approving it, and that the values for which we stand as a nation compel us to preserve the little wilderness we have for its own sake and as a heritage for future generations. On these ethical and cultural grounds, and in spite of their consumer preferences, the students opposed the Disney plan to develop Mineral King.

CONSUMER AND CITIZEN PREFERENCES

The consumer interests or preferences of my students are typical of those of Americans in general. Most Americans like a warm bed better than a pile of wet leaves at night. They would rather have their meals prepared in a kitchen than cook them over a camp stove. Disney's market analysts knew all this. They found that the resort would attract more than fourteen thousand tourists a day, in summer and winter alike, which is a lot more people than now hike into Mineral King.[3] The tourists would pay to use the valley, moreover, while the backpackers just walk in.

You might suppose that most Americans approved of the Disney proposal; after all, it would service their consumer demands. You could ride up the mountain and get a martini or watch TV. You could buy a burger and a beer at the gondola stops. The long Kaweah River might be transformed into a profitable commercial strip. Every red-blooded American with a camper, an off-road vehicle, a snowmobile, or some snazzy clothes and a taste for a little "action" might visit the Disney playland.

You might think that the public would have enthusiastically supported the Disney plan. Yet the public's response to the Disney project was like that of my students – overwhelming opposition.[4] Public opinion was so unfavorable, indeed, that Congress acted in 1978 to prohibit the project, by making the Mineral King Valley a part of Sequoia National Park.[5]

Were the rights of the skiers and scenemakers to act freely within a market thwarted by the political action of the preservationists? Perhaps. But perhaps some of the swingers and skiers were themselves preservationists. Like my students, they may themselves condemn the likely consequences of their own consumer interests on cultural or ethical grounds.

I sympathize with my students. Like them and like members of the public generally, I, too, have divided preferences or conflicting "preference maps." Last year, I bribed a judge to fix a couple of traffic tickets, and I was glad to do so because I saved my license. Yet, at election time, I helped to vote the corrupt judge out of office. I speed on the highway; yet I want the police to enforce laws against speeding. I used to buy mixers in returnable bottles – but who can bother to return them? I buy only disposables now, but to soothe my conscience, I urge my state senator to outlaw one-way containers.

I love my car; I hate the bus. Yet I vote for candidates who promise to tax gasoline to pay for public transportation. I send my dues to the Sierra Club to protect areas in Alaska I shall never visit. And I support the work of the American League to Abolish Capital Punishment although, personally, I have nothing to gain one way or the other. (If I hang, I will hang myself.) And of course, I applaud the Endangered Species Act, although I have no earthly use for the Colorado squawfish or the Indiana bat. The political causes I support seem to have little or no basis in my interests as a consumer, because I take different points of view when I vote and when I shop. I have an "Ecology Now" sticker on a car that drips oil everywhere it's parked.

I am not alone in possessing incompatible "consumer" and "citizen" preference orderings. Economists have long been aware of the existence of these conflicting preference-schedules in the average individual. Indeed, the distinction between consumer and citizen preferences has long vexed the theory of public finance. R. A. Musgrave, reporting a conversation he had with another economist, Gerhard Colm, states the problem as follows:

> He [Colm] holds that the individual voter dealing with political issues has a frame of reference quite distinct from that which underlies his allocation of income as a consumer. In the latter situation the voter acts as a private individual determined by self-interest and deals with his personal wants; in the former, he acts as a political being guided by his image of a good society. The two, Colm holds, are different things.[6]

Are these two different things? Stephen Marglin suggests that they are. He writes:

> The preferences that govern one's unilateral market actions no longer govern his actions when the form of reference is shifted from the market to the political arena. The Economic Man and the Citizen are for all intents and purposes two different individuals. It is not a question, therefore, of rejecting individual

53

...preference maps; it is, rather, that market and political preference maps are inconsistent.[7]

Marglin observes that if this is true, social choices optimal under one set of preferences will not be optimal under another. What, then, is the meaning of optimality? An efficient policy, let us say, is one that maximizes the satisfaction of preferences weighted by their intensity. If individuals possess conflicting preference-maps, however, how can we say what an efficient policy is?

Marglin jokes that economists, in order to preserve the coherence of the efficiency concept, "might argue on welfare grounds for an authoritarian rejection of individuals' politically-revealed preferences in favor of their market revealed preferences!" One might argue just the reverse as well, namely, that we may reject our market-revealed preferences to pursue politically revealed values!

Very few economists, if any, advocate an authoritarian rejection of either political or consumer preferences. Some would seek a way to combine both sorts of preferences on the same preference map. They might agree with Gordon Tullock, who observes that two assumptions about preferences are essential to modern economic theory.

> One of these is simply that the individual orders all alternatives, and the schedule produced is his total preference schedule. The second is that he will be able to make choices among pairs of alternatives, unless he is indifferent between them. ... From this assumption and a further assumption, that such choices are transitive, it is possible to deduce the preference schedule, and most modern economists have taken this route.[8]

If we make these assumptions, which are essential to the theory of welfare economics, it must be possible to infer, for any individual, a "meta-ordering" of his consumer and political preferences. Markets, to be sure, would *not* reveal this meta-ordering, for it includes politically expressed values. Yet economists, by using interview techniques and the like, might be able, at least in principle, to derive the individual's combined preference schedule and price environmental benefits on that basis.

Attempts to find a "combined" or inclusive preference ordering, however, are bound to fail. They will fail for logical, not merely practical, reasons. Individuals have a variety of often incompatible preference schedules they reveal in the contexts appropriate to each, for example, in markets, family situations, professional contexts, and political circumstances. To try to combine these preference schedules into one is to search for a single comprehensive role the individual plays; it is to ask for the individual to behave *not* as a parent, citizen, consumer, or the like but in all and none of these roles at once. The individual, in effect, must reveal himself or herself as the "rational man" of economic theory simply because economic theory demands it. As one commentator rightly points out, no such social role exists, unless it is the role of a social moron.[9]

In some roles – particularly that of a citizen or a member of a community – the individual states what he or she thinks the group should do; the individual makes a judgment that he or she would expect any member of the community to make insofar as that person reflects on the values of the community, not just on his or her own interests. In that situation, each member of the group judges, as it were, for all, and if they disagree, they must deliberate together to determine who is right and who is wrong. This way of finding the will of the community may require a vote; the vote settles a logical contradiction between beliefs, however, not necessarily a conflict among personal interests. Thus, analysts who attempt to shuffle citizen judgments and personal preferences into the same ordering commit a logical mistake. They confuse judgment with preference, that is to say, beliefs about what *we* should do with with expressions of what *I* want or prefer.

Some economic analysts attack the problem of split preference-orderings in another way. They note that efficiency analysis need not take into account the concerns of social equity or justice. Thus, one might rely on an individ-

ual's self-regarding market-revealed preferences to determine efficient social policies, for instance, by cost-benefit
analysis. Then one could rely upon altruistic or politically
revealed preference orderings to organize the redistribution
of opportunities and wealth.

This reply may be helpful insofar as consumer preferences
reveal a person's interests with regard to his or her own
consumption opportunities, while citizen preferences express his or her altruistic concerns about the distribution of
consumption opportunities in society generally. Yet citizens
advocate many ideal-regarding convictions and beliefs that
are not directed to the ways consumption opportunities are
distributed. Environmentalists are sensitive to the distributive effects of the policies they favor politically, but they do
not necessarily support these policies for the sake of those
effects.

One could speculate, indeed, that the distributive effect of
environmental protection is often to make the rich richer and
the poor poorer.[10] When land is removed from development,
housing becomes more expensive; consumer products also
cost more when corporations are required to pollute less. The
rich can afford to live in environmentally protected areas and,
therefore, arguably benefit more than the poor from environmental preservation. It has been very difficult for state
governments to site environmentally necessary hazardous-
waste treatment and landfill facilities; one often hears, however, that these tend to end up in the neighborhoods of the
poor. This would be another example of the way the poor
may pay the costs of environmental protection while the rich
reap the benefits.

I do not think any systematic relationship exists in fact
between the policies environmentalists favor and the relative
well-being of the rich and the poor or, for that matter, of
present and future generations. The speculations I have offered so far are just that – speculations. I know of no recent
empirical study that substantiates them. They suggest, however, that equality or justice is not the only ethical or cultural
goal that concerns us as citizens. We may also be concerned

as citizens with education, the arts and sciences, safety and health, and the integrity and beauty of the natural environment. These concerns cannot be assimilated to the personal, arbitrary preference-maps of consumers. Nor can they be entirely analyzed in terms of equity or justice.

ALLOCATION AND DISTRIBUTION

I want to approach my thesis in this chapter by way of an important distinction: that between the *allocation* and the *distribution* of resources. The allocation of resources has to do with how they are used; the distribution has to do with who uses them or benefits from their use.[11] The Mineral King Valley, as a matter of *allocation*, could be used as a ski resort, kept as a wilderness, or exploited in some other way. Some individuals or groups would be made better off as a result; some would be made worse off; the decision, in other words, would have *distributive* or *redistributive* effects. The resort, for example, would benefit skiers at the expense of hikers; it would be good for property owners in Tulare County but bad for property owners in Sun Valley. Some might argue in favor of the Disney project because it would produce tax revenues to support social welfare programs for the poor. This would be to argue in favor of an allocation because of a beneficial distributive effect.

Some economic theorists who write about the environment assume that natural resources should be used in the way a perfect market would allocate them: the way that maximizes efficiency, consumer surplus, utility, preference satisfaction, or wealth. For a given allocation, of course, questions of justice, fairness, or equality may arise with respect to the distribution of costs and benefits. Most analysts concede that ethical or political choices may have to be made concerning these distributive effects. They tell us, however, that the best way to produce wealth and the best way to divide it are separate issues best decided separately; they urge us, therefore, not to make an allocative decision on the basis of its distributive consequences.[12] Once the pie is as big as we can make it, we may distribute it in the way we then decide is just or fair.

Analysts who argue along these lines tend to collapse all discussion of regulatory policy into questions concerning efficiency in the allocation of resources and equity or fairness in the distribution of wealth. They argue, for example, that the allocation of fossil fuels should be left to the market, properly regulated for externalities. The inequalities that result may then be remedied, for instance, by a windfall profit tax used to help the poor pay their heating bills.[13]

Not all policy problems allow a neat separation between issues of allocation and issues of distribution; for example, any social transfer of wealth to the poor could increase the cost of labor and thus lead to an inefficient allocation of human resources. Many policy analysts speak, therefore, of a "trade-off" between equality and efficiency. They recommend, however, that policymakers use those two values to justify whatever decisions they make with respect to environmental and regulatory policy. Decisions that cannot be explained as rational attempts to make markets efficient, then, must be explained as attempts to distribute wealth more fairly.

Although some writers like to emphasize a "trade-off" between efficiency and equality, it is useful to recognize that these concepts complement each other and that the conflict between them, insofar as one exists, is largely overstated. Analysts who believe that efficiency is an important social value do so, in general, because they conceive of the social good as the satisfaction of preferences, weighted by their intensity, however arbitrary or contingent these preferences may be. Philosophers who emphasize the claims of justice or equity do not necessarily disagree with this conception of the good, but may in fact rely upon it. When the good is conceived in this way – when it is assimilated to the satisfaction of arbitrary preferences – then it is unsurprising that a conception of the right, that is, a conception of justice, should be prior to it. Some have argued that an adequate philosophy of right has yet to be written: one that shows how we should balance a conception of justice with a more appealing or more persuasive conception of the good than the notions of efficiency and preference-satisfaction imply.[14]

Many well-known writers (Ronald Dworkin is an example) argue that a conception of equality should be the criterion of public policy.[15] Other writers argue that the efficiency criterion should be the principal guideline. Most of the statutes and regulations that govern social policy, particularly for natural resources, public safety, and the environment, however, have fairly specific goals, like improving mine safety or protecting endangered species. These concerns of public policy stand on their own feet, as it were, and do not need to be supported by criteria or guidelines established by a priori philosophical or economic arguments.

What characterizes the debate between the "efficiency" and "equality" positions is not the touted conflict between them but the extent to which each is plausible only in comparison to the other. Both adopt the same vocabulary and conceptual framework; each assimilates all values either to essential human rights or to arbitrary personal preferences. They agree that any claim that is not based on a *right* must, then, simply state a *preference* or reveal a *want*.

Those who advocate the priority of equality find worthy opponents in those who defend the priority of efficiency.[16] They debate at length and without any apparent sense of tedium the extent to which rights "trump" interests because (1) rights go to the essence of free agency and personhood or (2) rights are justified, at a higher level of analysis, in relation to interests.[17] Once discussion takes off on this theoretical path, pitting "deontologists" against "rule utilitarians," it becomes irrelevant to officials and others who need a vocabulary adequate to the moral, aesthetic, historical, scientific, and legal considerations that matter in health, safety, and environmental policy.[18]

Congress, by rescinding the Disney lease, for example, made a decision based on aesthetic and historical considerations such as the argument that a majestic million-year-old wilderness is objectively *better* than a commercial honky-tonk. In this way, Congress responded to the opinions citizens backed up with arguments in public hearings and not to the wants individuals might back up with money in a market or the rights they might assert in court.

To speak bluntly, the problem with efficiency and equality as principles of social policy is that they have the smell of the lamp about them. Each approach assumes that academic economists and philosophers, by practicing deep thinking, discover the fundamental truths about Man, Civil Society, and the State from which the goals of social regulation may be derived. This assumption is false. The goals of social regulation are based in public values and are found in legislation.

Insofar as options are available under the law, policy decisions, often expressed in parts per billion, must be justified, as it were, from the bottom up, not from the top down. To make hard choices, public officials must organize the minute particulars involved in assessing risks, monitoring compliance, and litigating penalties. Discussions of the "trade-off" between efficiency and equality have become a useless academic pastime to which this book seeks to write an epitaph. These discussions have little to contribute to the practical and political concerns of social regulation.

THE RIGHTS OF FUTURE GENERATIONS

Some writers have suggested that the way we use the environment could change if we balanced our consumer interests with those of future generations. Some of these writers have worked hard to define a "social rate of discount"[19] to determine how we should take the interests of future consumers into account.

The rate at which we discount future preferences may make little difference, however, in the way natural resources are used. We can build resorts, highways, shopping centers, tract housing, and power lines to satisfy future as well as present demand. There are few decisions favorable to our wishes that cannot be justified by a likely story about future preferences. Even a nasty strip mine or a hazardous-waste

60

dump produces energy that will strengthen the industrial base left to future generations.

What are future generations likely to want? Will vacationers a hundred years from now want to backpack into Sequoia National Park, or will they prefer to drive their recreational vehicles in? I think the interests of future generations will depend largely on two things. The first is education, or advertising. I suspect that the Disney resort would always be jammed with visitors because Disney knows how to run an effective advertising campaign. Through the use of advertising, corporations typically ensure demand for the goods and services they create so that the product and the market for it are developed at the same time. Since what corporations want to sell is usually a good indicator of what consumers will be trained to buy, perhaps we should let the marketing departments of the top five hundred businesses tell us how to prepare the earth for future generations. The best way to create the bars and pizza palaces and motels and strips tomorrow's consumers will want may be to bring in the bulldozers today.

Second, the tastes of future individuals will depend not only on what is advertised but on what is available. People may come to think that a gondola cruise along an artificial river is a wilderness experience if there is simply nothing to compare it with. When I moved from a rural area to an urban one, I was appalled at the changes: noise, pollution, ugliness, congestion. People said I would get used to it – that I would come to *like* the convenience stores and the fast-food stands. They were right. This is what happens. If individuals in the future have no exposure to anything that we would consider natural or unspoiled, they will not acquire a taste for such things. What they will want will be determined more or less by what we leave to them, however dreary it may be.

Derek Parfit has constructed an argument that supports the point I wish to make. He argues that any policy we adopt today will make people born in the future better off than they would have been had we made some other decision. The reason is that these people would not even exist, and therefore could not be better off, had we made the other choice.

To show this, Parfit describes two policies, which he calls "High Consumption" and "Low Consumption." He then writes:

> If we choose High rather than Low Consumption, the standard of living will be higher over the next century. . . . Given the effects of . . . such policies on the details of our lives, different marriages would increasingly be made. More simply, even in the same marriages, the children would increasingly be conceived at different times. . . . this would in fact be enough to make them different children. . . .
>
> Return next to the moral question. If we choose High Consumption, the quality of life will be lower more than a century from now. But the particular people who will then live would never have existed if instead we had chosen Low Consumption. Is our choice of High Consumption worse for these people? Only if it is against their interests to have been born. Even if this makes sense, we can suppose that it would not go as far as this. We can conclude that, if we choose High Consumption, our choice will be worse for no one.[20]

The idea is that whichever policy we choose, future generations will have nothing to complain about, because but for that choice, different marriages would have been made and different children conceived. Whatever policy decision we make, therefore, determines who shall exist, and thus the policy we choose is better for those who will be born than any other policy would have been. Because these people will be all who exist, our choice will make no one worse off. Most people would agree that a policy that is the very best for all those it affects, and that makes no one worse off, is satisfactory from the point of view of distributive justice and efficiency. Thus, whichever policy we choose will be just and efficient with respect to the generations that come after us.

Parfit's argument does not clear us of moral responsibility with respect to future generations; rather, it helps us to understand what our responsibility is. It is not – if I may put it this way – a responsibility *to* the future as much as it is a responsibility *for* the future. If Parfit is correct, the major decisions we make determine the identity of the people who follow us; this, however, is not the only, or the most morally significant, consequence. Our decisions concerning the environment will also determine, to a large extent, what future people are like and what their preferences and tastes will be.

If we leave them an environment that is fit for pigs, they will be like pigs; their tastes will adapt to their conditions as ours might when we move from the country into town. Suppose we destroyed all of our literary, artistic, and musical heritage; suppose we left to future generations only potboiler romances, fluorescent velvet paintings, and disco songs. We would then ensure a race of uncultured near illiterates. Now, suppose we leave an environment dominated by dumps, strip mines, and highways. Again, we will ensure that future individuals will be illiterate, although in another way. Surely, we should strive to make the human race better, not even worse than it already is. Surely, it is morally bad for us to deteriorate into a pack of yahoos who have lost both knowledge of and taste for the things that give value and meaning to life.

Future generations might not complain: A pack of yahoos will *like* a junkyard environment. This is the problem. That kind of future is efficient. It may well be equitable. But it is tragic all the same.

Our obligation to provide future individuals with an environment consistent with ideals we know to be good is an obligation not necessarily to those individuals but to the ideals themselves.[21] It is an obligation to civilization to continue civilization: to pass on to future generations a heritage, natural and cultural, that can be valued and enjoyed without absurdity. These ideals are aesthetic; they have to do not with the utility but with the meaning of things, not with what things are used for but what they express. The programs that preserve them, however, are morally good. The moral good involved is not distributional; for it is not the good *of* individuals we are speaking of, but *good individuals*

63

who appreciate things that are good in themselves. The allocation of resources in environmental law need not always – it sometimes should not – be based on norms of distribution. The way we use resources may also be justified in the context of a reverence we owe to what is wonderful in nature; for in this kind of appreciation, aesthetic and moral theory find a common root.[22]

That political authority should avoid acts of paternalism has been a traditional theme of liberalism. Liberals since John Stuart Mill have argued that the state should restrict the freedom of one individual only to protect the welfare of another – not merely to prevent the individual from harming himself. Although this reluctance to interfere with a person "for his own good" is not absolute in liberalism (or even in Mill himself),[23] it is a consequence of the principle that the state should leave it to individuals to answer the moral questions and thus should not make their mistakes for them.

Yet, to protect a wilderness we may have to prohibit a resort; to provide a resort we may have to destroy a wilderness. So we must make decisions that affect the preferences or values future generations will have, not just the degree to which they can act on their own values or satisfy their preferences. To what extent should the possibility of one lifestyle be restricted to protect the possibility of another? What moral opportunities are worth providing? As we debate public policy for the environment, we must answer questions such as these. We cannot avoid paternalism with respect to future generations.[24]

Yet this paternalism, if that is what it is, is of a peculiar kind. It is not a paternalism about the welfare of future generations; for, as I have argued, whatever policy we choose is likely to be optimal for the individuals and the interests it helps to create. Rather, it is a paternalism about the character of future individuals, their environment, and their values. In short, it is a concern about the character of the future itself. We want individuals to be happier, but we also want them to have surroundings to be happier about. We want them to have what is *worthy of happiness*. We want to be able to respect them and to merit their good opinion. How may we do this except by identifying what is best in our world and trying to preserve it? How may we do this except by determining, as well as we can, what is worth saving, and then by assuming that this is what they will want?

What is worth saving is not merely what can be consumed later; it is what we can take pride in and, indeed, love. To protect wilderness and to restore the environment to meet shared ideals are not merely to show respect and concern for future generations but to show respect for ourselves as well.

To think about our moral responsibilities to future generations is to consider how resources should be used and not merely to consider who should use them. Ethics in allocation, in other words, is not a consequence of ethics in distribution. An environmental ethic cannot be derived entirely from a theory of justice.

THE CONFLICT WITHIN US

If an environmentalist wants to preserve parts of the natural environment for their own sake, he might do well to concede that this is his intention. The environmentalist must then argue that the principles of justice, fairness, and efficiency that may apply to the distribution of income in our society need not apply to the protection or preservation of the natural environment. The reason is that the conflict involved, for example, over Mineral King is not primarily a distributional one. It does not simply pit the skiers against the hikers. The skiers themselves may believe, on aesthetic grounds, that the wilderness should be preserved, even if that belief conflicts with their own consumer preferences. Thus, this conflict pits the consumer against himself as a citizen or as a member of a moral community.

The conflict, in other words, arises not only *among* us but also *within* us. It confronts what I want as an individual with what I believe as a citizen. This is a well-known problem. It is the conflict Pogo describes: "We have met the enemy and he is us."

The conflict is an ethical one. It is not ethical only because it raises a question about the distribution of goods to the rich or the poor, to the present or the future. The ethical question is not simply the distributional question. It concerns, rather, how we satisfy our interests and how we live by our beliefs. This sort of question could never arise in a society that made efficiency and equity in the satisfaction of consumer demand its only goals. That sort of society could deal only with the opposition between the hikers and the skiers. It could never respond to, act upon, or resolve the opposition between the skiers and themselves.

I do not want to comment on the ethical position my students, like many Americans, hold with respect to preserving the natural environment. I merely want to point out that it *is* an ethical position. It is also an opinion that is widely shared, deeply held, and embodied in legislation. I imagine that if the law were changed and the Disney resort were built, more than half the skiers in the lift line would agree, in principle, with my students. They might condemn the resort on ethical grounds. But money is money, and only money talks. The skiers would have paid a lot of money and gone to a lot of trouble to use the facilities. There could be no question – could there? – about what they want.

The problem is a general one. It arises not just because of our high regard for wilderness areas, such as Mineral King, but because of broad values we share about nature, the environment, health, safety, and the quality and meaning of life. Many of us are concerned, for example, that the workplace be safe and free of carcinogens; we may share this conviction even if we are not workers. And so we might favor laws that require very high air-quality standards in petrochemical plants. But as consumers, we may find no way to support the cause of workplace safety. Indeed, if we buy the cheapest products, we may defeat it.

We may be concerned as citizens, or as members of a moral and political community, with all sorts of values – sentimental, historical, ideological, cultural, aesthetic, and ethical – that conflict with the interests we reveal as consumers, buy-

66

ing shoes or choosing tomatoes. The conflict within individuals, rather than between them, may be a very common conflict. The individual as a self-interested consumer opposes himself as a moral agent and concerned citizen.

What kind of society are we? Do we admit into public consideration values of only two kinds: personal interests and distributive norms? Do we insist that the only political decisions we can make are those intended to distribute wealth or welfare, for example, by making markets more equitable and efficient, while every other choice – every allocative decision about the environment – should be left, if possible, for those markets to decide? Should we leave allocative choices to the tourist listening to his John Denver cassette as he pulls his recreational vehicle into the Automobile Reception Center at the Disney resort? Is this fellow the appropriate legislator of our common will?

Suppose *he* opens his mouth to express an ethical opinion – *horribile dictu* – about the use of the environment. Suppose he tells us that we should have kept Mickey Mouse out of the mountains. Must we shut our ears to him? Is that the kind of society we are? Is a perfectly competitive market all we wish to have?

I do not know the answers to these questions. I suspect, however, that most people are resigned, by now, to an affirmative answer to them. How else can one explain the reluctance of environmentalists to argue on openly ethical or political grounds? Why do they prefer to tell stories about the possible economic benefits of the furbish lousewort rather than offer moral reasons for supporting the Endangered Species Act? That law is plainly ethical; it is hardly to be excused on economic grounds. Why do environmentalists look for interests to defend, costs to price, benefits to enter – even if they have to go to the ludicrous extreme of counting the interests of the trees?

Americans, no matter how they shop, generally share the ideology of the environmentalists.[25] Indeed, most Americans might claim that they are environmentalists.[26] Why, then, are they reluctant to confess to themselves that they make

67

environmental law on the basis of shared ideals rather than on the basis of individual utilities? Why do they find it hard to concede that their society is more than a competitive market and that allocative efficiency and distributional equity do not exhaust their repertoire of public values? Why is it so difficult for them to say that one may allocate resources not always as a perfect market would but on substantive, normative, and frankly ethical grounds?

I think the answers have something to do with the insecurity many of us feel when we find ourselves without "neutral" theories and criteria against which to evaluate political, ethical, and aesthetic positions. It's scary to think about problems on their own terms; it's easier to apply a methodology; it's even more tempting to think about the problems raised by the methodology or to investigate the theory itself. Besides, if one side has numbers, the other may need numbers as well. Because developers tell stories about willingness to pay for recreational opportunities at Mineral King, environmentalists tell stories about option values and amenity costs.

As a result, public officials discuss the meaning of magnificent environments using a vocabulary that is appropriate to measure the degree to which consumers may exploit them. A principal purpose of an environmental ethic may be to help policymakers find more appropriate concepts they can use to think about the goals of public policy and to address the obstacles that stand in the way of those goals. The concepts associated with the principles of allocatory efficiency and distributive equity are not especially suitable for this purpose.

MONEY AND MEANING

The things we cherish, admire, or respect are not always the things we are willing to pay for. Indeed, they may be cheapened by being associated with money. It is fair to say that the worth of the things we love is better measured by our *unwillingness* to pay for them. Consider, for example, love itself. A civilized person might climb the highest mountain, swim the deepest river, or cross the hottest desert for love, sweet love. He might do anything, indeed, except be willing to pay for it.

The Church once auctioned off indulgences. It sold future shares in heaven at the margin with a very favorable discount rate. Was it a good idea to establish a market in salvation? Of course it was. How else can you determine how much an infinity of bliss, discounted by the probability that God does not exist, is worth?[27] The Church membership, however, grew a little disillusioned when it saw that the favors of the Lord were auctioned for silver and gold. This disillusionment was one cause of the Reformation.

The things we are unwilling to pay for are not worthless to us. We simply think we ought not to pay for them.[28] Love is not worthless. We would make all kinds of sacrifices for it. Yet a market in love – or in anything we consider "sacred" – is totally inappropriate. These things have a *dignity* rather than a *price*.[29]

The things that have a dignity, I believe, are in general the things that help us to define our relations with one another. The environment we share has such a dignity. The way we use and the way we preserve our common natural heritage help to define our relations or association with one another and with generations in the future and in the past.

Let me return, now, to the example with which I began. My students, as I said, are pulled one way when they are asked to make a consumer choice whether or not to patronize the Disney resort. That question goes to their wants and desires simply as individuals. They are pulled another way when asked to make a political decision whether the United States should turn wilderness areas into ski resorts. That decision calls upon their conception of the values we share or the principles we respect as a nation.

Should we base environmental policy on the interests individuals may act upon as consumers or on the values that they may agree upon as citizens? Our policy may be "rational" either way. We may have a "rational" policy in an economic sense if we limit the role of law to that of protecting

69

rights and correcting market failures. We should then assume that the ends of policymaking are simply "given" in the preferences consumers reveal or would reveal in a market. Alternatively, we might suppose that a "rational" policy advances a certain conception of equality – or meets some other condition or criterion laid down in advance.

We may have a policy that is rational in what we may call a deliberative sense, however, if we strive to base law on principles and ideals that reflect our best conception of what we stand for and respect as a nation. This kind of rationality depends on the virtues of collective problem solving; it considers the reasonableness of ends in relation to the the values they embody and the sacrifices we must make to achieve them. This deliberative approach respects the constitutional rights that make it possible for people to contribute as equals to the political process, but it asserts no a priori political theory about the purposes of public policy.

This approach assumes, on the contrary, that the values on which we base social policy are objects of public inquiry. They are not to be derived (as they would be in a market) by aggregating exogenous preferences, or (as they might be in a political philosophy) from metaphysical truths about the nature of persons. Thus, the general goals of public policy are to be determined through a political process in which citizens participate constrained only by rights of the kind protected by the Constitution. These goals are not known beforehand by a vanguard party of political economists or by an elite corps of philosopher-kings.

COMPROMISE AND COMMUNITY

The students in the class I taught had no trouble understanding the difference between the judgments they make as citizens and the preferences they entertain as individuals. They also understood the importance of their "positive" freedom to lobby for their their views politically and their "negative" freedom to pursue their personal interests without undue interference from the state.[30] Plainly, these freedoms, like these values and preferences, are bound to come into tension or conflict. If the nation preserves every mountain as a wilderness heritage, there will be no place for these young people to ski.

This tension has been a central problem for political theories of liberalism. As one historian writes: "Liberalism of all sorts [in America] is troubled by the seemingly contrary pulls of responsibility to individual and community, by the divergent demands of absolute adherence to the doctrine of individual integrity and the needs and potentials of the common life."[31] In Chapter 7, I shall deal extensively with the problems liberals face in reconciling communitarian goals, for example, protecting wildlife, with what some see as an individualistic political philosophy. I shall argue that liberals are not constrained by their political theory to support only those communitarian policies they can justify as necessary to satisfy the interests or protect the rights of individuals.

The students in my class found it fairly easy to resolve the tension between their consumer interests and their public values with respect to the example of Mineral King. They recognized that private ownership, individual freedom of choice, and the profit motive (to recall the remarks of Dr. Kneese I quoted in the Introduction) would undoubtedly lead to the construction of the Disney paradise. They reasoned, nevertheless, that we should act on principle to preserve this wilderness, which has an enormous cultural meaning for us, since the resort, though profitable, would not serve important social ends. The students argued that because there are a lot of places for people to party, we do not need to make a ski resort of Sequoia National Park.

But what if the stakes were reversed? What if we should have to make enormous financial sacrifices to protect an environmentally insignificant landscape? Suppose industry would have to pay hundreds of millions of dollars to reduce air pollution by a small, perhaps an insignificant, amount? The students in my class, by and large, answered these questions the way they answered questions about Mineral King.

71

Just as they rejected the dogma of the perfect market, they also rejected the dogma of the perfect environment.

The students recognized that compromise is essential if we are to act as a community to accomplish any goal, however pure or idealistic it may be. To improve air quality, for example, one needs not only a will but a way; one needs to express one's goals in parts per billion or, more generally, to deal with scientific uncertainties and technical constraints. The goal of environmental purity, like the goal of economic efficiency, can become a Holy Grail, in other words, suitable only as the object of an abstract religious quest. To make progress, we need to recognize that God dwells in the details – in parts per billion and in the minute particulars of testing, monitoring, and enforcement.

Although the students thought that social policy usually involves compromise, they kept faith with the ideals they held as citizens. They understood, moreover, that if we are to take these ideals seriously, we must evaluate them in the context of the means available to achieve them. To will the end, in other words, one must also will the means: One must set goals in relation to the obstacles – economic, political, legal, bureaucratic, scientific, technical, and institutional – that stand in the way of carrying them out. We do not become a functioning political community simply by sharing public goals and by celebrating a vision of harmony between nature and society, although ceremonies of this sort are a part of citizenship. To function as a community we must also reach the compromises necessary to move beyond incantation to political and economic achievement.

This is the reason that the Mineral King example – and the difference between citizen and consumer preferences it illustrates – may serve to introduce a course in environmental ethics, but it does not take us very far into the problems of environmental policy. The interesting problems arise when we move, in Winston Churchill's phrase, "from the wonderful cloudland of aspiration to the ugly scaffolding of attempt and achievement."[32] Then we must chasten our goals by adjusting them to economic, legal, scientific, and political realities. How can we do this and still retain the ethical and aspirational nature of our objectives? How do we keep faith with the values of the citizen while recognizing the power of the consumer?

The following chapters deal with these problems. I shall first review attempts to integrate citizen values and consumer preferences within the framework of economic theory. Later chapters will suggest another way to bring ideals into touch with reality, so that we will not lose them among the parts per billion and lose, with these ideals, the capacity to reach consensus on social regulation and environmental law.[33]

Chapter 4

Fragile prices and shadow values

In 1975, the Environmental Protection Agency, enforcing the Prevention of Significant Deterioration (PSD) requirement of the Clean Air Act, directed states to amend their implementation plans to protect air quality in areas where pollution exceeds national health and safety minimums. The regulation, in other words, intends to keep clean air clean beyond health and safety requirements; it may appeal to us, therefore, on aesthetic and on ethical grounds. Yet PSD requirements may also impede economic growth and development; for example, they may conflict with plans to locate a network of power plants in the Southwest, where coal and clean air are abundant. What to do? How shall we enforce idealistic regulations when they blink at important economic facts?

TANGIBLE AND INTANGIBLE VALUES

In a recent article, "An Experiment on the Economic Value of Visibility," three economists from the University of Wyoming tackle this problem. The authors attempt to interpret and to evaluate PSD requirements in economic terms. "Aesthetics," they say, "will play a major role. The PSD requirements amount to formal governmental admission that aesthetics, at least as embodied in atmospheric visibility, is a 'good' that might have a positive value."[1]

These writers point out that economists "generally have shied away from attempting to quantify aesthetic phenomena because they are usually defined as intangible."[2] This is correct. By and large, economists who engage in cost-benefit analysis assign prices only to goods and services of the sort that are typically traded in markets and thus that can easily be priced. These economists generally list other values as "intangibles" to bring them to the attention of the political authority. The "intangible" values involved in environmental, health, and safety policy may often be more important than the "tangible" ones, of course, since they include social, moral, aesthetic, and cultural goals that have carried the day before Congress – hence the PSD requirements of the Clean Air Act.

This is not to say that Congress gives regulators – for example, the administrator of EPA – a great deal of discretion in weighing "intangible" values against costs and benefits. On the contrary, legislation may instruct the administrator to preserve and protect environmental quality without regard to the effect on consumer markets. The Clean Air Act, to continue the example, requires that "economic growth will occur in a manner consistent with the preservation of existing clean air resources."[3] The law sets the prevention of significant deterioration of air quality, then, as a normative constraint on economic growth and development, at least in certain areas, such as those in and around national parks.

The Wyoming economists, however, apparently interpret the law differently. Evidently they believe that the law does not require that the administrator protect air quality in and around national parks against the "intrusions" of industrial civilization. Instead, they apparently read the law as instructing the administrator to strike a balance – as, perhaps, a market would – between the costs and benefits likely to result, for example, from protecting visibility or from providing more electric power. They suggest that if a means could be found to give "intangible" values an accurate "shadow" or surrogate market price, then this "balancing" might take place within the framework of cost-benefit analysis.

Accordingly, the authors write:

The perspective that aesthetic phenomena are unquantifiable employing economic analysis may be unduly pessimistic. Beauty, or aesthetic phenomena, given that some physical measure is available which is perceivable with human senses, should be measurable in economic terms. Further, PSD regulations indirectly necessitate quantification. How then, has the economist responded to the intangible which must of necessity become tangible?[4]

To solve this problem, the authors showed a variety of people photographs of scenes in the Southwest. In some of these photographs the air quality was better, or at least the visibility was greater, than in others. The authors asked the participants how much they would be willing to have added to their monthly utility bills to preserve the visibility depicted in one photograph rather than accept the level of visibility shown in the next. The economists attempted in this way to establish a surrogate market in which "intangible" aesthetic values could be priced.

Many statutes other than the Clean Air Act set strong normative constraints on commercial exploitation of the environment. The Endangered Species Act, for example, expresses this aspect of the national conscience.[5] It requires all agencies of the federal government to "insure that actions authorized, funded, or carried out by them do not jeopardize the continued existence of such endangered species."[6] As Chief Justice Burger wrote for the Supreme Court: "One would be hard pressed to find a statutory provision whose terms were any plainer than those . . . of the Endangered Species Act. . . . The language admits of no exception."[7]

Because the plain language, as well as the judicial interpretation, of the Endangered Species Act explicitly prohibits an interest-balancing or cost-benefit test, the statute has worked rather well. Developers, by and large, have found mitigating strategies to protect species their projects might otherwise eradicate. Conflicts have given way so quickly to deliberation and negotiation on a case-by-case basis, indeed, that a special Endangered Species Committee, set up to grant exemptions, has met only twice.[8] And very few cases have been litigated under the act.[9]

Many analysts, however, would take a different approach to endangered-species policy. "The existence of such statutes as the Endangered Species Act," Judith Bentkhover writes, "provides evidence that man values preservation of species and ecological diversity, although the art of converting those values into economic terms is relatively undeveloped."[10] Bentkover observes that economists have developed theoretical means for quantifying "intangible" benefits of this kind, but "the application of these methodologies is fraught with difficulties."[11] In recent years, economists, like the group from Wyoming, have dealt extensively with the methodological difficulties involved in assessing environmental benefits.[12] They have attempted, in this way, to place endangered-species and other forms of environmental policy on a "rational" and "scientific" basis.

TWO APPROACHES TO SOCIAL REGULATION

In this chapter, I wish to return to the two conceptions of rationality that I distinguished in the Introduction. There, I proposed that each of two ways of approaching social policy decisions might be described as "rational" and as "scientific." One approach uses mathematical criteria and methodologies, laid down in advance, to infer policy recommendations from independent or exogenous preferences in the client society. This approach conforms to a philosophy of science that stresses notions like "value neutrality," "replicable experiments," and "correspondence to an independent reality."

The second approach ties the rationality of the policymaking process to virtues, particularly the virtues of deliberation, like intellectual honesty, civility, willingness to see a problem in a larger context, and openness of mind. The problem-solving approach of the Endangered Species Act, which sets up a committee to mitigate conflicts, illustrates this ethical and juridical attitude toward social regulation.

Economists, in measuring the value of unpriced social and

77

environmental benefits, are deeply conflicted between these two conceptions of science and rationality. This conflict becomes apparent when analysts must decide how much information to present to subjects and how much discussion, deliberation, and education to allow as part of an experiment. As we shall see, an analysis or assessment can be "scientific" in the sense of "gathering data on exogeneous variables" only if it allows no discussion, education, or deliberation to take place. An approach that is "scientific" and "neutral" in this way, however, will not be "scientific" in the sense of being "reasonable," "civilized," or "intelligent."

The Wyoming researchers followed the economic literature in supposing that environmental preservation may have value in various ways to which consumer markets ordinarily do not respond. First, it may have recreational use value, and this may be estimated by reference to entrance fees, travel costs, and the like.[13] Second, a preserved environment may have "existence" value either because it gives people an option to use the resource or because it provides them with the ideological satisfaction of merely knowing it is there.[14] Hence, these economists write:

> Individuals and households who may never visit the Grand Canyon may still value visibility there simply because they wish to preserve a natural treasure. Individuals also may wish to know that the Grand Canyon retains its relatively pristine air quality even on days when they are not visiting the park. Concern about preserving air quality at the Grand Canyon may be just as intense in New York or in Chicago as in nearby states and communities.[15]

To speak more generally: The Wyoming economists treated visibility, in southwestern national parks, for example, as a pure public good, that is, a good any person can enjoy without thereby lessening the amount that may be enjoyed by others.[16] They were concerned, in part, with determining the "preservation" or "existence" value of visibility, that is, "the value assigned to the existence of a certain level of visibility

78

aesthetics at a site even though one does not *ever* intend to participate in activity at the site."[17] The economists wrote another questionnaire to determine how much *users* of parks would pay in additional entrance fees to protect air quality or visibility. In this way, they devised bidding games or "contingent" or hypothetical markets in which to estimate, on a willingness-to-pay basis, the value of an amenity resource.

The attempt to "price" aesthetic or "existence" values, however it might serve to buttress arguments for environmental protection, invites a variety of objections. I have suggested one: The law directs the administrator to keep clean air clean "in national parks, national wilderness areas, national monuments, national seashores, and other areas of special national or regional natural, recreational, scenic, or historic value." The PSD requirements as they stand (of course, they could be amended by Congress) do not just set goals but also make rules; they establish air quality as a normative constraint on economic development. Thus, the law does not indirectly or directly necessitate quantification of aesthetic "benefits." It does not ask us to make the intangible tangible. The Wyoming economists might lobby Congress to have the law changed, but until it is changed, it does not permit, much less require, a cost-benefit or "balancing" test.[18]

The Wyoming economists might plausibly reply that we cannot always take laws at their face value. Environmental legislation, in particular, sets lofty, noble, and aspirational national goals that we may not fully achieve without bringing the economy to a screeching halt. Any project that causes air pollution in the Southwest, for example, could arguably affect air quality in a national park. Yet no one would insist on forbidding all polluting activities in that area. The ideal of a perfectly unpolluted environment – like the ideal of a completely risk-free workplace – is a chimera. At some point, the administrator of EPA (and those of the other regulatory agencies) has to recognize not only the law of the land but also the law of diminishing returns. The question will then arise, How much safety, purity, or whatever are we willing to pay for? How much clean air – as opposed to other goods and services – is enough?

This reply makes an important point that everyone – even those who interpret environmental laws as strong normative constraints on economic development – must concede. We must acknowledge, however idealistic we may be, that clean air, workplace safety, and the like have a price, and at some point the additional amount of cleanliness or safety we may buy may be grossly disproportionate to the goods and services we must forgo in order to pay for it.[19] It hardly seems reasonable to ask industry to pay hundreds of millions of dollars, for example, to provide a tiny or insignificant improvement in workplace safety, yet it is surely appropriate to require companies to pay even large sums to prevent significant risks. But how to determine what is appropriate from an ethical point of view? What counts as a "significant" risk or a "significant" deterioration of air quality? When shall we apply the law of diminishing returns?

I have proposed that there are two approaches to solving these problems. One approach seeks to find answers by manipulating exogenous data. The data that economists study have to do with prices and with the preferences consumers reveal or express in actual and surrogate markets. Economic analysts may tend, then, to answer questions like "How safe is safe enough?" by collecting data about preferences – data that represent independent variables or exogenous states of the world. They then balance the benefits of environmental protection, measured in this way, against the opportunity costs of economic development.

The other approach uses a juridical or deliberative model to weigh various normative constraints, established by statute, against these opportunity costs. Public officials must recognize both the legal and the ethical force of these constraints, but at the same time they take account of technical, economic, and other realities, for no one can pursue a goal without adjusting to the obstacles that stand in the way of achieving it. Since there is no methodology for making this sort of judgment, public officials have only statutory language, judicial interpretation of that language, their general knowledge and experience, and the virtues of inquiry to rely upon. This is the reason statutes generally require that officials respond to views presented at public hearings, set policies that are reasonable and feasible, and create a record of their deliberations that can be reviewed by the courts.

Public officials, I believe, may often be undecided about which of these approaches to take in social decision making. If they take the first approach, they can hire economists as consultants to gather data and to apply the appropriate software to generate decisions that are rational in that sense. Public officials might also support theoretical research, for example, in "pricing" environmental benefits.

Public officials, alternatively, may view themselves more as a jury that must deliberate about a great many conflicting possibilities, relying on the ordinary virtues of public inquiry. Like a jury, these officials would be responsible to governing statutes. Accordingly, they would have to deliberate openly, on the record, and in good faith. They could not rely on cloistered expertise.

THE WYOMING EXPERIMENT

The Wyoming economists take the first approach. They try to show how the techniques of cost-benefit analysis can extend to ethical and aesthetic concerns that the public qua public cares about. Accordingly, these economists must find ways to identify exogenous preferences as data they can then analyze using the appropriate quantified methodologies. Intangible values, in other words, must be made tangible. How can this be done?

How valuable is atmospheric visibility in parks, wilderness areas, and so on? How important is it for us to be able to stand on a mountaintop in Yosemite and contemplate an "integral vista" free of power plants, hotels, highways, or other signs of industrial civilization? What are the expressive or symbolic values of nature untouched by man, and how much are these worth to us? How draconian should prohibitions on development be in order to keep the wilderness experience pristine?

Let us stick to the example of visibility in and near national parks. In measuring the value of visibility, we need to know, first, how a loss of atmospheric clarity or quality is caused. Mist or fog hanging on the mountains, for example, can be beautiful, perhaps more beautiful than a clear view, as the Japanese show us in their paintings. Mist or fog, then, need not impair aesthetic value. Even a volcano that distributes ash over hundreds of miles may be viewed as an aesthetic marvel; people will come from afar just to see it. If soot and precipitates from a power plant impede visibility, however, the resulting loss of air quality, even if indistinguishable from that caused by a volcano, has a completely different meaning. We no longer think of it as natural or compare it with aspects of nature and its beauty; we may perceive it, rather, as an assault on nature and as destructive of its integrity.

The same point may be made with respect to the aesthetic properties of landscapes. Many studies have attempted to define formal criteria for beauty in landscapes as if the aesthetic response to an object varied simply with its formal qualities, for example, its masses, shapes, and lines.[20] It is clear, however, that the expressive or symbolic qualities of what we see are at least as important: We are concerned not merely with the way a thing appears but with what it is and how it came to be that way. Thus, we might be enchanted by the song of a rare native bird we happen upon; we might resent the same sound, however, were it made by a mischievous boy hidden in the woods or by mechanical reproduction.[21]

The Wyoming economists faced something of a dilemma when they designed their experiment: They had to decide whether or not to explain to the participants how visibility would be lost in the vistas presented in the photographs. If they let the participants assume that the cause would be natural, for example, an approaching storm, then they might elicit a preference for *less* visibility, since oncoming storms in deserts may be considered beautiful. If the experimenters identified the cause as the belching smokestacks of Humongous Megawatt, a coal-fired utility, however, the respondents might reveal not aesthetic but political preferences. They might express opinions, for example, about the inefficiency of increasing supply as opposed to decreasing demand for energy through conservation. They might even offer legal arguments based on the PSD provisions of the Clean Air Act.

In fact, this is what happened. The Wyoming team (appropriately, I believe) informed the respondents that visibility would be obscured by pollution from a power plant. They described the amount of energy (in kilowatt hours) to be produced, the location of the facilities, the levels of emission of various pollutants, and so on. There is no evidence that the economists gave the subjects of the experiment information about the PSD requirements of the Clean Air Act; the respondents, however, may have had that information. The economists asked the subjects, first, how much they would pay (the "equivalent surplus," or "ES," measure of consumer surplus) to prevent the deterioration of visibility caused by the power plant. They then asked for "compensation surplus," or "CS," values, which is to say, the amounts that the respondents would accept to allow the power plant to emit that much pollution.

When the respondents were asked how much they would demand in compensation (the CS or willingness-to-accept [WTA] value) to permit the loss of visibility shown in the photographs, at least half of them used the question as an occasion to express a political opinion. The Wyoming experimenters report:

> The CS values . . . put the liability for maintaining visibility with the power companies and presupposes [sic] that the power companies will attempt to buy off consumers rather than cleanse the air. If respondents reject this concept of "being bought off to permit pollution" they might increase their compensation. Strategically, respondents may give large or infinite

valuations as an indication that this concept is unacceptable. This is partially supported in that slightly over one-half of the sample required infinite compensation or refused to cooperate with the CS portion of the survey instrument.[22]

The experimenters found even in their own experiment, then, that a majority of a sample of citizens rejected a cost benefit or "consumer surplus" approach to trade-offs between health, safety, or environmental quality and economic growth, an approach that also seems to be precluded by the Clean Air Act, the Occupational Safety and Health Act, and other legislation.[23] In attempting to make that approach practicable, if not legal, the Wyoming experimenters found themselves in a strange position. They asked citizens, in order to participate in the experiment, to accept the concept of trading dollars for pollution "rights" – a concept many citizens reject.[24] And most of the subjects responded by entering protest bids or by refusing to cooperate with the experiment.

Social scientists have long known that the human subjects of their experiments go to great lengths to follow instructions and to remain obedient to authority. The famous Milgram experiments, which showed that people would torture other people when instructed do so, established how willing subjects are to do what they are told.[25] Why, then, did the Wyoming economists experience such resistance to their experiment? I think the problem goes deeper than a refusal to trade pollution "rights" for dollars. I shall argue that this refusal is the symptom but not the source of the difficulty inherent in the visibility experiment.

THE PROBLEM OF INFORMATION

In an excellent paper on "Information Disclosure and Endangered Species Evaluation," a group of economists from Hawaii describe bidding games and surrogate markets, that is, the contingent valuation method (CVM), they used to determine citizen willingness to pay to preserve endangered species. The Hawaii group observed that WTP values are deeply influenced by the information subjects receive in the survey or experiment. These authors write:

> Willingness to pay (WTP) to preserve a particular animal is significantly influenced by information provided about the animal's physical and behavioral characteristics, and about its endangered status. While this proposition may appear obvious, it bears important implications for the proper type and amount of information disclosed in preservation valuation studies.[26]

In the Hawaii experiment, subjects were asked how much they were willing to contribute to a fund for preserving humpback whales, an endangered species. Then an experimental group saw *The Singing Whale,* a Jacques Cousteau film describing the humpback and the threats to its survival. A control group viewed a film unrelated to whales, *The Sixty Minute Spot: The Making of a Television Commercial.* All subjects were then asked to reevaluate or reconsider their bids. After seeing the films, one-third of the experimental group and one-fifth of the control group increased their bids. The authors note that this "lends support to the view that preferences are learned during the interview process, even in the absence of new relevant information."[27]

The Hawaii economists point out that relevant information can influence preservation bids in many ways. A person is likely to decrease his or her bid, for example, if he or she learns that the population of a particular species is so large that it will survive or so small that it will become extinct no matter how much he or she and others contribute. A reasonable person, in other words, is likely to apply some principle of triage to deal with the number and characteristics of endangered species. The economists conclude that "information disclosure can influence perceived marginal efficiency of investment in a preservation fund, and thereby result in changes in an individual's budget allocation strategy."[28]

The Hawaii experimenters recognized the importance of their results for the contingent valuation of preservation, amenity, and other benefits of environmental protection. They saw a methodological question in the extent to which respondents should be given information or otherwise allowed to educate themselves, discuss, or deliberate over the issues. Should valuation be based on the immediate, untutored, *ex ante* preferences of the respondents? Should valuation refer to their informed or educated judgment instead?

One alternative, the authors note, "is to accept the state of the respondents' ignorance about the resource as given, and provide only enough information about the resource to create a realistic market situation." This alternative has the advantage of keeping the response exogenous to or independent of the experiment. It has the disadvantage (as we saw in the Wyoming experiment), however, "that respondents may not readily accept operating in a hypothetical market situation with unknown payoffs and opportunity costs."[29]

At the other extreme, "the analyst could provide vast amounts of information to respondents about the resource being valued, along with complete information about its substitutes and complements." The respondents might discuss, in the visibility case, say, various alternatives to constructing power plants near national parks, for example, the possibility of energy conservation. They might try to size up or define the problem in terms that allow a different sort of solution. This kind of approach, the Hawaii economists point out, "could change the preference mappings of respondents and therefore make individual values endogenous to the valuation process."[30]

How should we choose between these alternatives? Shall we accept the first alternative, insisting that the valuation of environmental benefits be "rational" in the sense of being methodical, derived from exogenous variables, and determined by criteria laid down in advance? Should we prefer the second alternative, emphasizing the virtues of deliberation rather than the methods of derivation, and hence a conception of "rationality" that is less akin to the "methodological" than to the "civilized," "reasonable," and "sane"?

An analogy may help us answer these questions. Let us suppose that a person has been called to perform jury duty. The judge informs each juror that a Mr. Smith has been accused of robbing a liquor store. Then the judge asks each juror separately whether Mr. Smith is guilty. If the judge is methodologically sophisticated, indeed, he or she may ask how much each juror is willing to pay for the preferred verdict. The judge may then report the verdict in terms of the mean, the average, or some statistical transformation of the weighted average of the jurors' preferences.

If you were a juror, how would you respond to the judge? You might complain that the methodology is flawed: You might believe the judge should use the average rather than the mean bid to set the sentence. The judge may point, however, to a large literature that investigates all the ins and outs of the statistical methodologies – perhaps the software – used by the court. He or she may reply, moreover, that the verdict is scientifically accurate because it rests entirely on *ex ante* preferences that remain completely independent or exogenous to the decision-making process.

You might, on the other hand, ask the judge to let the jury hear the case – the evidence for and against – and to deliberate to reach a consensus in good faith. The judge could rule this out, since the verdict would then be biased by the means of obtaining it. What is more, no quantified methodology exists for reaching a verdict through deliberation on the evidence. To be scientific, so the judge might reason, the verdict must be derived from exogenous variables by quantified criteria laid down in advance. Jurors might be permitted to make use of any hearsay evidence they may have picked up beforehand from the newspapers. No further inquiry, however, may bias or prejudice preference.

If you were faced with this situation, what would you think? You would think that the judge is *crazy*. You would probably refuse to cooperate with this sort of "valuation."

You might protest, for example, or just vote to acquit Mr. Smith.

Economists often confront this kind of resistance to their surveys. Their subjects may reject cost-benefit balancing as an inappropriate and illegal framework for making social policy. Two resource economists observe:

> Bidding questions for changes in air quality are not always well received by respondents due to rejection of the hypothetical scenario, rejection of the implied property rights or liability rules presented in a situation, or rejection for moral and ethical reasons. . . . Rejection and protest bids have varied from 20 percent to 50 percent for specific applications of the bidding technique. *In these cases, respondents' true values remain unknown and unaccounted for.*[31]

I would contend that just the reverse is true: It is only in this way – by lodging a protest – that respondents can begin to make their values known. These respondents may perceive themselves not as bundles of exogenous preferences but as thinking beings capable of reaching informed judgments in the context of public inquiry and deliberation. They may regard themselves as a jury that might reach a considered judgment after discussion of all relevant views and information. The contingent valuation method, however, insofar as it tries to make respondents express preferences rather than deliberate about ideas, denies their status as thinking political beings. This is possibly the major reason that respondents so often enter protest bids or otherwise resist this sort of experiment.

MARKETS FOR MORALS

The Wyoming economists, however, may concede that the resistance of respondents to their experiment reveals a deep distaste for, and rejection of, cost-benefit approaches to public policy. The existence of legislation prohibiting cost-benefit and interest-balancing tests, moreover, shows that citizens value the idea that policies should result instead from ethical deliberation and the rule of law. Accordingly, the statutes indirectly necessitate quantification of this "intangible" cost of the cost-benefit methodology itself. How can we evaluate the cherished illusion that public policy rests on law and deliberation rather than on the application of a quantified methodology to exogenous variables?

Economists have studied and evaluated various "cherished illusions" – to use Abraham Tarasovsky's excellent phrase – which may cause citizens to suffer dissatisfaction when ideological wants are frustrated.[32] There are many examples of this phenomenon. Citizens may suffer anguish, for example, when they see a policeman act unjustly or when they learn that a judge discriminates against defendants who are black. This anguish shows that acts of injustice and prejudice have important third-party costs. These acts, therefore, may be inefficient because they create emotional externalities that markets may fail to price.

Likewise, citizens may object – as they apparently do – when CVM experiments threaten cherished illusions about themselves and their relation to their government. Citizens may express concern about the integrity of the political process, *ex parte* contacts at the Office of Management and Budget, and the availability of a public record reviewable by the courts; they may express other misgivings related to feelings they cherish about democracy and the rule of law. These concerns seem naive in the day of Executive Order 12,291; nevertheless, they exist, and cost-benefit analysts must find ways to take them into account. The "intangible" value of democracy must be made tangible. How can this be done?

Many policy analysts, law professors, and others have suggested answers to this question. In one study, Thomas Heller, who teaches law, deals generally with the sort of "amenity" and "existence" values the Wyoming economists attempted to measure. Americans, many of whom call themselves environmentalists, tend to oppose politically the transformation of their most beautiful and expressive landscapes into amusement parks and honky-tonks. Heller asks how policymakers may take this political opposition into account.

"An important element of the demand for preservation, nowhere manifested in market prices," Heller observes, "may derive less from its instrumental utility than from its symbolic meaning."[33] He argues that symbolic and normative concerns should not be dismissed when markets fail to price them. "For some, a serious loss of well-being at stake in the development of second homes results from a broadly held commitment to the normative position that nature is a source of value not because it is used but because it continues to exist."[34]

Heller describes accurately and eloquently what this "normative position" consists of. He writes:

> For those who find an imminent imagery in nature, a technological quietism flows from a reluctance to tamper. They assert that the role of man is to study, steward, and wonder at what envelops him. In treating nature as an instrumental object existing for the satisfaction of human wants instead of as a realm of intrinsically valuable coequal forms, it is believed man distorts his ability to grasp the meaning of his own existence.[35]

The "normative position," then, argues that certain environmental resources ought to be treated not as means to ends (e.g., consumer satisfaction, efficient allocation) but as ends in themselves. They are essential, in other words, to the process by which we create our values, not to the process by which we satisfy them.

How shall we deal with this "normative position"? The solution, according to Heller, is to regard convictions and arguments of this sort as "externalities," that is, costs and benefits that markets fail to price. Heller suggests that we should "internalize the externality," which is to say, we should give these arguments and opinions a fair market price.

Heller identifies a way to do this. We might determine how much preservationists are willing to pay for an "increase in the industry output of preservation services."[36] This would help to measure the increment in the economic surplus produced by preservationist policies. "The minimal measure of this increment is a surplus amounting to the difference between what preservationists would be willing to pay and what they do pay for the preservation use of the resources."[37]

Problems may arise, of course, in "the regulatory agency's attempt to discover a surrogate measure of the value of each of the components of consumer preservation surplus."[38] One might wonder, for example, whether environmentalists' support for legislation is a true indication of their consumer surplus or willingness to pay. This is a difficult question. Yet it may not be insurmountable. The value of preservation, based on various measures, may be shown to exceed the threshold value of consumer and factorial surplus realized by development. "A widely shared environmental ethic, even if only made up of small willingness to pay per individual, could, in the aggregate, exceed this threshold value."[39]

The attempt to construe moral principles and political convictions as market externalities and thus to deal with them by assigning them a market price does not stop with the environment. On the contrary, several recently published articles analyze slavery,[40] poverty,[41] slums,[42] and other social evils not in moral terms *as evils* but in economic terms *as externalities*. One paper by Guido Calebresi, for example, argues that it is *inefficient* to allow people to sell themselves into slavery; he shows this by referring to uncompensated third-party effects suffered by bleeding hearts who are made unhappy merely by knowing that people are enslaved.[43] As one astute commentator points out, the invocation of third-party costs "can miraculously convert . . . a value judgment into a datum of economic science."[44]

Why do markets and market analyses fail to capture or to price political opinions and ethical beliefs? Why are many economists content to leave these "intangible" values unpriced so that the decision makers may deal with them in political and ethical rather than in economic terms? Is the problem simply technical – nobody knows how to create property or other rights in these values; no one knows how to establish a market in political and moral costs and benefits? Should we think of the Wyoming economists as pioneers, then, whose experimental devices may have been primitive but who blazed paths in the right direction?

Is the problem, on the other hand, not technical but logical? Is it a matter of principle, not merely of methodology, that the beliefs and opinions of citizens are usually listed and treated separately from their consumer interests and preferences? Is it a logical or conceptual truth, in other words, that ideas or convictions that can be supported by reasons in the political process are to be considered by the decision maker as different from consumer wants and interests that may be satisfied in markets? If so, if the limitation is logical, if political and ethical debates are conceptually different from economic analyses, then we must infer that efforts to shadow-price "intangible" or "fragile" values must fail – not for any technical or empirical reason but because they rest on a logical mistake. The next section explains what I suppose this mistake to be.

A CATEGORY MISTAKE

The idea of "pricing" moral and ideological beliefs as if they were externalities might look attractive, at first, to environmentalists. A wilderness lover might find it heartening that his hand-wringing and teeth-gnashing are not entirely in vain. His misery will be priced among the costs of any commercial plan to exploit the nation's forests and parks. Such an environmentalist, indeed, may find an incentive in this to tear his hair a little more than otherwise, thinking, perhaps, that every strand will be weighed in the final cost-benefit account.

I understand that meters that measure gooseflesh and sweaty palms have been used by firms to determine the emotional response to their advertisements. Perhaps galvanometers, along with electrodes that measure brainwaves, could be used by analysts to measure the ethical costs and benefits of public investments. Public policy could then be based on neutral, scientific, and objective evidence about exogenous visceral and neurological states.

However neutral and scientific this approach may appear to be, however, the environmentalist should be wary of it. It may turn out that no matter how much gooseflesh, sweat, or migraine the partisan of preservation generates, compensating consumer benefits may, nevertheless, justify a controversial project. The environmentalist may be told it is cheaper for him to avert his gaze or forget his commitment than it is for society to give way to his frenzy. Then the environmentalist is left defending "intangibles" that seem rather conjectural in comparison to the hard-cash value of development.

The ability to find "free rider" problems, unpriced values, and transaction costs in every doorway and under every stone, moreover, undermines the credibility of market analysis. I think Professor Heller's article suggests that a clever analyst could justify any law or rule as efficient. If a constituency exists for a law, then, I should suppose, there are a lot of people who want it. The rest is easy. All you need to do is identify a "moral" externality, talk about free-rider problems, aggregate willingness to pay, and then say that the benefits of the legislation exceed the costs.

This criticism, however, may be construed as simply a technical one: It may only show that the attempt to shadow-price public values or "citizen" preferences faces insuperable problems in measurement. This objection, by now, is commonplace, and it is not the one I wish to make. I wish to argue that the attempt to shadow-price public values as externalities of private transactions involves a category mistake.[45]

This is the kind of mistake you make when you predicate of one concept another that makes no sense in relation to it. If I say that the square root of two is blue, for example, I have not uttered a meaningful sentence but an absurdity, since color concepts are not of a logical type that can meaningfully be predicated of numbers. Likewise, if I tell you the window wants to be closed, you would not take me literally to attribute a psychological state to an inanimate thing, which would be an absurdity. Again, to ask for the name and address of the average American family is to ask a silly question. It is to be confused about the qualities that can meaningfully be attributed to an object and to commit, in that sense, a category mistake.

Private and public preferences also belong to different logical categories. Public "preferences" involve not desires or wants but opinions or views. They state what a person believes is best or right for the community or group as a whole. These opinions or beliefs may be true or false, and we may meaningfully ask that person for the reasons that he or she holds them. But an analyst who asks how much citizens would pay to satisfy opinions that they advocate through political association commits a category mistake. The analyst asks of beliefs about objective facts a question that is appropriate only to subjective interests and desires.

When an environmentalist argues that we ought to preserve wilderness areas because of their cultural importance and symbolic meaning, he or she states a *conviction* and not a *desire*. When an economist asserts that we ought to attain efficient or optimum levels of pollution, he or she, too, states a belief. Those who argue in favor of or against a public policy likewise wish their views to be heard and understood; they seek a response to the arguments they make. What is more, they may believe that their citizenship in a democratic society gives them the right to such a hearing and response, and this is not what happens even in the most efficient market.[46]

People who argue for or against the teaching of creationism in the public schools, for example, believe that the scientific views they contend about are crucial. What matters is how well these views are supported by the objective evidence. The creationists are able to raise a great deal of money, but no one, not even they, contend that the intensity with which

94

people hold beliefs or the money they spend to publicize them indicates the cogency of their intellectual position. It is the cogency of the arguments, not how much partisans are willing to pay, moreover, that offers a credible basis for public policy.

THE DEMOCRATIC ALTERNATIVE

The blurring of the distinction between private interests and the public interest – and, therefore, between the competition of preferences and the contradiction of ideas – produces results that we should do well to avoid. First, the policymaker, employing the willingness-to-pay criterion, attempts to remain neutral among contending positions. As a result, the analyst would grant equal initial credibility to every position. For example, the policymaker, if "efficiency" is his goal, should take creationism seriously because its partisans are willing to pay a great deal for it to be taught in public schools. This approach, indeed, may favor the silliest views over the most sensible because, as Yeats wrote, "the best lack all conviction, while the worst are full of passionate intensity."[47]

The analyst, however, is unlikely to recognize silly, preposterous, or violent beliefs; he or she is unlikely to shadow-price preferences like those of Oscar the Grouch. Indeed, the analyst may rule out of consideration, either because they are "envious" and "meddling"[48] or, perhaps because they are "misinformed," views that are plainly ludicrous, malevolent, or stupid. These attempts to "launder preferences," to use Robert Goodin's excellent phrase,[49] may merely mark an underlying confusion between preferences that may be "priced" and values that are to be heard, considered, criticized, and understood. Once we recognize this distinction, we may no longer need to find technical grounds for "screening" preferences. We can dismiss racist, superstitious, and downright preposterous ideas as such.

Second, the willingness-to-pay approach to public policy removes the basis of legitimacy from the political process. I do not mean merely that it crushes the "cherished illusion" that policy comes from the minds of elected officials in Congress rather than from the computers of economists in the back room. I refer, rather, to the fact that cost-benefit approaches deal only with values or preferences already extant in society. A political process – a process of debate and compromise – is supposed to be creative. The ability of the political process to cause people to change their values and to rise above their self-interest is crucial to its legitimacy. Political participation is supposed to educate and elevate public opinion; it is not, like economic analysis, supposed merely to gratify preexisting desires.

A third likely consequence in public policy may be the most disastrous. Economic analysis tends to limit conflict to those parties who have something at stake for which they are willing to pay. This approach would prevent the socialization of conflict that is crucial to the functioning of a democracy.

Consider an example. Suppose a corporation proposes and an environmentalist group opposes the building of a shopping center in a rural area just outside of town. An economist might make a recommendation based on prices assigned to the various wants or preferences of relevant interest groups. This would effectively limit conflict to the immediate parties who know about and are affected by the project. The genius of democracy, however, is to let the conflict spread to a larger audience.

The institutions of democratic government – legislatures, agencies, parties, courts, and the press – depend and thrive on the potential for conflicts of this kind to widen beyond their original bounds. This happens when one side – usually the side that otherwise would be defeated – finds a public issue (e.g., a "snail darter") and moves the conflict into the press, the legislature, and the courts. The decision-making process then may become a kind of public good, since it allows everyone who participates in it the feeling of relevance, importance, and community-consciousness flowing from that participation.

This might seem grossly inefficient, and perhaps it is, but it is what democratic government is all about.[50] An alternative

– technocracy – quarantines or localizes conflict so that it can be resolved by the application of some mechanical rule or decision procedure. Cost-benefit approaches to public policy, if taken to their extreme, would do this, and thus they would substitute themselves for the processes of democratic government. The genius of cost-benefit analysis is to localize conflict among affected individuals and thereby to prevent it from breaking out into the public realm.

This suggests that the reason industry favors economic approaches to public policy is not necessarily the obvious one, namely, that cost-benefit analysis is sensitive to the costs of regulation. The deeper reason may be that cost-benefit analysis defines a framework for conflict that keeps the public qua public and the citizen qua citizen out. This characteristic of the cost-benefit framework – that is is antithetical to democracy – seems to have led analysts to try to take "citizen" values into account. This attempt fails, however, to get at the bottom of the problem. The deliberative rationality of democracy is just not like the interest-balancing rationality of markets.

CONCLUSION

Environmental law poses a severe test for economic approaches to public policy. "Disagreements over degrees of environmental protection," one writer has correctly surmised, "are not about relative costs and benefits but about the validity of economics itself as a form of interaction – its basis in exchange, costs, and cash – as a measure of the way we ought to relate to one another."[51] To notice that statutes like the Endangered Species Act, the Clean Air Act, and so on are not cost-beneficial is to recognize the obvious. That is the *point* of these laws, and of much of our environmental legislation.

These laws demonstrate that we are not consumers simply bent on satisfying every subjective preference. We insist upon our role as citizens as well. And, as citizens, we adopt a model of government and a vision of political life that allow us to posit collective values and to give effect to our national conscience and common will.

I do not pretend to assess the merits of the argument I have made here. I only want to point out that it *is* an argument. I did not treat the position many policy analysts defend as if it were merely their private preference. I did not survey economists to find out how much they were willing to pay to have their views about efficiency implemented. Why, then, do some economists survey environmentalists to find out how much they would pay to keep a vista clear or a river pure? Why do these economists believe that opinions that oppose theirs deserve a price and not a reply?

The role of the policymaker, indeed, of the legislature – and derivatively the role of the courts – may be to balance what we believe in and stand for as a community with what we want and need to achieve as a functioning economy. The problem may be to devise some way that we can relate to one another as members of a community in search of common ideals and, at the same time, compete and cooperate with each other in a market to satisfy individual interests.

The future of social policy rests on the resolution of conflicts of this kind. It is not just a matter of balancing interests with interests; it is a matter of balancing interests with morality and balancing one morality with another morality. In later chapters, I shall offer some suggestions about how *this* sort of balancing may be done.

Chapter 5

Values and preferences

A *New Yorker* magazine cartoon depicts the Devil introducing newcomers to hell. "You'll find there's no 'right' or 'wrong' here," he tells them, "just what works for *you.*"

This cartoon could serve as a frontispiece in a textbook that introduces students to policy analysis and management. In *A Primer for Policy Analysis*, Edith Stokey and Richard Zeck-hauser, for example, put forward the principle (ironically like the caption of the cartoon) that "individual welfare is all that matters in policy choices."[1] The individual's preferences, these authors say, constitute the standard or criterion by which we are to judge his or her well-being. "In the United States, we usually take the position that it is the individual's own preferences that count, that he is the best judge of his own welfare."[2]

The Devil and the policy analyst agree, then, that individual welfare is what matters in social regulation. The Devil tries to make people as miserable as possible; his goal is to defeat or frustrate preferences insofar as he can. The policy analyst, on the contrary, strives to increase overall welfare insofar as possible by recommending policies that maximize the satisfaction of preferences over society as a whole. Might the recommendations of the policy analyst be good, then, for the very reasons that the Devil's actions are evil?

This chapter discusses whether efficiency, as a goal or as a criterion for social regulation, has a normative or an ethical basis. I shall consider whether the efficiency criterion has any connection with a substantive conception of welfare, for example, and whether it has a foundation in the ethical theory of utilitarianism.

I shall argue, first, that the symmetrical view of the Devil and the policy analyst – one bad, the other good for the same reason – is mistaken. The Devil does evil things to his victims: He thwarts their autonomy, frustrates their freedom, and unless they are masochists, makes them terribly unhappy as well. By satisfying preferences, however, the policy analyst does not necessarily do anything good; he does not show himself to be right where the Devil is wrong. On the contrary, virtues like benevolence and justice that make it bad as a matter of policy to defeat the preferences of individuals do not make it good as a matter of policy to satisfy them. The Devil may justify his actions, moreover, as retributive: He punishes people for their sins. The policy analyst, however, may not claim even this justification: He tries to give people not what they deserve but what they desire instead.

I shall argue, second, that social regulation should be based on communitarian or public values, not on the personal preferences of individuals, once basic needs are met. Public values are goals or intentions that people ascribe to the group or community of which they are members; such values are theirs because they believe and argue they should be theirs; people pursue these values not as individuals but as members of the group. They then share with other members of their community *intersubjective* intentions or, to speak roughly, common goals and aspirations, and it is by virtue of these that a group or community *is* a group or community.[3]

When individuals participate in the political process to determine the common values and purposes that hold them together as a community or as a nation, they regard themselves as judges of public policy, not merely as channels or locations at which wants can be found. Debates in which individuals or their representatives discuss and decide upon public values need have no analogy, then, with markets where individuals determine and pursue personal preferences. In a democracy the application of a cost-benefit formula cannot replace the public discussion of ideas; it is not just what the person *wants* but what he or she *thinks* that counts.

WHY SATISFY PREFERENCES?

Many novels – *The Great Gatsby* is an example – criticize those of us who find little to do but to satisfy our consumer appetites. Gatsby likes to drive an expensive automobile. This is what he wants to do, and he is free to do it. Is it the goal or purpose of social policy to satisfy this sort of preference? Having a preference gives the person who has it a reason to try to satisfy it. Has the government, however, a reason to try to satisfy that preference?

Plainly, social policy should be concerned with the basic needs of citizens – but this is a matter not of efficiency but of justice. Similarly, regulation may strive to make the conditions under which people live and work cleaner, safer, more natural, and more beautiful, because these goals reflect public values and represent a shared conception of what we stand for as a nation. These are also sensible goals, and they are not hard to justify on ethical or aesthetic grounds. Textbooks in policy analysis suggest that social policy should be based not on legislated goals like these but on the principle of the satisfaction of preferences and demands. Is individual welfare, in this sense, what matters in social regulation?

The thesis that "individual welfare is all that ultimately counts in policy choices" may seek support from consequentialist political theories (usually called utilitarian) that start from some conception of what the good is: utility, welfare, happiness, potential Pareto improvement, wealth, GNP, whatever. Utilitarians a century ago defined the good in terms of pleasure or happiness and thought it to be the appropriate goal of public policy and law. These utilitarians did not have much trouble saying why happiness *is* good, since they believed, plausibly, that it is intrinsically valuable. Many of us would agree that happiness is a good thing in itself, although we may not agree that it is the only thing that is intrinsically good.

Utilitarians today speak of utility or welfare, by which they mean, generally, not a state of the individual (like pleasure) but the degree to which the preferences of the individual, as he or she ranks them, are satisfied. These preference utilitarians, as we may call them, confront the task of explaining why welfare in this sense is valuable, why it is good. Is the satisfaction of preferences an intrinsic good, like pleasure or happiness, or is it good instrumentally because it leads to consequences that are good in themselves?

It cannot be argued that the satisfaction of preferences is a good thing in itself, for many preferences are sadistic, envious, racist, or unjust. Preferences may also be coerced or adapt to coercive circumstances; these express not the autonomous choice of the individual but a process that preempts autonomy.[4] Many preferences – for example, some that are endogenous to consumption, like the urge for a cigarette – are despised by the very people who have them. Why should we regard the satisfaction of preferences that are addictive, boorish, criminal, deceived, external to the individual, foolish, grotesque, harmful, ignorant, jealous, . . . or zany to be a good thing in itself?

It may be good in itself that certain preferences be satisfied, namely, preferences that are good in themselves. In these instances, the primary value attaches to the preference, for example, because it is noble or just, and that is the reason its satisfaction is also valuable. Ordinary consumer preferences, however, are usually regarded not as intrinsically good but as arbitrary from a moral point of view. People should be free to pursue these preferences, to be sure, but why should it be an intrinsically good thing that they succeed in satisfying them?

Policy analysts may reply that the satisfaction of preferences is not an intrinsic good but an instrumental one, insofar as it increases the welfare, well-being, or utility of the person whose preferences they are. This seems to be true, however, only in a trivial sense, for economists define "welfare," "utility," and "well-being" in terms of the satisfaction of preferences. If "welfare" was given a normative sense, if it was defined in terms of self-realization, for example, what connection would it then have with the satisfaction of preferences? None comes to mind, unless one then defines self-realization in terms of satisfying preferences, which is to trivialize, not to understand that concept.

Likewise, it is unhelpful to argue that a person becomes "better off" to the extent that his or her preferences are satisfied. If "better off" simply means having more preferences satisfied, then we have argued in a very small circle once again. If "better off" means something like "happier," however, then we may wonder why we do not return to the old, original utilitarianism, producing happiness any way we can, not just through the satisfaction of preferences.

A contemporary preference utilitarian may reply that we should strive to satisfy preferences because this is what the people who have them prefer or want. This answer, besides inviting an infinite regress, however, is ambiguous. If it means that a majority of citizens favor preference satisfaction as a national goal, it is plainly false.[5] If it means that each person wishes his or her own preferences to be satisfied, it is false again. A person wishes his or her preferences satisfied at the moment he or she has them, but often changes his or her mind, regrets they were satisfied, or is grateful they were not.

A reflective person, asked if he or she is better off in his or her own estimation because some preference has or has not been satisfied, will hardly know how to answer, since he or she cannot presume to judge what his or her life might otherwise have been like.[6] How would Ulysses evaluate his early preference not to go to Troy? He would tell you one thing when he was in the cave of Cyclops, another when in Circe's bed. Was he *better off* because he went to war? What a question! He can only answer: "I am a part of all that I have met."[7]

Although a person may not be able to judge among alternative lives, he or she may be the best judge of his or her own welfare in another sense. That person, recognizing that it is "better to be Socrates dissatisfied than a fool satisfied,"[8] may reflect upon and then strive to improve his or her tastes and preferences. The improvement or education of taste – rather than the arbitrary satisfaction of whatever desires one has – may then be a goal of public policy that can be justified on classical utilitarian grounds. "The chief thing which the common sense individual actually wants," Frank Knight observes, "is not satisfaction of the wants he has, but more, and better wants. . . . true achievement is the refinement and elevation of the plane of desire, the refinement of taste."[9]

HAS THE EFFICIENCY CRITERION A BASIS IN UTILITARIANISM?

Those who defend the efficiency norm in public policy could appeal, perhaps, to the old Benthamite principle of maximizing pleasure or happiness, but they rarely do. Welfare theorists know, first, that the "greatest happiness" principle for public policy invites many devastating objections now standard in the philosophical literature, where they can be found.[10] What is more, there is no convincing evidence to show that the satisfaction of preferences leads to or increases satisfaction in the sense of happiness or contentment, once basic needs are met.

The evidence, in fact, runs the other way. In polls, people report a negative correlation between material improvement and perceived happiness.[11] Literary and empirical studies amply confirm what every mature adult discovers: Happiness and well-being are more likely to spring from overcoming or outgrowing many of our desires than from satisfying them.[12] One commentator explains: "Progress produces dissatisfaction because it inflates expectations faster than it can actually meet them. And this is virtually inevitable because the faster preferences actually *are* met, the faster they escalate."[13]

Although most welfare economists recognize only a historical relationship between the efficiency criterion and utilitarianism as a moral or political theory, some believe that a conceptual or logical connection exists. George Peterson and

Alan Randall write, "The benefit cost criterion is not an alien intruder from the economic arena into the political environment. Rather, it is directly derived from one particular, utilitarian, political philosophy."[14]

Utilitarianism, however, judges the value of actions according to the degree to which their consequences increase or decrease happiness, pleasure, or some other substantive conception of the good. Any criterion that derives from utilitarianism must, therefore, be consequentialist and must connect in some empirical or conceptual way with happiness or some other substantive ideal.

The version of preference utilitarianism found in current welfare economics meets neither of these tests. First, this kind of "utilitarianism" measures welfare or utility in terms of the expectations that lead to actions ("expected" utility) not the consequences ("actual" utility) that result from them. On this approach, a decision maker allocates resources to those willing beforehand to pay the most to use or consume them. There seems to be no concern with, or even reference to, the consequences of that allocation for those individuals.

Romeo's famous transaction with the druggist – "Oh, honest apothecary!" – illustrates the difference between expected and actual utility. The parties entered this transaction freely and were "fully informed as to the quantitative and qualitative characteristics of goods and services and the terms of exchange among them."[15] From the perspective of welfare economics, Romeo benefited from this exchange – but it was a horrible tragedy from a utilitarian point of view. Sophisticated analysts point out, therefore, that the "most important thing to bear in mind about the concept of value [in the welfare economist's sense] is that it is based on what people are willing to pay for something rather than the happiness they would derive from having it."[16]

I have now argued, first, that the efficiency criterion, because it refers only to the expectations that lead to a transaction rather than to the consequences that follow from it, has no basis in a consequentialist philosophy like utilitarianism. I have argued, second, that the efficiency criterion has no demonstrable connection with any substantive or normative conception of welfare – a conception, in other words, that is not simply defined in terms of it. Someone might suppose that when preferences are satisfied (in the sense of "met" or "fulfilled"), individuals become satisfied (in the sense of "happy" or "content"). No one has provided evidence that this is so. Social scientists have often observed, on the contrary, that "acts of consumption, . . . which are undertaken because they are expected to yield satisfaction, also yield disappointment and dissatisfaction."[17]

Fred Hirsch offers the following partial explanation. He argues that consumers, after their basic needs are met, tend to want "status" or "positional" goods.[18] Plainly, the satisfaction of these "status" preferences cannot be maximized, any more than one can maximize the number of people who are first in line or win a race.[19] Hirsch concludes that the satisfaction we take in consumer goods depends more on their scarcity than on their abundance. This is the reason, he says, that "economic advance [has] become and remained so compelling a goal to all of us as individuals, even though it yields disappointing fruits when most, if not all of us, achieve it."[20]

Mary Douglas has observed that as societies rise above the poverty level, goods are valued more for their social or cultural meaning than for their use; this meaning, moreover, is largely determined by their distribution.[21] Thus, as goods are more widely distributed, they may lose both their meaning and their value. When everyone stands on tiptoe, as Hirsch put the idea, no one sees any better.[22] These observations suggest that the "greatest happiness" principle of classical utilitarian theory and the efficiency criterion of contemporary welfare theory have a tenuous connection at best. To think otherwise is merely to confuse the satisfaction of preference, which policy analysts propose, with the old utilitarian preference for satisfaction.

To summarize: The efficiency criterion and the political theory of welfare economics from which it is derived have no basis in utilitarianism because, first, they evaluate actions by reference to the conditions that precede rather than the consequences that follow them; and because, second, they have no demonstrable relation to happiness or to any other substantive conception of the good. It is reasonable to conclude from this and from the argument I present in the next few pages that the efficiency criterion has no normative basis at all.

In drawing this conclusion, I do not assert that rights associated with equality or justice override the goal of economic efficiency in certain circumstances. This contention presupposes that efficiency has an independent justification; it supposes, in other words, that allocative efficiency is itself a good thing, even though other values, like distributive equity, may outweigh it. This presupposition is false. Efficiency has no merit or worth to begin with and therefore cannot be balanced against substantive values like equality or justice. I do not argue, then, that rights "trump" efficiency. I argue, rather, that efficiency has no normative claim or moral worth; therefore a "trade-off" between efficiency and equality is conceptually not in the cards.[23]

DO WE CONSENT TO THE EFFICIENCY NORM
IN PUBLIC POLICY?

Arguments that seek to justify allocatory efficiency as a policy objective generally refer to *social* costs and *social* benefits; they speak of the welfare or well-being of *society* and of the interests of society *as a whole*. Stokey and Zeckhauser, for example, write, "The purpose of public decisions is to promote the welfare of society."[24] The term "society" functions in this sentence the way the words "the average American family" function in the sentence "The average American family has 1.4 children." There is no family in the Middle West somewhere that has exactly 1.4 children. Likewise there is no entity called "society" out there, the welfare of which one can strive to promote.

A cost-beneficial policy may benefit the individuals whose interests it happens to satisfy; it may be advantageous to *them*, at least in a tautologous sense. Even if the winners could compensate losers and still be winners, the policy benefits winners and is preferable only from their (not from society's) point of view. Even if there are no losers – if at least one person prefers and no one opposes the policy – it is preferable just from that individual's point of view. The idea that it is preferable from *society's* point of view either means nothing or begs the entire question. Why should a policy that benefits *some* be considered, in addition, to benefit *society* or to command the consent of *society* as a whole?

In 1953, Gunnar Myrdal observed that contemporary utilitarianism presupposes a "harmony of interests" or a "communistic fiction" about the oneness of society.[25] According to the contemporary version of this fiction, society as a whole has a single interest, namely, the general welfare or the general good, as may be defined by efficient markets or, since these do not exist, by cost-benefit analysis. This communistic ideal "amounts to the assertion that society can be conceived as a single subject"[26] and may be assumed, on the basis of an argument known to the enlightened, to consent as one person to policies that serve "its" interest.

Judge Posner, Professor Zeckhauser, and other members of a vanguard of policy analysts express this collectivist faith by contending that society gives its unanimous "hypothetical" or "counterfactual" consent to the programs they advocate. Judge Posner argues that consent is the "operational basis" of the efficiency norm in policy analysis. He reasons that "consent to efficient solutions can be presumed."[27] In discussing the allocation of risk, Herman Leonard and Richard Zeckhauser write, "Cost-benefit analysis . . . would gain the hypothetical consent of the citizenry. We know of no other mechanism for making policy choices that has an ethical underpinning."[28]

Is this correct? May we assume that citizens in the United States consent, at least hypothetically, to a cost-benefit approach to public policy for the workplace, consumer product safety, human services, health, and the environment?

Policy analysts recognize, of course, that legislation in

these areas, for example, the Occupational Safety and Health Act, prohibits a cost-benefit test.[29] They sometimes complain of a "discrepancy," moreover, between the approach they take to regulatory policy and the approach taken by nearly everybody else.[30] If the cost-benefit approach in regulatory policy is both illegal and unpopular, as it seems to be, how can it have our hypothetical consent?

The answer apparently depends on a familiar, if metaphysical, conception of human nature. According to this view, a rational individual is essentially a self-interested maximizer of utility; in short, he or she is the "Economic Man" of welfare economic theory. Once one accepts this metaphysical premise about people's essential nature, the rest of the argument is easy. Leonard and Zeckhauser propose that people would contract with one another to adopt the cost-benefit approach, at least if they did not know their particular social identities. These authors write:

> What mechanism for making decisions would individuals choose if they had to contract before they knew their identities in society or the kinds of problems they would confront? Our answer is that, on an expected value basis, cost-benefit analysis would serve them best, and hence would be chosen.[31]

These authors conclude that "consent and the cost-benefit criterion are equivalent, and . . . cost-benefit analysis can be thought of as a form of 'hypothetical' consent by the community."[32]

Posner and Zeckhauser are not alone, of course, in claiming the "hypothetical" consent of society to controversial political programs. Marxist theoreticians have argued that we would consent to the policies they advocate if we were purged of our corrupt bourgeois ideology. Religious zealots might likewise dismiss dissent as ignorance, for who would not agree with them, once he understood his need for salvation or had seen the divine light? Libertarians I have spoken to have occasionally assured me that I would agree with their views if I only understood the true nature of freedom.

And so on. Conceptions of rationality, neutrality, freedom, equality, truth, and progress abound in our society, and we are the richer for them. An advocate of any of these conceptions of the common good or the common will might argue that we would surely agree with him, if only our heads were screwed on right.

The difficulty with hypothetical consent arguments of this sort is that there are so many of them. There are as many behind-a-veil-of-ignorance hypothetical consent arguments of this kind as their are a priori or metaphysical conceptions of liberty, personhood, or the meaning and purpose of life. Once one becomes convinced of one's own insight into the human condition, one expects others who take an impersonal point of view to make the same judgment. If they do not, they are ignorant or they may be perversely or irrationally predisposed against one's views.

The principal problem in political theory, however, is not hypothetical agreement but real disagreement. The problem is to structure mechanisms of social choice in a way that is as fair as possible between every legitimate conception of our intrinsic natures, common goals, and shared aspirations. The problem is not necessarily to determine which of these conceptions is correct, a task as old as Plato, but to understand how to structure social institutions so that people with contradictory metaphysical positions can go about the business of trying to convert one another under terms congenial to all.

Well before it was written, the Leonard–Zeckhauser "hypothetical consent" argument had been refuted by John Rawls, whose veil-of-ignorance technique it ironically parodies. Rawls argues persuasively that a liberal theory of justice, if it is to serve the purpose of providing a fair and congenial framework for social interaction, must be political, not metaphysical.[33] It will depend, then, not on metaphysical views about man but on a reflective equilibrium among values and lessons that arise as a result of our history, experience, and culture.

In political theory, arguments presented from an impersonal, detached, behind-a-veil-of-ignorance point of view primarily serve a practical purpose. They are intended to help us determine the basic social structures in which individuals who differ sharply in their economic interests and philosophical opinions can live together and secure the advantages of social cooperation. Since individuals who stand behind a veil of ignorance do not know what their interests or their opinions will be, they are likely to agree to structure institutions in a way that is fair among whatever preferences they may possess and political views they may espouse. Presumably, a free market economy and a representative legislature – that is, the institutions of a modern democratic state – provide the kind of structure that can be fair among competing interests and beliefs and, therefore, the kind of structure on which these individuals might agree.[34]

It is precisely because every zealot, ideologue, and academic with a theory to defend knows that he or she is right, and therefore that every rational agent will agree with him or her, that the Rawlsian emphasis on politics rather than metaphysics is necessary.[35] We must understand that the deliberation through which we determine our collective will is political, not metaphysical; it is actual, not hypothetical. It takes place at town meetings, in state assemblies, before regulatory agencies, and in Congress, not in the metaphysical speculations of political and economic theory. The way to get better social regulation is not to spend the next two thousand years seeking the theoretical conception of rationality. It is to encourage the virtues of inquiry and deliberation in legislatures and regulatory agencies.

MARKETS, EFFICIENCY, AND CHOICE

Allen Kneese, in the testimony from which I quoted in Chapter 1, speaks of efficiency in the context of individual choice. He argues, as we saw in Chapter 2, that an efficient allocation of resources always results from the free and informed choices individuals make in perfectly competitive markets. Since such an allocation results from free choice, we might

111

argue that it is freely chosen, or at least that the people consent to the allocation. And if people would choose or consent to an efficient allocation in perfect markets, then we may assume their consent to this same allocation even when the government, because of some form of market failure, must intervene in order to achieve it.

This argument – which ties efficiency not to preference but to choice – is based on two major premises. It asserts, first, that individuals choose (and therefore consent to) not only the transactions they make but also the outcomes of those transactions, at least within a perfectly competitive market. Second, it claims that what a perfect market would do is what people would choose or consent to. The conclusion follows that people at least hypothetically choose or consent to the use of the efficiency criterion in social regulation, if it achieves the same results they would have themselves reached under ideal market conditions.

Both premises in this argument are plainly false. First, it is simply not true that someone who makes a choice either chooses or consents to the consequences of that choice. If you buy a lottery ticket and lose, for example, it may be fair that you lose, and you may have no reason to complain about the loss; but you do not choose to lose, nor do you necessarily consent to do so. If you take a risky job and are seriously injured, you neither choose nor consent *ex ante* to your injury. Indeed, it may be unfair that you are injured if, for example, your employer could easily have maintained safer conditions.

Even if we concede the first premise for the sake of discussion, the second premise of the argument is false. What a perfect market *would* do is not necessarily what people *would* consent to. People might instead regard a market, however perfect, as inappropriate or as irrelevant to the decision or allocation in question. They may think in the circumstances that some other decision-making framework – a jury, a play-off, a coin toss, a consensus reached after discussion, voting, binding arbitration, or just letting the chips fall where they may – is the appropriate instrument of collective choice.

To see this, suppose the problem is to rank football teams

or to determine which ones are better than others. To establish a ranking, analysts might ask a random sample of citizens how much they are willing to pay to have each team win the Super Bowl. The teams could be ranked on this willing-to-pay basis, and the top team could be declared the national champion. No games need be played. The final order, moreover, would have the hypothetical or implicit consent of the citizenry, since it reflects the choices they would have made in a perfectly competitive market.

This approach to allocating victory to football teams presents a number of interesting methodological problems. How can we determine a fair sample from cities with and without a football franchise? (Even people outside major cities – people who live near the Grand Canyon, for example – may have preferences for which they are willing to pay.) Should we survey for willingness-to-accept-a-loss (WTAL) prices, or for willingness-to-pay-for-a-win (WTPW) prices – and how to balance them? I need not multiply the many methodological issues that analysts may resolve through stimulating theoretical research.

The problem with this market approach to allocating victory, however, is not methodological. The problem is that it is *crazy*. People want to see the football games; they do not want to choose the victor, as it were, in a market. Respondents would therefore scoff at the "contingent valuation" survey. They would protest that this is not the sort of decision or choice for which a market or a cost-benefit analysis is at all relevant.

The same is true, *mutatis mutandis*, with respect to social regulation. Questions like "How safe is safe enough?" and "How unpolluted is unpolluted enough?" go to our conscience and character as a nation. We expect our political representatives, therefore, to deliberate over these questions and to make wise and virtuous decisions on scientific, moral, aesthetic, economic, and legal grounds. The question whether to keep national parks as "sacred" refuges from civilization or to clutter them with the debris of economic progress, for example, is primarily an ethical not an economic question. That is the reason respondents to the Wyoming survey I discussed in the preceding chapter entered protest bids or refused to cooperate with the experiment.

THE GOOD SOCIETY

Political theorists who write within or against the utilitarian tradition generally agree that it is for the individual, not the government, to choose among conceptions of the good life. As long as individuals respect the freedom of others, they should be free to plan their own lives and to pursue the lives that they plan. The government, then, must "avoid any assessment of the relative value" of different people's lives.[36] It must make its decisions so far as possible "independent of any particular conception of the good life and what gives value to life."[37]

Writers in the liberal tradition – for example, Bruce Ackerman and Ronald Dworkin – argue persuasively that the political decisions of a good society are as neutral as possible among conceptions of the good life. I do not mean that neutrality, for these writers, serves simply as a negative criterion political decisions must meet. Decisions and decision-making procedures, for example, coin tossing, if they were utterly arbitrary or random, could possibly pass such a test. These authors argue, rather, that conceptions of neutrality and equality form the basis of political decisions in a good society. They show this particularly well in connection with policies intended to provide opportunities to individuals and to redistribute wealth.

With natural resource policy, particularly the regulation of pollution, it is different. Analysis of conceptions of neutrality and equality will not tell us what the exposure standard should be for vinyl chloride or benzene; these ideals, while urgently important in many areas, do not entail a wilderness policy or a consumer product safety policy or a policy for food and drugs. The answer to the question "How safe is safe enough?" is not to be drawn simply from the duty of society to respect the right of free and equal individuals to live their own lives. It turns also on the independent obligation of government to preserve the environment individuals share and to protect public safety and health.

When citizens discuss environmental issues from a public point of view, that is, as members of society rather than from the perspective of their own private interests, they are likely to express what Ronald Dworkin calls "impersonal preferences," which are preferences people have "about things other than their own or other people's lives or situations."[38] Dworkin notes that "some people care very much about the advance of scientific knowledge, for example, even though it will not be they (or any person they know) who will make the advance, while others care deeply about the conservation of certain kinds of beauty they will never see."[39] Many people believe that pollution should be strictly controlled, wilderness areas preserved, and the safety of workers ensured not because these goals promise advantages to them but because they conform to their conscientious idea of what a good society stands for or obliges itself to do.

How should impersonal preferences or values such as these enter into political decisions to preserve the environment or protect public safety and health? In a democratic political process, citizens have an opportunity, at least in theory, to present their views before legislatures. Democracy, as everyone knows, is susceptible to abuse and has all kinds of problems, but I know of no other mechanism for making policy decisions that has this ethical underpinning. The powers of a majority to make law must be limited, of course, by the rights of minorities to participate in the political process and to be safe from tyranny. Within these well-known constraints, however, democracy allows citizens to debate and act upon impersonal views on their merits, rather than forcing them to disguise these views as personal wants or preferences.

Consider working conditions. Suppose we were to determine for cost-benefit purposes a value-per-life-saved from *unregulated* but otherwise efficient markets – markets as they were, for example, at the turn of the century. Suppose, in other words, that we were to set an economic value on safety on the basis of the amount traded for it in markets not severely constrained by humanitarian regulation. It might be a very low value indeed. A hundred years of compassionate legislation has produced conditions in which economists can now argue that voluntary markets set an appropriate value on worker safety. This is a result not of more efficient markets but of persistent ethical regulation.

Cost-benefit analysis is often criticized because it is conservative. It preserves the status quo by valuing resources, such as safety, at prices currently paid for them, with a lot of methodological discussion, of course, about discount rates for future generations. These prices, however, result by and large from social regulations now in place; heaven only knows what prices would be like in unregulated markets. Thus cost-benefit accounts of the value of socially important goods – safety, clean air, and so on – probably have no serious relation to prices that might be paid in a market that has not been already constrained by social regulation. There is simply no way – and probably no reason – to find out how much, for example, children would be paid now to "hurry" coal in mines.

Social regulation itself has become a public good, as it were, because anyone can enjoy debating about it, while not decreasing the same opportunity for anyone else. Sometimes participation in public controversy may be more satisfying than the pursuit of one's personal preferences. In our world, as A. O. Hirschman points out, "men think they want one thing and then upon getting it, find out to their dismay that they don't want it nearly as much as they thought . . . and something else, of which they were hardly aware, is what they really want."[40] This "something else" often turns out to be participation in public life, the pursuit of a public rather than a private happiness.

The pursuit of private satisfactions, except for the committed hedonist, soon becomes disappointing or boring, and we look for some public cause, like saving the whales, that does not benefit us personally but appeals to our conscience.

We wish to govern ourselves according to a conception of the good society that we decide upon together; we are not willing to resign ourselves simply to pursuing our several conceptions of the good life.

According to Hannah Arendt, this is the reason Thomas Jefferson and other colonists rebelled against the king. On Arendt's interpretation, Jefferson understood tyranny as an abridgment as much of "positive" as of "negative" freedom: A government becomes tyrannical when it inhibits efforts to attain either private or public ends. Jefferson conceived tyranny as a form of government in which the ruler

> ... monopolized for himself the rights of action, banished the citizens from the public realm into the privacy of their households, and demanded of them that they mind their own, private business. Tyranny, in other words, deprived of public happiness, though not necessarily of private well-being, while the republic granted to every citizen the right to become "a participator in the government of affairs," the right to be seen in action.[41]

If you envision political relationships in terms of cooperation and competition among self-interested individuals, you will never fathom American regulatory or environmental law. That vision of law may help you understand what the courts have done over the past thirty years to defend individuals against unfair treatment and to secure their right to live their own lives in private. The New Deal experiment with public law, during the same time, has moved in an opposite but complementary direction. The legislative effort to preempt private with public law (and thus to replace the norms of competition with the norms of community) defines a sphere of public values – particularly concerning public health, safety, and the environment – that help to determine the identity of Americans. In pursuing these values, Americans do not necessarily pursue their advantage as individuals. Rather, they express the kind of people they are and the sort of society they wish to be.

King George III ranked among the more liberal rulers of his day: He did not dictate religious adherence or meddle otherwise in the colonists' personal lives. Parliament had long since chosen the course of toleration. More recently, British bureaucrats have shown themselves adept at decision theory and policy analysis; they know how to respect personal rights while making markets efficient. If that is what government ought to do – to act as a prophylactic on markets – why should people maintain democratic institutions? Why not call off the American Revolution? It is not too late. King George is alive and well and teaches at the Kennedy School of Government.

THE CONCEPT OF COMMUNITY

I suggested earlier that the term "society" functions in the phrase "the welfare of society" in the way the words "the average American family" function in the sentence "The average American family has 1.4 children." To suppose that society exists as an entity giving its consent to policies that increase its welfare is to commit what philosophers know as a category mistake. As well suppose that the average American family lives in Nebraska or Iowa raising its 1.4 children.

I wish to argue, however, that there is a radical difference in the concept of society as it occurs in the framework of policy analysis and the idea of society or community we may use when we think about public policy and law in a more appropriate way. The concept of society in policy analysis refers only to an aggregate of individuals or, more precisely, an aggregate of preferences. From the point of view of welfare economics, as many commentators point out, individuals count simply as locations or channels at which preferences may be found. "Persons do not count as individuals in this any more than individual petrol tanks do in the analysis of the national consumption of petroleum."[42]

It is possible, however, to think of community in another way, namely, as the logical subject of intentions or policies of a certain kind. A person may say, for example, that we should not support right-wing dictators abroad even if they are anti-Communists. I think President John F. Kennedy once announced a national intention to "make the world safe for diversity." Statements such as these are not meant to express the "subjective" judgment or intention of the individual who utters them, even if he is the president. Rather, they are meant to describe the judgment or intention of the nation as a whole. It is for the community, through the political process, to ignore, endorse, or reject these statements.

I want to argue that members of any community – it could be a family, a team, or a nation – may conceive goals and aspirations that, like their perceptions and beliefs, are *intersubjective*. The group or community exists or has a life of its own – it is not simply a logical aggregate – insofar as its members participate in these intersubjective intentions.

Only a skeptic would doubt the objectivity or intersubjectivity of perceptions and beliefs. When you and I perceive the same table, for example, our *perceivings*, being acts or states of mind, are subjective; what is *perceived*, the "content" of the act of perception, however, exists objectively, as what we both see. Thus, even though acts of perceiving are subjective, the object perceived is intersubjective, belonging to a world that is not *mine* or *yours* but *ours* in an epistemological sense. Thus, if I say the table has three legs and you say six, one of us is mistaken, and by investigating the object further, we can usually determine who it is.

What is true of perception is likewise true of belief. If I believe the earth is flat, while you believe it is round, there is a fact of the matter and a method for determining the fact. To say the shape of the world is "subjective" simply because people have believed different things about it is simply to deny, as the skeptic does, that knowledge is possible of anything at all.

Intentions, superficially, resemble perceptions and beliefs. If I intended to do something, such as kick a field goal, then my intention qua act of intending is subjective, while what I intend to do – the act the intention is about – is objective, for example, my visible attempt to kick a field goal. Yet, on analysis, we can see that the objects of my beliefs and perceptions are intersubjective in a way that the objects of my intentions are not. The objects of my beliefs and perceptions are states of the world we share, but the objects of my intentions, it seems, must always be *my own actions*. I cannot intend the same acts you intend, it seems, although I can see and believe the same things you see and believe.

Suppose, for example, we are married to each other and have a child who we both intend shall have the best education possible. I shall say, "I intend Jared to have the best education possible." You will likewise say, "I intend Jared to have the best education possible." The acts we intend, however, will be uniquely our own, even if we mean the same thing by the "best education possible." I may try to make enough money to send Jared to private school. You may spend a lot of time helping him with his homework. The acts we intend are different even if the general outcome we envision – the consequences of these intended acts – is the same.

Now suppose that in some matters we determine our intentions not individually but together. We ask ourselves what *we* shall do about Jared's education. We discuss what *our* policy should be and then set out tasks for each of us to accomplish. We might decide that you should earn the money while I help with the homework, or some such thing.

We might then express our shared intention by each saying, "*We* intend Jared to have the best education possible." Wilfrid Sellars points out that statements of this kind "in the first person *plural* have the interesting properties that (a) they express the speaker's intention, yet (b) the intentions expressed are in the strongest sense the same."[43] The *acts* of intending are subjective and therefore two in number, but the *content*, what is *intended*, is the same. In these circumstances, intention may be as intersubjective as perception and belief.

The general intentions set out in public law, for example, to make the environment cleaner or the workplace safer, have this intersubjective form. They are goals we determine for ourselves as a community, goals we could not conceive, much less achieve, as individuals trading in markets. A community is not an aggregate of individuals or a set of preferences to be satisfied; people in communities know purposes and aspirations together they could not know alone. A nation is not an aggregate but a community that in the purposes it seeks to accomplish, however limited, has a life and a character of its own.

INTEREST AND IDENTITY?

When you turn your attention to conditions in the workplace or in the environment, or when you consider the way wealth is distributed in society, you may feel responsible for the evil you see because you are a member of that society. You may be ashamed as an American, for example, for the racism in American society. You may have done nothing personally of which you are ashamed; shame, rather, touches what you are, not what you do; it touches you because you are a member of a profession, community, religion, or nation that practices discrimination. Similarly, you may be pained whenever the practice of a community of which you are a member falls far beneath its principles or, even worse, when those principles conflict with your moral intuitions and ethical sentiments. Then, insofar as you identify yourself as a member of that community, you will feel some obligation to improve things if you can – for example, by arguing for reforms needed to bring the practices of the group more in conformity with its principles and its principles more in line with one another and with ordinary virtues and moral intuitions.

The goals a society chooses should be consistent with a sense of decency and compassion for which there is no analytical or methodological substitute. They will also depend on the place of that society in the historical progress of humankind and on the lessons it has learned from experience. The goals we choose should also represent a reflective judgment on what other societies have done and tried to do. We "know to some extent what is thought right or wrong in other communities now, and what has been thought in other times; and this leads to a notion of goodness not of any particular time or country."[44] The "cosmopolitan morality" we gain from reflection on history and human experience can inform political judgment and is neither arbitrary nor absolute.

According to Jean-Jacques Rousseau, the "cause of human misery is the contradiction . . . between man and the citizen; make man one and you will make him as happy as he can manage to be."[45] I believe that this contradiction, far from being the cause of human misery, is a major source of human freedom. As individuals, we are free to live our own lives, but as citizens we are also free to share in a larger life: We are no longer confined by the logic of interests. This is not simply because we are free, if we like, to be irrational – to fly in the face of our interests; nor is it merely because, once understanding our interests, we are better prepared to deal with them.

It is because we are not forced to accept the vision of society associated with contemporary economic theory; we are not required to adopt that conception of morality and rationality in preference to some other list of moral, cultural, or historical values. This is not merely to say that we can, in an act of will, replace one morality with another. It is to insist, rather, that we can see things differently, that we can see the good not as an object of preference but as an object of shared belief, insight, and affection.

Statutes enacted during the 1960s and 1970s reflect public *attention* to the workplace and the environment; they resulted from political deliberation about what a decent, self-respecting society with a particular history would do about the workplace, the environment, civil rights, and public safety and health. These laws express a common perception of ourselves and the values we stand for as a moral community; they are not intended to satisfy personal preferences. When we make public law and public policy, we put both the Devil and the policy analyst behind us, for we are to consider shared values and common intentions, not simply personal interests. Public issues must be discussed in public terms. What counts in public policy is a conception of right and wrong – a conception of the good society – not just what works for *you*.

Chapter 6

Nature and the national idea

Perry Miller, the great American historian, dropped out of the University of Chicago in 1923, his freshman year, to seek what he called the "boon of adventure," which World War I had provided for his older contemporaries.[1] He traveled during the next three years to an isolated mountain cabin in Colorado, to Greenwich Village, where he worked as an actor, and to the Belgian Congo, where he was a seaman on an oil tanker.[2] There, while he unloaded naval stores from America, he experienced an "epiphany (if the word be not too strong) of the pressing necessity of expounding my America to the twentieth century."[3] At the edge of the jungle of central Africa, Miller writes, he had thrust upon him "the mission of expounding what I took to be the innermost propulsion of the United States, while supervising, in that barbaric tropic, the unloading of drums of case oil flowing out of the inexhaustible wilderness of America."[4]

Miller, through his books and, until 1963, when he died, through his lectures, acquainted thousands of younger Americans, many of them immigrants or the children of immigrants, with the culture they had inherited as Americans. He found in the errand of puritanism in the American wilderness the fundamental themes of American history, which he interpreted to those who looked for a sense of national purpose and character, for the "innermost propulsion" of the United States.

Anyone who wishes to understand American environmental law – certainly anyone who hopes to reform it – must

124

recognize in it the purposes and aspirations of a nation that exploited a wilderness to achieve what it thought or hoped were worthy ends. The responsibilities we share on account of the changes we have made and are making upon the land – the success and failure of an American errand into a morally inexhaustible but physically exhausted wilderness – should lie at the heart of environmental policy. I shall review a little of this history, not to add anything to what is already known but to make what is known more available to those concerned with making and implementing environmental law and social regulation.

In earlier chapters, I argued that environmental policy should be based on ethical, aesthetic, cultural, and historical considerations and, therefore, should be the subject of political deliberation, not just economic analysis. In this chapter, I shall attempt to explain, by way of example, what I take some of these normative considerations to be.

AMERICAN HISTORY AND NATURAL HISTORY

Of the hundred or so persons who landed with the *Mayflower*, November 11, 1620, at Plymouth, William Bradford tells us that more than half died in the first two or three months, "especially in January and February, being the depth of winter and wanting houses and other comforts."[5] The environment, as Michael Wigglesworth described it in 1662, was a "Devil's den":

> A waste and howling wilderness
> Where none inhabited
> But hellish fiends and brutish men
> That devils worshiped.[6]

Bradford and the Pilgrims, Wigglesworth and those who migrated to New England during the latter part of the seventeenth century, the fur traders after them, the killers of Indians, the homesteaders, the empire builders – all learned what we would learn if we visited, even for a short while, an uncivilized place: that nature – and nature meant the wilderness for those people – is

> ... marvelous, fantastic, beautiful; but it is also terrifying, it is also profoundly sinister. There is something in what, for lack of a better word, we must call the character of great forests ... which is foreign, appalling, fundamentally and utterly inimical to intruding man.[7]

This is the attitude of the explorer, but when he becomes a settler and has a farm and home, he loses the sense of awe. As Marx once wrote: "Nature becomes ... purely an object for men, something merely useful, and is no longer recognized as a power working for itself."[8] In America this change of attitude was early and abrupt. For three or four years the Pilgrims recognized nature as a power working for itself; then they made it work for them by clearing it of trees and fertilizing it with dead fish.

Every Thanksgiving Americans celebrate their forefathers' success. They celebrate the fact that in America, nature is the antithesis of hostile, inimical, or foreign; all you have to do is replace the forests with farms and cities, and it nicely serves the purposes of man. The Puritans in America understood this perfectly; they looked on the wilderness with dread and thanked God every time some of it was destroyed. They also understood that when forests go down, profits go up; and they thanked God for that as well. "I think it fair to say," writes Perry Miller, "that the founders had no qualms about doing harm to nature by thrusting civilization upon it." He continues, "They reasoned in terms of wealth, comfort, amenities, power, in terms which we may conveniently call, though they had not been derived from Bentham, 'utilitarian.'"[9]

In the first century or century and a half of settlement, Americans did think this way. From the moment when Bradford stepped from the *Mayflower* into a "hideous and desolate wilderness," the attitude of the American toward nature was, to quote the historian Roderick Nash, "hostile and his dominant criteria utilitarian. The *conquest* of the wilderness was his major concern."[10]

Over the next two hundred years, this attitude underwent a remarkable, even incredible, change. At first, Americans thought of the civilized nations of the world, notably England, as the regions blessed by God, while they considered their own environment a howling waste. In 1702, for example, Cotton Mather, while eulogizing a woman, said she had left an "earthly paradise" in England to "encounter the sorrows of a wilderness" in America. Eventually, she "left that wilderness for the heavenly paradise."

A hundred years later, Americans came to see the wilderness as the equivalent of Eden, a paradise "fresh as it were, from the hands of the Creator."[11] The city, whether in Europe or America, had become the Devil's den.

A causal connection surely exists between our attitude toward nature and our desire to alter it or keep it as it is. There also is a logical connection between our aesthetic description of nature – whether we say the wilderness is a heaven or hell – and the conclusion we draw about changing or preserving it. The history of the idea of nature and of the natural environment in America, then, is surely relevant to the nation's environmental policy. How, then, is this connection to be understood?

The aesthetic qualities of natural objects, for example, the power of a river or the inviolability of the moon, are to some extent cultural creations, just as the entrance of the pope into Saint Peter's is a cultural creation. Those who share in the culture learn to perceive the mightiness of the river, just as Catholics learn to perceive the holiness of the pope. These objects, indeed, function within a culture as paradigms of the qualities they express. Accordingly, although the determination of the expressive properties of an object depends largely on cultural history, the perception is immediate and personal. Our feelings may function cognitively – they help us describe the world – like our organs of sense.

The idea that the wilderness and the objects in it, given

our cultural history, serve us as examples of the qualities we most cherish – freedom, innocence, courage, strength – is not itself a sufficient condition for preserving those objects; very often we are forced to sacrifice the things we most admire. Likewise, the purity and cleanliness of air and water mean something to us and matter to us, even if we cannot always protect them, since other goods, which mean less, may matter more. An environmental policy, however, must attend to the meanings things have for us, for example, the meaning of pollution, not simply the magnitude of the risks it may pose. The meanings or expressive values we discover in our environment involve a kind of self-discovery; what a nation recognizes in its natural environment it identifies in itself.

American history is continuous with the natural history of North America; it is a history of what settlers from other continents have done with the wilderness and with farms and cities that arose from the wilderness, and what that experience did to them. To this experience Americans trace their national character and conscience; they share a sense of responsibility to one another and to the land they inhabit. This is the kind of responsibility, I believe, Perry Miller recognized in 1926 while unloading case oil from the then and still inexhaustible American wilderness.

THE END OF AN ERRAND

Except for Thanksgiving and the bathetic experience of John Alden, the Pilgrims gave us little to remember. Unlike the later Puritans who came with the Great Migration of 1630, to run "an errand into the wilderness,"[12] the followers of Bradford left England to escape persecution, not to make history. And so it is with the landing in Salem, June 12, 1630, of John Winthrop and his group of immigrants, or perhaps with his speech "A Model of Christian Charity" aboard the *Arbella*, that Americans' consciousness as a nation began.

In his lay sermon, Winthrop told his people that they came to America not to get a better station in life but to form a

better community "both civil and ecclesiastical"; that God
had appointed them to do so and "wee are entered into a
covenant with him for this work"; and that according to the
covenant, if "wee shall . . . embrace this present world and
prosecute our carnall intentions seeking greate things for our
selves and our posterity, the Lord will surely breake out in
wrathe against us . . . and make us knowe the price of the
breache of such a covenant." If, on the contrary, they did
the work and so built a just commonwealth, God would
reward them: "He shall make us a prayse and glory, that
men shall say of succeeding plantations: the lord make it like
that of New England: for wee must consider that wee shall
be as a City upon a Hill, the eyes of all people are upon
us."[13]

Needless to say, Winthrop was entirely mistaken. His peo-
ple failed to do what he thought was the work of God in
America – and yet they achieved an enormous prosperity.
They had not intended to become prosperous, and yet they
did; prosperity, as John Higginson told the Massachusetts
General Court in 1663, had become a remarkable fact of life.
In his inaugural sermon, he said:

> When the Lord stirred up the spirits of so many of his people
> to come over into the wilderness, it was not for worldly wealth
> or better livelihood for the outward man. The generality of the
> people that came over professed the contrary. Nor had they
> any rational grounds to expect such things in wilderness. Thou
> God, hath blessed His poor people and they have increased
> from small beginnings to great estates . . . Look upon your
> towns and fields, look upon your habitations shops and ships
> and blessings of land and see. Have I been a wilderness to
> you? We must need answer, no Lord thou has been a gracious
> God, and exceeding good even in these earthly blessings. We
> live in a more comfortable and plentiful manner than ever we
> did expect.[14]

At first, Puritans accepted Winthrop's suggestion that their
prosperity came as a reward for their labors. By 1660, however, they followed Higginson in citing God's free benevo-

lence. Finally, in the 1670s, the continued "sweetening" of life in New England could only be regarded as evidence that God did not know what was going on there. Even Higginson included a warning in his sermon. In words much quoted thereafter, he reminded the court that they were "originally a plantation of Religion, not a plantation of trades. Let merchants and such as are increasing cent per cent remember this."[15]

The warnings increased in severity; sermons took on the form of jeremiads, which they were called; and every shipwreck, flood, or drought was recognized as an omen that at last God's vengeance was on its way. When King Philip's War (1675) failed, for all its horror, to make God's will known to his people, the ministers formed a synod and published as its *Result*, in methodical fashion, the crimes against which they had declaimed for years in their jeremiads. Although some of the sins mentioned there are solid even by today's standards, there was a clear emphasis on the connection between the first, a "cooling of former life heate in spiritual communion," and the tenth, an "inordinate affection to the world."[16]

Looking back at these events, we can surmise that the land speculation, dissension, inflation, lessening of religious ardor, and other complaints listed by the synod were not sins but necessities. They represent the attempt of a second and third generation to deal with the social problems their fathers, immersed in the political and theological disputes that had brought them from England, had not confronted or even expected. The jeremiads, the halfway covenants, the revivals, and the like did not restrain so much as exorcise these activities. By offering a ritual *mea culpa*, the young people could get on with the business of life.

But still beneath this was the fact – unacknowledged at the time but always sharply felt – that New England had lost its audience. Cromwell and the Independents, in whose cause the Puritans had come to America, grew more concerned about improving their army than their theology, and when they noticed the Americans at all, it was only to tell them

that their zeal was an embarrassment, because they themselves had determined upon a course of toleration. Consequently, the settlers of New England were left with a sense
of having a mission – but no idea what it was or from whom;
a covenant – but no assurance of God's interest or understanding of its terms; and a national identity – but no idea
what that was or who they were. As Perry Miller put it:
"Having failed to rivet the eyes of the world upon their city
on the hill, they were left alone with America."[17]

America was the wilderness, but what was that? How
would a Puritan people describe it? As their history suggests,
they were not utilitarians in a philosophical sense; on the
contrary, their Protestant background would have made
them resist a pleasure–pain philosophy. Accordingly, while
they did reason about their environment in terms of wealth,
power, comfort, and amenity, they valued these advantages
not as ends in themselves but as means to, or as rewards
for, religious accomplishments; and if they taught themselves
to pursue happiness, it was happiness within a new social
order and not individual success for its own sake.

When their religious errand failed and no new social order
materialized, although there was an abundance of individual
success, Americans began to question whether they any
longer had a mission of such importance that it merited tearing down a wilderness. They began to ask whether they were
corrupting their environment – but only after they discovered, as we have seen, that their environment had corrupted
them.

The wilderness that had served them had also seduced
them, and in destroying it, they destroyed something of their
hopes, something of their history, and something of their
future as well as of their past. They saw that their prosperity
was also an apostasy, their nationalism was also a secularism,
and their happiness was also an emptiness. And while they
reasoned in terms of wealth, power, comfort, and amenity,
they had nothing to serve but themselves.

If, after this time, Americans have remained materialistic,
if they have emphasized personal acquisition and wealth,

they have done so *faute de mieux*. It is a part of their national character to want a devotion to noble purposes, a respect for great symbols, a commitment to important ideals. Of course, they had only one place to look. If they found collective symbols of freedom, intelligence, virtue, courage, and strength, they did so because a puritan people ascribed these qualities to nature itself.

NATURE AS SYMBOL

In imposing civilization on so vast a landscape, Americans were, in fact, doing what had never been done. They had a mission – if not the one that brought them – and the world watched. They had become conscious of new symbols, stories, and beliefs, and so they had begun to unite themselves, without relying on the traditions, memories, and myths of their European origins. In a word, Americans started to describe nature in a way that could help them describe themselves.

It is hardly surprising that this search – the attempt to locate in nature the symbols of national character and destiny – was first conducted in religious terms. In 1755, Jonathan Edwards, then a missionary to Indians at the frontier town of Stockbridge (Northampton had expelled him in 1750, correctly surmising that it was not good for business to worry as much as he did about the wrath to come), published a *Dissertation Concerning the End for which God Created the World*, in which he set forth some of his reasons for opposing the rationalist theology of Boston. Although Edwards did not say that God is an artist rather than a clockmaker, he has been interpreted as if he did, and properly so, for this clearly was part of his intention. Here is what he said:

> Thus it appears reasonable to suppose, that . . . the disposition to communicate himself, or diffuse his own FULNESS, which we must conceive of as being originally in God as a perfection of his nature, was what moved him to create the world. But here, as much as possible to avoid confusion, I observe, that

there is some impropriety in saying that a disposition in God to communicate himself *to the creature*, moved him to create the world. For though the diffusive disposition in the nature of God, that moved him to create the world, doubtless inclines him to communicate himself to the creature, when the creature exists; yet this cannot be all.... Therefore, to speake more strictly according to truth, we may suppose, that a disposition in God, as an original property of his nature, to an emanation of his own infinite fulness, was what excited him to create the world.[18]

This was not entirely new. Puritans had long considered nature to be not only a creation but also an expression of the power of God. A century earlier, John Cotton, for example, had described nature as "a mappe and shaddow of the spiritual estate of the soules of men."[19] And Edwards himself had encountered in nature the "images or shadows of divine things."[20] The *Dissertation* is unusual, however, even startling: first, because it refuses to go along with Cotton Mather and others in finding the glory of God expressed primarily in the mechanical perfection of the Newtonian universe and, second, because it does not hesitate to use such Neoplatonic terms as "diffuse," "emanate," and "communicate" to describe God's relation to the world.

This is a real departure. Instead of studying science of theology, indeed, instead of staying within the conventions of Calvinism, Americans could find in the experience of nature the condition of spiritual awakening. The revivals were founded on this belief. Nature is a symbol of the divine; therefore, the wilderness assures Americans of their special relation to God.

But how is this symbol to be understood? Edwards himself tried to blunt the impact of his words – God does not communicate himself chiefly for the benefit of man – and therefore the symbol is in a foreign character, a faint clue and indirection, a shadow on the wall of a cave. But take away the Calvinist theology, remove the doctrine of original sin, of which Edwards, of course, was a major exponent, and the conclusion would follow from the passage quoted that God, nature, and man, being of one substance, are equally divine. In that case, like may respond to like, and we may all become transcendentalists, immediately interpreting the messages of God.

If you think Emerson drew this inane conclusion, you are obviously right; the theme that flows through him is Jonathan Edwards's old Puritan conviction shorn of its theological restraint:

> There is no great and no small
> To the Soul that maketh all:
> And where it cometh all things are;
> And it cometh everywhere.[21]

The easy, all too easy, manner in which the "unfallen" Emerson went about reading the character of God in Nature offended at least some of his contemporaries: Walden Pond, for example, was 2 miles from Concord center and 12 feet deep, and Moby-Dick was farther away and deeper than that. But whether with the majority of Americans you read Emerson and the great slush of Romantics, and thus saw Nature as the paradigm of joyful innocence and God as essentially benevolent, or you chose Melville, Hawthorne, Poe, or, later, Twain and were made aware of the ancient distances in the deep seas and dark forests, you recognized nature as an aesthetic symbol before you considered it in economic terms.

In order to understand nature as an aesthetic symbol, you had to decide upon its metaphorical character; is it virtuous, independent, mighty, and free, or is it inimical, wrathful, and ambiguous? Now, these qualities belong to nature, if they belong at all, no less than properties of age or chromosome count; metaphorical possession is possession nonetheless.[22] It is just that the conventions for establishing age or chromosome count are well entrenched in the history of science, whereas the conventions for determining metaphorical qualities are less well entrenched.

The commonsense properties of an object are settled by ordinary perception – indeed, this is what makes them commonsensical; the metaphorical qualities, or, if you prefer, the aesthetic or expressive qualities, of things are determined primarily by literature, music, and the arts. No wonder the first conservationists – Audubon, Catlin, Cole, Muir, Olmsted – were not pioneers, businessmen, or politicians; they were artists. Only by recognizing the metaphorical or expressive features of nature can one understand the moral dimension of the fact that America has torn the wilderness down.

THE FALL: FORTUNATE AND UNFORTUNATE

The opinion in New England and New York, as represented, let us say, by Emerson and Thoreau in the one and Melville and Whitman in the other, that nature has sublime qualities that can be read or at least translated into the American national character received support – it was entirely paralleled, in fact – in the writing of Thomas Jefferson and the thinking of the first settlers of Virginia and the South. Although those who lived south of New York tended to visualize America as a garden rather than as a wilderness, and thus their imagery reflects a lower latitude, their emulation of nature was much the same.

"What then is the American, this new man?" wrote Michel de Crèvecoeur, a French-born New York farmer who corresponded with Jefferson and, through his popular *Letters from an American Farmer*, with the world. "He is an American," Crèvecoeur continued, "who, leaving behind him all his ancient prejudices and manners, receives new ones from the new mode of life he has embraced."[23]

That "new mode of life" was, of course, to be bucolic – the rural life of independent freeholders. Jefferson's distrust of the cities – which he regarded as belonging spiritually to Europe, wherever they were – is well known, as is his reliance on virtues nourished by the land. In *Notes on Virginia*, Jefferson wrote, "Those who labour in the earth are the chosen people of God, if ever he had a chosen people, whose breasts he has made his peculiar deposit for substantial and genuine virtue." He went on: "Corruption of morals in the mass of cultivators is a phenomenon of which no age nor nation has furnished an example."[24] Of this sentiment, one historian, Leo Marx, has written, "By 1785, when Jefferson issued *Notes on Virginia*, the pastoral ideal has been 'removed' from the literary mode to which it traditionally had belonged and applied to reality."[25]

The pastoral ideal presented as a priori a scheme as the covenant theology of Winthrop, and one that fitted reality as badly; apparently, cultivators are no less susceptible to corruption than the same number of merchants. Worse than that, they could not remain cultivators; once the tide of civilization, as it is always called, moved west, those who moved with it had to become woodsmen, hunters, traders, soldiers, or whatever was needed to turn an inhospitable environment into a more comfortable, if more ordinary, place to live. They would have to reinterpret America's religious errand in this new frontier. The images of Arcady were of no use to them, and the banalities of Emerson reflect a man on the Chautauqua circuit, not the Oregon Trail.

Those who moved west in their successive waves – to keep within Frederick Jackson Turner's metaphor – felt the old American antipathy toward the wilderness, and anyway they were concentrating on something else. Alexis de Tocqueville says of them:

> In Europe people talk a great deal of the wilds of America, but the Americans themselves never think about them; they are insensible to the wonders of inanimate nature and they may be said not to perceive the mighty forests that surround them till they fall beneath the hatchet. Their eyes are fixed upon another sight: the American people view its own march across these wilds, draining swamps, turning the course of rivers, peopling solitudes, and subduing nature. This magnificent image of themselves does not meet the gaze of Americans at intervals only; it may be said to haunt every one of them in his least as well as in his most important actions and to be always flitting before his mind.[26]

In 1840, the *New York Review*, in a feature typical of the time, advised all foreigners in America to watch out for the symbols of the future:

> A railroad, a penitentiary, a log house beyond the Mississippi, the last hotly-contested elections – things rather heterogeneous to be sure, and none of them at first glance so attractive as the wonders of the old world – are in reality, and to him who regards them philosophically, quite as important, and as they connect themselves with the unknown future, quite as romantic.[27]

Here is the hope that new symbols – a railroad, for example – could take the place of the forest in expressing the freedom and power of the new nation. Here once again is the expectation that Americans would build their city on the hill, that they would replace the great forests with a greater civilization. Even Thoreau felt this fever. In the roar of a railroad train he heard a promise he knew would not be kept. "When I hear the iron horse make the hills echo with its snort like thunder," he wrote, "it seems as if the earth had got a race now worthy to inhabit it." The disappointment follows immediately:

> If all were as it seems, and men made the elements their servants for noble ends! If the cloud that hangs over the engine were the perspiration of heroic deeds, or as beneficent to men as that which floats over the farmer's fields, then the elements and Nature itself would cheerfully accompany men on their errands and be their escort.[28]

This is the dilemma that confronted the nation in the nineteenth century. Can the railroad train, the log cabin, the penitentiary, and the last hotly contested election express the ideals of national character and destiny as well as the objects of nature do? Do they represent a nation whose deeds are so heroic and whose ends are so noble that it is worthy to inherit a wilderness? Or are they merely the servitors of destruction, rapine, and luxury? You guessed it: the last; and so the celebration of nature turned quickly to eulogy and lament.

Nobody reads James Fenimore Cooper anymore – Mark Twain's view of his writing is too accurate[29] – but in the nineteenth century the *Leatherstocking Tales* and the hundreds of dime novels modeled after them provided a sort of elegy on the wilderness. Natty Bumppo, the hero of Cooper's romance, is, needless to say, everything the son of nature should be: strong, honest, innocent, just, a good shot, and so on. He is up against the force of civilization, cast in the form of Judge Marmaduke Temple, who owns most of the visible landscape and whom Bumppo respects, mostly because Temple has working for him the arts of law and theology. In short, it is the Siegfried legend, but in western New York and during the Washington presidency.[30]

Bumppo thus comes into conflict with a number of Alberichs – the Skinners in *The Spy* and Ishmael Bush in *The Prairie* – who, by robbing the land of its wealth, attempt to set up an empire to rival the judge's own. In one memorable scene from *The Pioneers*, Bumppo comes upon some frontiersmen massacring flocks of passenger pigeons by spraying them with buckshot from a cannon. Leatherstocking responds as would any hunter who values nature: A cannon, he says, suits "them that don't know how to put a ball down a rifle barrel, or how to bring it up again with a true aim; but it's wicked to be shooting into flocks in this wasty manner, and none do it who know how to knock over a single bird."[31] When Bumppo is himself sentenced for killing a deer in violation of the new game laws and eventually exiles himself to the prairie, no one can miss the point: The New World would take its manners and prejudices from the old.

The conventional oppositions between the head and the heart, the city and the country, the guilty and the innocent, the past and the future, the dark and the blond, the European and the American, the sublime and the beautiful – all of which are found in *Leatherstocking* and in the thousand romances that surrounded and imitated it – set the terms by which Americans in the nineteenth and twentieth centuries have come to understand the expressive significance of nature and the environing wilderness. Anyone who wants can abandon these conventions. One can see, if one likes, the hand of God not in the woods, as Bumppo did, but in a parking lot. But if we wish to get some agreement about the expressive features to be found in our national landscape, if we hope to move from an arbitrary to a historically justified way of describing these things, then we must begin with a careful examination of the description available in literature, religion, music, and art.

As everyone knows, a single interpretation of America's cultural history – indeed, of anything in it – will not emerge easily; works of art are open to an indefinite number of interpretations. This is so, however, because we have not often recognized the need to look into our cultural history and traditions for ways to describe ourselves and to justify our decisions. After all, we are not a plantation of arts but a plantation of trades.

The question of land policy, however, forces the issue. Historians of culture should put together the best sense they have, based on literature and art, of the concepts we value and the objects in nature that express these concepts. Historians may surprise us with the consistency of our cultural inheritance.

AMERICA'S COVENANT WITH NATURE

"Appreciation of wilderness," writes Roderick Nash, "began in the cities. The literary gentleman wielding a pen, not the pioneer with his axe, made the first gestures of resistance against the strong currents of antipathy."[32] The pastoral imagery of the South combined easily with the biblical associations of the North: Arcady merged with Eden; the American was cast as Adam; and technology became the Edenic tree. Once again we stood at the dawn of civilization, as Emerson put it, "the plain old Adam, the simple genuine self against the whole world."[33] "And now," observes Adam in Hawthorne's "New Adam and Eve," "we must again try to discover what sort of world this is and why we have been sent hither."[34]

It did not require the literary gentleman wielding a pen – or the artist – to find out that the New World was not heathen, cursed, desolate, or ungodly; it was, as anyone, even the foreigner Tocqueville, could see, "the most magnificent dwelling place prepared by God for man's abode" and offered, as he said, "an immense booty to the Americans."[35] Americans did not need artists to tell them this. They needed their artists and writers to provide the litany of confession, in which Americans engaged to a ferocious extent during the nineteenth century, so that they could take hold of this immense booty without feeling too much guilt about the magnificent abode. Where a hundred years earlier there had been jeremiads, halfway covenants, and revivals, there were now novels, newspaper editorials, and revivals – and in the wake of the revivals came the courts.

"The astonishing fact about this gigantic material thrust of the early nineteenth century," as Miller says, "is how few Americans would any longer venture, aside from their boasts, to explain, let alone to justify, the expansion of civilization in any language that could remotely be called that of utility." Miller continues, "The more rapidly, the more voraciously, the primordial forests were felled, the more desperately poets and painters – and also preachers – strove to identify the personality of this republic with the virtues of pristine and untarnished, or 'romantic' Nature."[36]

Miller is right; writers, artists, and preachers not only exorcised the nation's guilt but also recognized its responsibility; for while the nation saw nature as a source of prosperity, they experienced it, following the Puritans and the Jeffersonians before them, as a symbol of virtue as well. And so they had a purpose other than economic; although the nation destroyed most of the wilderness, it would not do so frivolously. Expiation followed exploitation. The nation had second thoughts. Even while it tore down the wilderness it kept nature alive in the symbolism of religion, literature, and art.

The contribution of artists, writers, and preachers from the time of Edwards to Melville to Fitzgerald and Faulkner was to discover in nature, then, the symbols of virtue, or, to be quite strict in the matter, to find in nature the attributes of God – his strength, intelligence, integrity – exemplified. It was to confront man with these attributes as ideals, and thus it was to compel him, as Fitzgerald wrote, "into an aesthetic contemplation he neither understood nor desired, face to face for the last time in history with something commensurate with his capacity to wonder."[37]

In describing what sort of world this is, our artists, writers, and preachers have also told us why we had been sent hither: to conquer nature, surely, but to achieve also a national character that becomes it – so that our personality as a people will justify our prosperity and our prosperity will not have to justify our personality. How does this differ in any important respect from what Winthrop told his followers aboard the *Arbella*? The covenant is now with nature, no longer with nature's God, but this, in retrospect, may not be an important difference. Since nature may provide the best samples we have of the attributes of God, the terms of the covenant are the same.

The covenant we have made with nature, which is as much an obligation to use well our natural environment as to protect it – and, in any case, not to destroy it wantonly or in a wasteful manner – historically had religious rather than economic or even literary and artistic origins. Ever since Edwards in *The Nature of True Virtue*, published together with his *Dissertation* in 1755, defined true virtue as "benevolence" or "love for being in general" and distinguished it sharply from love or benevolence for the things that pertain to oneself, including beauty, family, country, and the like,[38] we have been found to recognize that our virtue as a people depends to a large extent on our benevolence toward our natural environment.

But "benevolence" may be distinguished into two kinds. The first is the benevolence of Ben Franklin, an economic analyst at heart; it is a willingness to countenance the interests of all creatures (except in the most inconvenient cases) against one's own. It asks, "Which wants have I satisfied today?" Second, there is the benevolence described by Jonathan Edwards; this benevolence respects things enough to let them be. It is not indifferent to suffering – pain should be relieved – but it would allow an animal to die, if to feed it would deprive it of its independence and strength. This kind of benevolence appreciates the character of things and allows objects their own integrity by restraining the interference of man. This is a reverence for all things on which we might base an acceptable environmental ethic: It respects nature enough to leave it alone.

This kind of benevolence does not reason in terms of benefits and costs; and it does not blush at the terms "guilt" and "responsibility." What benefits we received, for example, from slaughtering Indians and tearing down the wilderness, explain but do not justify our acts; they may even add to the severity of the crime. The point would be to recognize our responsibility not only to what survives of the past but also to what we have destroyed. The recognition of what we have done – it is guilt – is a great resource to us: It provides a more human and more satisfactory motivation than does the simple pursuit of prosperity. Why does this sound strange? It is as old as Adam. It is the oldest thought in the world.

HISTORY AND RESPONSIBILITY

Our responsibility to the wilderness is a recognition of its qualities both present and past; and it requires us to imitate these qualities. We wish to preserve them where we can and, where we cannot, to assume the character of what we have destroyed. In *Big Woods*, William Faulkner's hero, Ike McCaslin, as a twelve-year-old, goes on his first hunt and, following the directions of Sam Fathers, an Indian guide, kills a deer. Years later, McCaslin remembers:

> I walked to the buck lying still intact and still in the attitude of magnificent speed and bled it with Sam's knife and Sam

dipped his hands into the hot blood and marked my face forever while I stood trying not to tremble, humbly and with pride too though a boy of twelve could not actually have phrased it: "I slew you; my bearing must not shame your quitting life. My conduct forever afterward must become your death."³⁹

"I believe," Thoreau wrote, "that Adam in paradise was not so favorably situated on the whole as is the backwoodsman in America." Then he added, it "remains to be seen how the western Adam in the wilderness will turn out."⁴⁰ This is the point. If he remains Adam, an innocent, a backwoodsman, a cost-benefit analyst, he will have his riches, his prosperity. Like F. Scott Fitzgerald's creation Jay Gatsby, he will have no history and no responsibility, but he will be in some respects a Titan, and he will fill with excitement many otherwise empty lives. "The truth was," Fitzgerald wrote, "that Jay Gatsby of West Egg, Long Island, sprang from his Platonic conception of himself. He was a son of God . . . and he must be about his Father's business, the service of a vast, vulgar, and meretricious beauty."⁴¹ The future, one imagines, is with Gatsby, not McCaslin.

At the end of Faulkner's story, McCaslin, now eighty-one, returns to the remnant of the woods along with a few younger people on his last hunt. On the first morning, his great-nephew, Roth Edmonds, shoots two deer, both female, and therefore killed in violation of the law, and with buckshot, not with "the rifle which he had used ever since he had finally seen that a man with a steady eye and hand owed more to the bear or the buck than to shoot it with a blind handful of pellets." McCaslin, too sorrowful to be furious, manages to get the man to pick up the animals and feed them to the dogs – one doe is too old and tough for humans – and he asks Edmonds why he used a shotgun. Edmonds replies with the innocence of the frontiersman who defended to Natty Bumppo the efficiency of a cannon. It is a cost-benefit answer. "You said last night you want meat."⁴²

Herbert Croly notes that "had it not been for . . . the virgin wilderness, the United States would never have been the Land of Promise." He continues:

> If its promise is anything more than a vision of power and success, that addition must derive its value from a purpose; because in the moral world the future exists only as a workshop in which a purpose is to be realized . . . Only by a better understanding of the popular tradition, only by an analysis of its merits and difficulties can we reach a more consistent and edifying conception of the Promise of American Life.[43]

In other words: To know your policy, you must know your purpose; and to get your purpose, you have to know your history. Do not think, however, that policy characterized by efficiency is completely ahistorical. On the contrary, it is the outcome of a certain kind of history, that is, history written in a certain way. It follows from the economic approach to history – the epistemological or perhaps metaphysical view that considerations of wealth, power, comfort, and amenity must determine human action and the interpretation of events. When history is written that way, it is "scientific" in a sense. It makes everything conform to criteria, guidelines, and a priori concepts laid down in advance.

The economic approach to explanation has not been limited to historians. Frank Norris and the American Realists in their novels and paintings anticipated Charles and Mary Beard. But then the conventions of history always reflect those of fiction; the Beards owe as much to writers like Norris as they owe to Marx. George Bancroft in the 1820s took his perspective from the pastoral writing of his own day, and so on through the history of history.

If our literature at present has become psychoanalytic and associative, our historical writing has also changed. Treatises on the progress of bathtub manufacture in Rhode Island have yielded gradually to a large-scale journalism of ideas. In the work of Perry Miller, undoubtedly America's greatest historian, and in that of Henry Nash Smith, R. W. B. Lewis, Bernard Bailyn, Leo Marx, and scores of others, policymakers

144

can find a more consistent and edifying conception of the American past – and therefore the basis of a more consistent and edifying conception of the promise of American life.[44] Or they can obtain a sense of America's purpose by watching television and by seeing what is advertised in *Time*.

The choice comes down to this: not what ideals we shall serve, because we know these – freedom, integrity, justice, intelligence, power – but what we shall mean by them. And this question is answered in our symbols. The paradigm, the symbol, if you will, of freedom has been the wilderness, a deer, a bear, an eagle, a rapid river. It could be a washing machine, a coffee percolator, a breakfast food. It might then amount to leisure and efficiency. It's Gatsby's motor car: "the spontaneous fruit of an Edenic tree."[45] It's the shotgun pellets; it could be the cannon. Our symbols of freedom could close with those of law and order; they may be the penitentiary and the machine gun. And they will change our understanding of what freedom is. There is a threat here, and one that makes Winthrop's warning mild by comparison. And so the covenant analogy is complete.

"This land," says the old hunter in Faulkner's story, "No wonder the ruined woods I used to know don't cry for retribution. The very people who destroyed them will accomplish their revenge."[46]

Chapter 7

Can environmentalists be liberals?

Classical liberalism, as Brian Barry notes, comprises many ideas, but one is "certainly the idea that the state is an instrument for satisfying the wants that men happen to have rather than a means of making good men (e.g., cultivating desirable wants or dispositions in its citizens)."[1] The state, on this view, seeks to ensure that all its citizens will be able to pursue personal interests and private preferences under conditions that are convenient and equitable to all. "The state, on the liberal view," Barry summarizes, "must be capable of fulfilling the same self-effacing function as a policeman on point duty, who facilitates the motorists' getting to their several destinations without bumping into one another but does not have any power to influence those destinations."[2]

Once liberalism is defined in this way, as an individualism, it merges easily with the value premise on which many economists base the cost-benefit or efficiency criterion in public policy. "The value premise," as Kneese and Bower state it, "is that the personal wants of the individuals in the society should guide the use of resources in production, distribution, and exchange, and that these personal wants can most efficiently be met through the seeking of maximum profits by all producers."[3]

Liberal political theory, likewise, may construe values as "personal wants of the individuals in the society"; thus it may regard public values as a peculiar kind of personal desire. In that case, political theory may dismiss idealistic, impersonal, or community values as illegitimate meddling in other people's affairs, or it may treat them as a weird sort of "intangible" that deserves a surrogate market price. "What underlies this view," as Brian Barry explains, "is a rejection of any suggestion that an ideal-regarding judgement should be treated as anything other than a peculiar kind of want."[4]

Those who support a cost-benefit approach to social regulation, as we have seen, consider the welfare of the individual to be the major desideratum of public policy. They often appeal for support to individualistic concepts that are central to the institutions of a liberal society, such as private property, personal freedom, and individual choice. Environmentalists, as I have argued, would base social regulation largely on shared or public values, which may express not our wants and preferences as individuals but our identity, character, and aspirations as a community. Environmentalism may seem, then, to involve a sort of communitarianism that is inconsistent with principles traditionally associated with a liberal state.

On the one hand, environmentalists (e.g., the Greens in Germany) apparently belong to the political left. On the other hand, they cannot (as I have argued) derive their policies simply from considerations of efficiency or equality, interests or rights. Where, then, do environmentalists fit into the political spectrum? Are the policies they propose consistent with the concepts and principles on which the institutions of a liberal society are based?

TWO KINDS OF ENVIRONMENTALISM

"Conservation," Aldo Leopold wrote, "is a state of harmony between men and land."[5] Leopold supposed that natural communities possess an order, integrity, and life that command our love and admiration and which, therefore, we should seek to protect for their sake and not simply to increase our own welfare. The National Environmental Policy Act of 1969 (NEPA) echoes Leopold's concern with the ethical and aesthetic relations between man and nature. The statute seeks to encourage a "productive and enjoyable harmony between man and his environment."[6] According to one observer, "NEPA incorporates the basic principle of the Leopoldian ethic."[7]

This "ethic" contrasts with the economic approach to environmental policy advocated by early conservationists like Gifford Pinchot. "The first great fact about conservation," Pinchot wrote, "is that it stands for development."[8] He added, "Conservation demands the welfare of this generation first, and afterward the welfare of the generations to follow."[9]

The difference between the positions of Leopold and Pinchot may be summarized as follows. Both recognize that only human beings (so far as we know) have values; in other words, only human beings make judgments of the kind: "This is valuable" or "This is good." Leopold and Pinchot agree, then, that human values and only human values count in resource policy. They disagree, however, over which values are important. In that sense, they disagree about *what is valuable.*

Leopold argued that land use and environmental policy ought to respond to the love, admiration, and respect many of us feel for the natural world. Love, admiration, and respect are human values, of course, but they do not necessarily involve human welfare. Rather, these values (although they arise in human beings) may be directed to the well-being and integrity of the rest of nature. Values such as these engender a widely shared attitude of aesthetic contemplation and moral altruism, for example, toward other species, for love typically seeks benefits not for itself only but also for its object.[10] Thus, the values Leopold emphasized, although they are human values, are directed toward the good of nature, not toward Leopold's own good or the good of humanity.

Pinchot, on the other hand, apparently believed that resource policy should serve the good of humanity and therefore should attempt to maximize social welfare as this is understood in economic theory. Pinchot assumed that only human welfare – and therefore nothing else in nature – can be valued for its own sake or have intrinsic worth. On this view, the reverence and respect people feel for nature do not endow it with intrinsic value; rather, these attitudes simply represent preferences the satisfaction of which will contribute to human "satisfaction."

Thus, Leopold and Pinchot agree that only human beings have values; only humans, so far as we know, value things. Those in the tradition of Pinchot, however, assert that the only object that can have intrinsic value or worth – the only goal that can be considered an end in itself – is human welfare. This differs from the view of Leopold and his followers, who assert that nature, as an object of reverence, love, and respect, itself has a moral worth and therefore should be protected for its own sake and not simply for the "satisfactions" or "benefits" it offers human beings.

I shall be concerned in this chapter with environmentalism as a movement that follows Leopold in espousing on ethical grounds the political goal of maintaining harmony between people and their environment. This movement asserts the importance of the cultural, historical, aesthetic, and religious values I described in the preceding chapter; it attempts – at times successfully – to embody these values in legislation. This sort of environmentalism rejects the individualistic view that society is essentially an "assemblage associated by a common acknowledgment of right and community of interest."[11] Instead, it visualizes society as a nation or people, which is, in Augustine's phrase, "an assemblage of reasonable beings bound together by the objects of their love."[12]

The tradition of classical liberalism, in emphasizing the importance of the individual, may support Pinchot's view that individual welfare is what matters in policy choices. It is easy, for example, to show how Locke's conception of property might justify the idea that perfectly competitive markets define the best or most valuable uses of land. In the next chapter, I shall discuss this use of Locke's theory. Here, I need only refer to the kinship many commentators have noted between traditional statements of liberal political theory, for example, in John Locke and Adam Smith, and classical economic theory. "The classical liberal view of individuality merged easily with economic rationality, and together these two ideologies spoke against any intervention" by the government except to ensure the fair and efficient functioning of markets.[13]

Today, many liberal political theorists emphasize the importance of state neutrality among the competing goals, values, or ends individuals may seek to achieve.[14] Bruce Ackerman, for example, argues for a "Neutrality Principle" according to which no one can argue for a social arrangement by claiming "that his conception of the good is better than that asserted by any . . . of his fellow citizens."[15] Likewise, Ronald Dworkin contends that the liberal state "must be neutral on what might be called the question of the good life" and that "political decisions must be, so far as possible, independent of any particular conception of the good life, or of what gives value to life."[16]

Liberals strive to prevent "moral" majorities from imposing ethical views and religious beliefs on minorities, for example, with respect to abortion, homosexuality, and school prayer. Environmentalists, however, may be said to constitute a moral lobby, if not a moral majority, of a sort, insofar as they advocate laws that embody ethical and perhaps even religious ideals concerning the way we ought to treat our natural surroundings.[17] If the laws and policies supported by the environmental lobby are not neutral among ethical, aesthetic, and religious ideals but express a moral conception of people's appropriate relation to nature, can environmentalists be liberals? May liberals support environmental laws even when these conflict with the utilitarian and egalitarian goals we usually associate with liberalism?

TWO KINDS OF LIBERALISM

Let me begin to answer these questions by presenting a view of what liberalism is. Liberalism is the political theory that holds that many conflicting and even incommensurable conceptions of the good may be fully compatible with free, autonomous, and rational action. Liberals contend, therefore, that political and social institutions should be structured to allow free and equal individuals the widest opportunities, consistent with the like opportunities of others, to plan their own lives and to live the lives they plan.

Liberals differ in this respect from conservatives, who believe that social institutions should reward virtue and punish vice, as these are conceived within a particular cultural or religious tradition, and that these institutions therefore should not be neutral among the ways people may choose to live.[18] The conservative will favor the conception of the good life associated with the religion and culture of his or her community, for example, with respect to prayer, pornography, and sexual behavior, and he or she may wish to enforce that conception with the steel of the law.

Socialists differ from liberals because they, like conservatives, subscribe to a conception of virtue they would oblige citizens to practice. Socialists would officially discourage a hedonic or bourgeois life-style, for example, in the classless society they expect to flourish after the Marxist revolution. The socialist derives his or her conception of virtue and vice, however, from a priori arguments and philosophical theories, of the sort known to a political vanguard. In this the socialist differs greatly from the conservative, whose view of the good life is much less esoteric and rests in familiar religious and cultural traditions.[19]

Liberalism has been understood historically in terms of a distinction between two imaginary entities: civil society and the state.[20] According to this picture, individuals are joined in civil society to pursue their own interests, whatever they may be, by cooperating and, if necessary, by competing with one another within a system of rights that is fair to all. Individuals are joined as citizens in the state strictly for the purpose of enforcing those rights. The liberal state does not dictate the moral goals its citizens are to achieve; it simply referees the means they use to satisfy their own preferences.

It respects the right of each person to pursue his or her own conception of the good life as long as his or her actions do not infringe on the same right of others.

It is common nowadays to sort liberal political theories under two headings: deontological (or "Kantian") and utilitarian. These theories differ essentially in the way they construe the relationship between the *right* and the *good*. *Rightness* is a quality that attaches to actions, for example, insofar as those actions are just or meet some other ethical criterion. *Goodness* attaches primarily to the consequences of actions, for example, insofar as these consequences increase happiness, satisfy preferences, or achieve some other goal assumed to be worthwhile.

Deontological approaches to liberalism, which I shall discuss presently, hold that a legal or political decision is right insofar as it is just and fair and respects the fundamental equality of persons. For the deontological liberal the principles of justice are established independently of social interests and preferences, and "against these principles neither the intensity of feeling nor its being shared by the majority counts for anything."[21] Deontological liberals argue, therefore, that policies that advance justice, fairness, and social equality "trump" claims that may be made on behalf of the general welfare.[22]

Utilitarian political theories argue, on the contrary, that a policy or decision is right not independently of its effect on social welfare but precisely because of it. The utilitarian liberal may argue, indeed, that rights themselves are justified only because they maximize overall welfare when consistently enforced over the long run. A utilitarian may concede, then, that the rights secured by a theory of justice "trump" the claims of social welfare in specific cases. Nevertheless, the utilitarian will argue that, at a higher level of analysis, the principles of justice are themselves to be justified in relation to their consequences for social welfare.[23]

Utilitarian liberalism differs from deontological liberalism, then, primarily because it takes the right to be subservient to the good. By this I mean that utilitarians consider an action or a decision to have the moral quality of rightness to the extent that it leads to (or is derived from rules that lead to) the maximization of good consequences, conceived in terms of social welfare or utility, over the long run.

Deontological liberals may agree with a conception of the good that ties it to social welfare, wealth maximization, or utility, insofar as such a conception remains arguably neutral among the values that preferences, desires, or satisfactions express. The deontological liberal insists, however, that the rightness, fairness, or justice of decisions cannot be analyzed at any level in terms of the satisfaction of preferences or the maximization of utility. In that sense the deontological liberal takes the right to be prior to the good.

We are now in a position to understand more clearly the logic of the conflict or "trade-off," which we discussed in Chapter 3, between efficiency and equality as criteria for social choice. It is a thesis of deontological liberalism that no such trade-off makes conceptual sense. Those who take the deontological position hold that since the rights secured by justice and equality are prior to goals like preference satisfaction and efficiency, they cannot be balanced against them. As John Rawls puts this point:

> Each person possesses an inviolability founded on justice that even the welfare of society as a whole cannot override. . . . Therefore in a just society the liberties of equal citizenship are taken as settled; the rights secured by justice are not subject to political bargaining or to the calculus of social interests.[24]

Liberals argue for this lexical priority of the right over the good on various grounds. Charles Fried, for example, asserts that concepts of right and wrong "establish our basic position as freely choosing entities."[25] The norms that ensure the equality, freedom, and inviolability of persons are thus "absolute in respect to the various ends we choose to pursue."[26] The goal of social equality, because it ensures the integrity or autonomy of the person who forms preferences, must be prior to the goal of social efficiency, which concerns only the extent to which those preferences are satisfied. This is the fundamental reason that a trade-off between efficiency and equality – roughly a trade-off between preferences and the persons who have them – is conceptually not in the cards.

Earlier this century, utilitarian liberals joined conservationist movements to advocate the prudent use and wise exploitation of natural resources. As one commentator observes, conservationist movements

> were mostly concerned with making sure that natural resources and environments were used in a fashion that reflected their true worth to man. This resulted in a utilitarian conception of environments and in the adoption of means to partially preserve them – for example, cost-benefit analysis and policies of multiple use on federal lands.[27]

The environmental, or "ecology," movement that arose in the 1960s and 1970s differs from conservationism in defending a nonutilitarian conception of man's relationship to nature. Environmentalists often refer to a dictum of Aldo Leopold's to describe this relationship. "A thing is right when it tends to preserve the integrity, stability, and beauty of the biotic community. It is wrong otherwise."[28] Speaking of actions insofar as they affect the environment, commentators add that "the good of the biotic *community* is the ultimate measure of the moral value, the rightness or wrongness, of actions,"[29] and that "the effect on ecological systems is the decisive factor in the determination of the ethical quality of actions."[30]

If environmentalists take a moral position about environmental policy, as they seem to do, and if, therefore, they would not regard preference satisfaction or welfare as the desideratum of social choice, can they be liberals? To answer this question, we shall next consider deontological liberalism and its relation to environmentalism.

We shall find in the course of this discussion that the deepest questions are not those that concern the relation between liberalism and any particular ideological cause, such as en-

vironmentalism. They concern, rather, the perplexing relations among political theory, public policy, and law.

DEONTOLOGICAL LIBERALISM AND ENVIRONMENTALISM

Deontological, or "Kantian," liberalism may best be understood as a reaction to liberal political theories associated with
utilitarianism.[31] Deontological liberals typically argue that
utilitarianism fails to respect the boundaries between individuals and the fact of their separate existences; they claim
that utilitarianism replaces persons with their pleasures or
preferences, all of which it then combines, in a fungible way,
into a single social aggregate.[32] Utilitarians treat persons with
equal respect and concern, so this criticism goes, by treating
them with no respect or concern but only as locations where
pleasures may be produced and preferences may be found.[33]

The deontological approach, on the contrary, recognizes
that justice, equality, and autonomy are the irreducible conditions under which freedom is possible, and persons may
be said to choose and not merely to channel their preferences
and desires.[34] A utilitarian state, its critics further contend,
fails to treat its citizens as ends in themselves but regards
them merely as means to be dedicated to the maximization
of social welfare or utility. And thus a utilitarian government
will sacrifice the interests of some individuals unfairly in
order to confer greater benefits on others or on society as a
whole.[35]

Utilitarian liberals are by now familiar with this criticism,
and many respond that intuitions about justice and equality
are, indeed, important; therefore, a trade-off or balance must
be struck between equity and efficiency.[36] As deontological
liberals are quick to argue, however, goals like "allocatory
efficiency," "preference satisfaction," and "wealth maximization" are not to be considered as independent ideals, to
be weighed or balanced against other ideals, namely, distributional justice and equality, which unfortunately conflict
with them.[37] Rather, an efficient allocation of resources, in-

sofar as it differs from an equitable one, has no value to begin with and therefore has no moral claim against which to balance the claims of equity.[38]

This argument goes back to Kant, who considered wants, desires, and preferences to be mere "inclinations," which may be arbitrary or contingent from a moral point of view, and thus the satisfaction of which per se has no value or moral significance.[39] As John Rawls puts this point: "The satisfaction of these feelings has no value that can be put in the scales against the claims of equal liberty."[40]

Many environmentalists, agreeing with this critique of utilitarianism, have tried to make common cause with deontological liberalism. They have attempted to do this in two ways. First, environmentalists have appealed to the rights of future generations as reasons to protect wilderness and other natural areas.[41] This appeal fails, however, because it amounts to no more than the conservationist principle that we should exploit environmental resources wisely to maximize the long-run benefits nature offers humankind. Utilitarianism itself may treat present and future interests, pleasures, and preferences on an equitable basis, moreover, by insisting that cost-benefit analyses employ a social discount rate that balances the welfare of future individuals fairly with our own.[42]

Second, some environmentalists, seeking deontological arguments for preserving the natural environment, have appealed to the rights and interests of animals and other natural things. Indeed, a few scholars have explored the possibility that natural objects, like animals and trees, might have rights of the sort that give them legal standing or, failing that, interests that might be entered into the cost-benefit analyses on which social regulations may be based.[43]

These suggestions proved futile, however, in part because only individuals, that is, particular plants or animals, could possess rights or interests, but it is collections, such as species, communities, and ecosystems, that environmentalists are concerned to protect. As Joel Feinberg observes, species cannot be a proper object of moral concern in the context of a theory of rights, fairness, or justice. "A whole collection, as such, cannot have beliefs, expectations, wants or desires. ... Individual elephants can have interest, but the species elephant cannot."[44]

To protect a few members of one species, it may be necessary to seal the fate of many more of another, for example, the millions of krill eaten by a single whale. To preserve the healthy functioning and integrity of an ecosystem, it might be necessary again to let many individual creatures perish – deer, for example – that might easily be saved from starvation by human intervention or might even prosper in a managed environment.

Although the animal rights movement correctly emphasizes the important truth that man ought not to be cruel to animals and thus has insisted, quite properly, on humane conditions for pets and livestock, it is unclear how the rights or interests of animals and other natural objects can be systematically connected with the goals and values of environmentalism. Accordingly, the rights and interests of animals, although important in the domestic context, will not allow environmentalism to hitch its wagon to the star of either deontological or utilitarian liberalism.[45]

From the point of view of the environmentalist, indeed, there may be little to choose between utilitarian and deontological liberalism, for all the controversy between them. The controversy comes down to this: The utilitarian allows certain trade-offs the deontological liberal refuses to permit. As Brian Barry observes:

> On the surface, rights theories stand in opposition to utilitarianism, for rights, whatever their foundation (or lack thereof), are supposed to trump claims that might be made on behalf of the general welfare. The point here is, however, that the whole notion of rights is simply a variation on utilitarianism in that it accepts the definition of the ethical problem as conterminous with the problem of conflicting interests, and replaces the felicific calculus (in which the interests are simply added) with one which does not permit certain interests to be traded off against others.[46]

The environmentalist does not define the ethical problem as "conterminous" with the problem of conflicting interests. The environmentalist analyzes the ethical problem, insofar as it concerns our relation to the natural environment, in terms of cultural, aesthetic, and moral responsibilities or in terms of national ideology, character, and pride. This is not the same thing as asserting an interest; rather, it is to assert a conception of the good that is not based on a calculus of interest. Nor is it to affirm a right that "trumps" conceptions of the good, for it is itself a conception of the good. The trade-offs environmentalists would prohibit are not the same as those deontological liberals are concerned to prevent.

POLITICAL THEORY AS A POLICY SCIENCE

More than a century ago, Christopher Columbus Langdell, then dean of the Harvard Law School, wrote that it "was indispensable to establish at least two things: first, that law is a science; secondly, that all the available materials of the science are contained in printed books (of judicial opinions)."[47] The task of the legal scholar, according to Langdell, is to unify the data found in judicial decisions by discovering the few underlying principles by means of which these opinions may be explained and predicted and aberrant decisions may be criticized and overturned.

Now, more than a century later, the search for a "Comprehensive View" of the law continues as a primary task of legal philosophy and scholarship. Bruce Ackerman describes a "Comprehensive View" as "a relatively small number of principles describing the general abstract ideals which the legal system is understood to further."[48] Ackerman proposes that judges, in adjudicating cases brought before them, act either as "Ordinary Observers," by grounding their decisions on precedents and other institutionally based norms and expectations, or as "Scientific Policymakers," by deriving decisions from a Comprehensive View. The function of a Comprehensive View, Ackerman adds, "is to provide a set of standards by which policymakers may determine the proper legal content of legal rules and evaluate the performance of the legal system as a whole."[49]

The distinction Ackerman draws between "Ordinary Observers" and "Scientific Policymakers" parallels the distinction I have drawn between two conceptions of rationality. The Ordinary Observer would base decisions on deliberation constrained by various intellectual virtues, like openmindedness, clarity, publicity, and attention to detail. The Observer does not rely on esoteric theories or on terms of art; rather, he or she appeals to precedents and to commonplace ideas that are based on the good sense and reasonable expectations of the general public.

The Scientific Policymaker, on the contrary, construes rationality to require a Comprehensive View, replete with principles, criteria, and definitions laid down in advance. The Policymaker reaches decisions by applying these principles and criteria to data, which is to say, the circumstances of a given case. Ideally, the Policymaker should have a methodology that deduces the policy solution from the data mechanically, which is to say, simply by applying formal rules to the relevant phenomena. Apparently this was Langdell's view of how judges in an ideal legal order would behave.[50]

Bruce Ackerman, in discussing Scientific Policymaking, describes two Comprehensive Views on which social policy may be based.[51] The first makes efficiency or the maximization of wealth the criterion for social regulation; the second bases political decisions on a conception of rights, justice, and the equality of persons instead. Such criteria correspond roughly to the principles of utilitarian and deontological liberalism. These two forms of liberalism, then, would have an important characteristic in common. They each would require public officials to deduce the right answer or the correct decision by applying the standards and criteria contained in the Comprehensive View to the circumstances involved in any particular policy or legal question. They would therefore not allow citizens or their representatives, who may have their own moral views and ethical agendas, to work out policy through political deliberation.

159

Democracy, therefore, would be a problem for each of these forms of liberalism – as it would likewise be a problem for socialism or conservativism, insofar as these set out standards and criteria on which they would base policy decisions. The problem for all Scientific Policymaking is that legislatures are full of Ordinary Observers, which is to say, people who either do not understand or are perversely opposed to the true criteria, methodologies, and principles of collective choice. Accordingly, both utilitarian and deontological liberalism must explain away, reverse, or somehow account for a lot of statutes that have no apparent connection with the Comprehensive View on which public policy, if it is Scientific, must be based.

Utilitarian legal theorists are aware of the importance of public or statutory law, which since the New Deal has increasingly preempted private or common law adjudication. A "Scientific Policymaker" might square this orgy of statute making (as Grant Gilmore calls it)[52] with utilitarianism, however, in one of two ways. First, contemporary utilitarians, following in the tradition of such political scientists as Truman[53] and Bentley,[54] may regard the legislative process as a method by which competing interest groups work out compromises by bargaining for votes. Statutory bargains of this sort, to be sure, would soon become obsolete, and after a few years, a more efficient compromise might better be struck by the courts.

Second, a utilitarian may argue that Congress attempts or should attempt to judge what an efficient or a wealth-maximizing policy would be. Congress would not itself be a market, then, but it would attempt to correct the failure of markets.[55] Either way, judges could legitimately review legislation on utilitarian or cost-benefit grounds, since, on the utilitarian view, courts and legislatures would engage in essentially the same business, namely, the socially necessary task of balancing interests, allocating resources efficiently, and maximizing social wealth.

Deontological liberals also believe that the courts should

play an active role in reviewing legislation. They assert, however, that judges should enforce the principles of fairness, equality, and justice insofar as these conflict with the principles of welfare economics. Ronald Dworkin goes farther: He argues that the Bill of Rights "must be understood as appealing to moral concepts."[56] He therefore calls for a "fusion of constitutional law and moral theory."[57] To apply constitutional law, a court must "decide where moral progress lies."[58] It must be an activist court, "in the sense that it must be prepared to frame and answer questions of political morality."[59]

Dworkin means that judges should frame and answer questions of political morality not the way a utilitarian, a socialist, or a fundamentalist Christian or Muslim would but the way a philosopher schooled in the Kantian tradition, particularly one who has read *Taking Rights Seriously*, would frame and answer them. Just as utilitarian liberalism apparently makes the judicial decision an exercise in economic theorizing, so deontological liberalism may make it an exercise in moral theorizing. Is this what Langdell intended? In order to make law "scientific," would he close the law schools and instruct lawyers to study economics and philosophy instead?[60]

In an important book, *A Common Law for the Age of Statutes*,[61] Guido Calabresi observes the difficulty democratic legislatures pose to those who would have the courts base their decisions on a Comprehensive View of public policy. The problem is that a legislature may fail to adopt a Comprehensive View, it may adopt one that is incorrect, or it may express conflicting Views in different statutes. What is more, even if the legislature recognizes the efficiency criterion, social welfare, or some other acceptable "scientific" rationale, the statutes it enacts may soon become obsolete and may therefore inhibit rather than advance the purposes they are intended to serve. Accordingly, Calabresi argues that the courts should have the power to review on subconstitutional (e.g., efficiency) grounds statutes they "deem out of phase."[62] "At times this doctrine would approach granting to courts the authority to treat statutes as if they were no more and no less than part of the common law."[63]

Can environmentalists be liberals? To ask this question is to ask whether the constitutive political philosophy of liberalism is tied to a Comprehensive View and to making all policy decisions conform to "scientific" principles and criteria laid down in advance. It is to ask whether liberalism must regard every value that is not a *right* as an *interest* or a *preference* and therefore a mere feeling or inclination, utterly arbitrary and contingent from a moral point of view. If so, then we may conclude that liberalism defines every policy question as one of maximizing utility or enforcing rights. If liberalism makes these assumptions – which, perhaps, it need not – then it is plainly incompatible with environmentalism. And it appears to be incompatible with democracy as well.

DEONTOLOGY AND DEMOCRACY

The essential normative principle of democracy, Charles Fried writes, "requires that the democratic process be seized of moral questions as readily as that process is seized of political questions; the democratic citizenry has the *moral* right to seek to understand and implement moral arguments."[64] Environmentalists, peace advocates, feminists, welfare activists, veterans, and many other citizens' groups all give moral reasons why society should adopt the policies they support. A democratic society has the right to reject these policies in favor of ones that maximize utility, or it may reject policies that maximize utility in order to benefit the poor, protect the environment, reward veterans, or whatever it finds a moral reason to do. Liberal political theory cannot commit a democracy beforehand to adopt any general rule or principle that answers the moral questions that confront it; if political theory could do this, it would become autocratic and inconsistent with democracy.

Comprehensive moral views, even those associated with Kant and Mill, therefore, do not provide an appropriate foundation for liberalism as a democratic political philosophy. This is true, in part, because public agreement on these views and all they entail about the nature of the good could not be achieved without the autocratic use of state power. That is the reason, as John Rawls says, no such conception can provide the basis for political judgment in a modern democratic state.[65] Political philosophy must rely on a concept of justice that makes legitimate political judgment possible without the autocratic use of state power. It may not prescribe, then, what public choices should be; it may only describe the basic structure of social institutions in which free and equal individuals may make those choices.

If liberalism insists on a utilitarian conception of the good in social policy, it is not only inconsistent with democracy, but it undermines its own neutrality and credibility as well. Michael Sandel observes, "If the good is nothing more than the indiscriminate satisfaction of arbitrarily-given preferences regardless of worth, it is not difficult to imagine that the right . . . must outweigh it."[66] The morally diminished status of the good, Sandel argues, calls into question the status of rights, insofar as these are defined simply in opposition to it. "Given a conception of the good that is diminished in this way, the priority of the right would seem an unexceptionable claim indeed."[67] When deontological liberalism accepts a utilitarian conception of the good, it invites the question whether the right could sustain its priority over a less impoverished conception. Would the rights of individuals still "trump" legislation intended to reflect a fuller, richer, more plausible conception of human striving and achievement?

Deontological liberalism has a reply to this question that at once disengages its death grip on utilitarianism and shows it to be consistent with democracy as well. Liberalism as a political philosophy may concern itself simply with the problem John Rawls, among others, has addressed. This is the problem of structuring social institutions so that individuals and groups, likely to differ fundamentally in their moral beliefs and commitments, can nevertheless live peacefully together and secure the benefits of social cooperation. The fundamental problem for a liberal theory of justice, then, would be that of defining the basic structure of political institutions in a modern democratic state.

The rights secured by such a conception of justice do not take their status from their opposition to a utilitarian or any other particular conception of the good. Rather, respect for these rights would provide the basic structure in which free and equal individuals may join in diverse groups and communities, each with its own full, moral, and constitutive conception of the good, and still cooperate with one another to make collective decisions under arrangements that are fair to all.

We are now in a position to distinguish two different questions. We may ask, first, how liberalism would determine the basic structure of social and political institutions. Because society is likely to contain many communities, each with its own full, constitutive conception of the good, this structure must allow for their peaceful and harmonious coexistence. Such a structure will allow individuals of all persuasions to participate as free and equal citizens in the democratic process. The rights this social structure guarantees, then, must be preserved, for example, because they are constitutive of the democratic decision-making process itself. Rights that preserve the integrity of structures – the processes of a free market and of a representative legislature – must "trump" any conception of the public interest that emerges from those structures.

Second, we may ask what particular conceptions of the good liberals will advocate not in their political theory, which must be neutral among all such conceptions, but in their social policy. We may ask, in other words, about the political program rather than the political philosophy of liberalism. We know that liberals cannot deduce their program from their philosophy, for otherwise their political philosophy would fail to maintain neutrality among many incompatible and incommensurable conceptions of the good. On the other hand, the program should be close enough to the philosophy so that we can understand why it should be called "liberal."

I cannot describe in any detail here the political program of liberalism or its relation to the constitutive political theory of liberalism. In the next sections, however, I shall try to characterize this program well enough to explain, insofar as I can, its relation to the moral principles of environmentalism.

LIBERALISM AND PUBLIC POLICY

Liberalism, as I understand it, relies on two distinctions, the first of which, as I have said, divides the state from civil society. We need not interpret this distinction as drawing a sharp division, however, between rights and preferences or between the rules that govern competition and the interests that motivate it. We might better understand the distinction in relation to its provenance in the separation between secular and religious authority – *imperium* and *sacerdotium* – and the attendant difference between matters of legitimate public concern and matters to be left to the conscience of the individual.

It is essential to liberalism that the state not try to improve upon, or even influence, the intimate, personal, or religious activities of its citizens, provided that the freedom of conscience of one person does not infringe on the like freedom of another. In this respect – in matters of personal morality and private conscience – the state must strive for strict neutrality, and its decisions, insofar as possible, should be independent of any particular conception of the good life. The reason for this neutrality, incidentally, need not depend on a metaphysical thesis about the separateness and inviolability of persons. It may rely instead on the pragmatic lesson of history: When a government tries to establish a religion in a heterogeneous society, it is likely to produce civil insurrection instead.

This tells us nothing, of course, about the relation between liberalism and environmentalism. Environmental decisions, by and large, have to do with what goes on out of doors not indoors; they concern the character and quality of the public household not of the private home. Environmental policies, in general, restrict what corporations and municipalities may do with their investments and effluents – not what individuals may do with their lovers, co-worshipers, or friends. Thus the content of environmental policy rarely becomes relevant to the kind of neutrality essential to liberalism.

Accordingly, the distinction between civil society and the state, at least as I interpret it, need not prevent environmentalists from being liberals. This distinction, moreover, need not prevent liberals from endorsing even those environmental policies that are based on particular ethical, cultural, or aesthetic convictions. These convictions must not infringe on the right of every citizen to make his or her own intimate decisions, for example, with respect to choices of friends, religion, and sexual relationships. I cannot think of any environmental statute that restricts these personal choices and beliefs.

The second distinction on which an understanding of liberalism depends divides between the basic structure of institutions and the social policies that emerge from those institutions. Liberal political theory concerns only the former, that is, the basic structure of social arrangements. At this level, liberals insist on structures that are fair among the individuals who participate in them. These arrangements must be neutral among conceptions of the good and treat individuals as equals independently of their race, sex, color, preferences, principles, or beliefs. Thus, liberal theory as a Comprehensive View applies at the level of social structure, not at the level of social policy.

This is not to say that liberals, as liberals, have no view of the good society and no particular conception of what social policy should be. What I suggest is simply that liberal social policy cannot be inferred from liberal political theory. Instead, liberals endorse, for a variety of reasons, social policies that provide a lively, diverse, and hospitable environment in which people can develop their own values and exercise their talent and imagination. No theory, of course, tells liberals what kind of environment this is. Liberals depend, at the level of policy, not on a Comprehensive View about neutrality and equality but on aesthetic judgment, moral intuition, human compassion, honesty, intelligence, and common sense.

What distinguishes liberalism at the level of social policy is not the absence of a particular conception of the good society but an openness to a variety of such conceptions and a willingness to experiment with and judge each on its merits with respect to particular issues. What distinguishes liberalism at the policy level, then, is its freedom from the toils of ideology, policy science, and political philosophy. This tolerance for competing views makes liberalism particularly compatible with democratic institutions, in which individuals and groups may argue for the policies they favor and may advocate various conceptions of the good. Because liberalism is liberal in this way, it is open-minded; it attends to the views individuals express, and not simply to their rights and their wants.

ENVIRONMENTALISM, LIBERALISM, AND THE NATIONAL IDEA

The word "liberal" rarely appeared in political discussion in America before the New Deal; when it was used politically, it was usually used pejoratively, to refer to freethinking secularism and an irresponsible attitude toward time-tested ideas and traditions. Then, when Franklin Roosevelt became president, his administration preempted its critics by proudly describing itself as liberal. Writers, politicians, and the general public quickly followed in using the term "liberal" to describe the outlook and policies of the New Deal.[68]

What was essential to the outlook of the New Deal, as Samuel Beer has argued, was not just its progressive economic policy; it was also a *national idea*. Beer explains:

> The national idea is not only a view of American Federalism, but also a principle of public policy. As a principle of public policy, it is a doctrine of what is commonly called "nation-building." Its imperative is to use the power of the nation as

a whole not only to promote social improvement and individual excellence, but also to make the nation more solidary, more cohesive, more interdependent in its growing diversity; in short, to make the nation more of a nation.[69]

In order to make the nation "more of a nation," New Deal liberals supported a nationalism of shared ideals and aspirations. For New Deal liberals – one would include, for example, Hubert Humphrey – the Democratic party was the nationalistic party, the party of Hamilton not Jefferson, insofar as it opposed regionalism and the competition of special interests. Yet the common purposes New Deal Democrats sought to achieve were those of a peace-loving society and had nothing to do with the militarism that dominated the nationalistic movements in Europe.

Among the unifying goals and aspirations that New Deal Democrats emphasized, environmental protection was prominent. "When Franklin Roosevelt became President," as Stephen Fox points out, "the organized conservation movement was controlled by members of the opposition party."[70] After the New Deal, "most conservationists were democrats."[71] Under the leadership of Harold Ickes, Roosevelt's secretary of the interior, moreover, conservationism began to merge with environmentalism. "I do not happen to favor the scarring of a wonderful mountainside," Ickes said after two years in office, "just so we can say we have a skyline drive."[72]

After the New Deal, the Democratic party continued to identify itself with nationwide as opposed to special and regional interests; it became the party of a strong central government as distinct from what it once was, the party of states' rights. The goals of the Democratic party comprised progress in civil rights, entitlement programs, full employment, support of the sciences and arts, and environmental protection. These goals are consistent with an emphasis on the welfare of the individual, but they are also "nationalizing" in that they provide a cultural, economic, and political basis on which groups that had been excluded from the national community have been integrated into it. In the goals and doctrines of New Deal liberalism, as Sam Beer observes, "the national idea worked to integrate the pluralism of the twentieth century."[73]

For a more recent example of the importance of the environment in the "national idea," one may read the farewell address of President Carter. The president began this address by describing the national idea:

> Today, as people have become ever more doubtful of the ability of the Government to deal with our problems, we are increasingly drawn to single-issue groups and special interest organizations to ensure that whatever else happens, our own personal views and our own private interests are protected. This is a disturbing factor in American political life. It tends to distort our purposes, because the national interest is not always the sum of all our single or special interests. We are all Americans together, and we must not forget that the common good is our common interest and our individual responsibility.[74]

President Carter then spoke of the three issues that he thought most concerned our common good or common interest. He included "the threat of nuclear destruction, our stewardship of the physical resources of our planet, and the preeminence of the basic rights of human beings." He spoke of "the destruction of beauty, the blight of pollution" and of "our most precious possessions: the air we breathe, the water we drink, and the land which sustains us." In discussing the nuclear threat, the importance of human rights, and the protection of the environment, President Carter emphasized that these issues were not just national but international concerns. He urged the country to forgo its national regionalism to identify its common interest with that of the rest of the world.

"What the Western world has stood for – and by this I mean the terms to which it has attributed sanctity," T. S. Eliot writes, "is 'Liberalism' and 'Democracy.'"[75] Eliot observes that these concepts are neither identical nor inseparable. If we think of liberalism as a kind of individualism, then

169

we may surely think of it not only as distinct from, but also as opposed to, social integration and, therefore, environmentalism and democracy.

Yet we need not believe that liberalism must insist on a granular conception of society or an atomic conception of the person: It need not push pluralism into individualism. Rather, by balancing pluralism with integration, individuality with community, liberalism makes itself consistent with democracy. If either is to have any value for us, we must have both.

Chapter 8

Property and the value of land

For ten years now, a friend of mine has refused to shop at the mall on the outskirts of our town. If you want to go to the cinema there, she will not go with you. The county condemned a little piece of property she owned to make a highway to the mall; even though she was paid a pretty penny for her land, she still opposed the mall when it was built. She was fond of the farms and the trees it displaced. She believes that her personal consumer boycott makes an important political statement.

The rest of us are not so priggish. We recognize that one makes political statements politically; consumer choices hardly express the views one might defend as a citizen. Once the trees went down and the Montgomery Wards, Penneys, Discount Records, and the like went up, therefore, we gave in. Besides, it is easier to shop in the suburbs than downtown. So we do. But it is unlikely that the farms will reappear downtown where we used to shop.

The problem is this: Almost all of us in town share the values of my friend. We hated to see the trees cut down and the mall built. But it really is a convenient place to shop. So we follow each other through the electric fountains and the potted plastic palms. This is just what the developers predicted. And thus they justified – on our behalf – the erection of Pyramid Mall.

Twelve years ago, the mayor of our town and his council had to make a decision. What would serve the public interest?

The developers pointed out that the mall would be a terrific moneymaker. It is. They said it would contribute mightily to the tax base. It does. So the mayor had his answer, and as a result, you can buy fifteen kinds of pizza where there were once only woods and farms – and see six movies as well. This is the kind of decision that serves the public and, curiously, outrages it at the same time.

Many of us thought that the farms and trees were somehow more valuable (if less profitable) than the shoe stores and parking lots that replaced them. How can we understand this? Wonderful as open land may be, Julian Simon observes, it may have "greater value to the economy as a shopping center, which is why the mall investors could pay the farmer enough to make it worthwhile for him to sell."[1] The land may have greater value for the economy when it grows stores, restaurants, and cinemas than when it grows trees and corn. May we conclude, then, that it has greater value for the public and for the nation as well?

In this chapter, I want to discuss the following questions: To what extent is the value of land reflected in the price of property? Will markets in which consenting adults freely exchange property allocate land to its most beneficial uses? In what does the most beneficial use of a parcel of land consist? How is this use related to the ways land can be developed or exploited most profitably?

I am particularly concerned about the transformation of the American landscape into commercial blight and suburban sprawl. Commercial strips and tract developments threaten to make the entire nation not only ugly but ugly everywhere in exactly the same profitable ways. To protect amenity and other public values, the government relies on zoning and other ordinances to restrict severely the manner, however profitable, in which property may be developed. Is centralized planning of this sort justified? How can we reconcile aesthetic and other "elitist" values with property rights and free markets?

LOCKE ON PROPERTY

Let me begin with the idea that land has value primarily not *as land* but *as property*. This idea can be traced to John Locke, particularly, to Chapter V of the *Second Treatise of Government*. There, Locke writes:

> God, who hath given the World to Men in Common, hath also given them reason to make use of it to the best advantage of Life, and convenience. The Earth, and all that is therein, is given to Men for the Support and Comfort of their being. And though all the Fruits it naturally produces . . . belong to Mankind in Common, . . . yet being given for the use of Men, there must of necessity be a means *to appropriate* them some way or other before they can be of any use, or at all beneficial to any particular Man.[2]

Locke rests his argument on the observation that land has little or no value except when labor changes its character and thus, as it were, forces its favors. Locke says:

> Land which is wholly left to Nature, that hath no improvement of Pasturage, Tillage, or Planting, is called, as indeed it is, *waste*; and we shall find the benefit of it amount to little more than nothing.[3]

And, again:

> *Labour makes the far greatest part of the value* of things, we enjoy in this World: And the ground which produces the materials, is scarce to be reckoned in, as any, or at most, but a very small part of it.[4]

And, again:

> *Tis Labour . . . which puts the greatest part of Value upon Land.*[5]

Although Locke adheres to a labor theory of value, he does not deny that there are moral limitations on land ownership.

To be sure, Locke contends that land, water, and other resources are virtually worthless in their natural state. Yet he does not infer from this that a person may rightfully possess *any* unowned resource into which he "mixes" his labor. Locke restricts ownership, at least at first, to what an individual can use without waste or spoilage.[6] Second, Locke allows a rightful original claim to land only when there exists "enough and as good" for others.[7] If all, or almost all, of a resource is already owned, then an individual has arrived late: He must buy from others. And this he can do if he has *money*.

If the labor theory causes Locke to place these two moral limitations on the acquisition of property, the theory of money allows him to overcome these restrictions. As soon as people can trade for money, scarcity and spoilage no longer limit the amount of property one person can accumulate. As for the spoilage limitations, a person may possess more of a commodity than he can himself consume because he will sell the surplus before it spoils. Locke says:

> A man may fairly possess more land than he himself can use the product of, by receiving in exchange for the overplus, Gold and Silver, which may be hoarded up without injury to any one, these materials not spoiling or decaying in the hands of the possessor.[8]

The use of money, Locke argues, also permits a person to acquire resources rightfully even after they have become scarce. A person has only to buy them from someone who has a rightful title. And that a person will do, at least in theory, if he can make a more profitable, and in that sense more beneficial, use of the resource. Accordingly, Locke reasons that people may "heap up" as much land and other resources as they like, since they will either use those resources or sell the "overplus" to those who will use them in profitable and, therefore, beneficial ways.

The concept of allocatory efficiency – the idea that resources should be allocated to those who derive the greatest benefit from them – is not mentioned by Locke explicitly. Locke seems to believe, however, that people will sell property for the sake of profit – that is, they will generally accept the highest bid unless they would pay more themselves to acquire that property. Accordingly, a free-market system would generally transfer land and other resources to their most profitable, most highly valued, or most beneficial uses. Something like this idea allows Locke to transform a natural right to the property one needs into an unlimited right of acquisition.

The theory by which Locke justifies the acquisition and transfer of property relies, then, on two principles. The first asserts that an individual has a "natural" right to enjoy his property as he wishes, to sell or not to sell it, as long as he respects the same right of others similarly to enjoy their property without intrusion or invasion. The second principle holds that property rights should flow to those who are willing to pay the most for them and who will use them, in that sense, in the most valuable and beneficial ways. This second principle assumes that people will transfer rights to maximize profit. That is the reason they will not use the "overplus" they own wastefully or allow it to spoil.

To see how these two principles are likely to come into conflict, consider the example of a cement plant that locates near farmland. Since cement manufacturing produces a lot of dust, fumes, and noise, the farmers may soon find they cannot live in their houses or make their land produce crops. They may bring an action to enjoin the plant from polluting their property. How should the court respond?

According to Locke's first principle, which respects the right of individuals to be secure in their persons and their property, provided they respect the same right of others, the court should grant the injunction. The cement company would then have to reach an accommodation with the farmers to which they agree, or it would have to cease polluting and, as a possible result, cease producing cement. The com-

175

pany could not simply coerce the farmers off their land by paying them for the privilege. The farmers would have the right to refuse any offer the cement company might make.

If a court routinely awarded injunctive relief in nuisance cases of this sort, it would take property rights seriously. It would not transfer these rights from A to B without A's consent, even if B could compensate A handsomely and still emerge with a profit. The court, then, would validate only bargains that are Pareto superior, which is to say, bargains that at least one right-holder favors and none opposes. It would not approve a transfer of an entitlement without the owner's consent, even if that transfer easily met a Kaldor–Hicks or "potential" Pareto improvement test.

The sanctity and inviolability of personal freedoms and property rights, which might appeal to us (as it appeals to libertarians) for ethical reasons, may trouble us on economic grounds. The routine availability of injunctive relief in nuisance cases, after all, apparently gives those who suffer pollution a veto over the economic activities of those who cause it. This veto or injunctive power could bring the economy to a screeching halt. As Richard Posner writes: "Literal adherence to the Pareto-superiority criterion could be paralyzing."[9] Accordingly, he rejects the routine award of injunctive relief – or the insistence on the consent of all concerned – on straightforward utilitarian grounds.

In order to avoid the economic paralysis Posner mentions, we might appeal to Locke's second principle, which would allocate resources to those willing to pay the most for them, preferably with, but if necessary without, the consent of those who happen to own them. On this approach, those who want property can take it from those who have it, as long as they are willing to pay the "going" price as determined by a court or by some other competent agency of the state.

To see this, suppose that the farmers make no profit from their land: The price of wheat and soybeans is so low that they lose money. Across America, farms are facing foreclosure. From one point of view, the cement company may be

doing the farmers a favor by offering to take their land off
their hands. The land in question, we may assume, is worth
a lot more as a catchment area for pollution than as a place
to grow crops.

Noting this, the court may set the liability of the cement
company at the losses the farmers sustain, for example, because they cannot grow crops and have to move from their
homes. A court that routinely awards damages instead of
granting injunctions in nuisance cases, however, may seem
to establish a dangerous principle. The operator of the cement company, a sheepherder, a developer of a shopping
mall, or whoever wanted to take over the farmers' land might
move his pollution, sheep, or bulldozers in, litigate against
the farmers, and eventually pay the price a court determines
the property is worth. The cement company, or whoever,
could make the farmers an offer they could not refuse. It
could coerce the farmers from their property by paying a
price determined by an agency of the government.

If the court takes this second path – if it awards damages
rather than injunctive relief – it may justify its decision as
the socially efficient one. It is not efficient in the "Paretian"
sense that requires consent from all of the parties to a transaction. Rather, it is efficient in the sense that it yields a "potential" Pareto improvement by passing a Kaldor–Hicks
compensation test. I commented in earlier chapters on the
value and justification of efficiency of this sort as a criterion
of public policy. Here I wish only to emphasize that it has
little to do with free markets in which people can prevent
other people from invading or taking their property rights
without their consent.

So far, I have argued that Locke's two principles pull in
opposing directions. The first principle, which takes property
rights seriously, demands that courts provide injunctive relief in nuisance cases. This could lead to economic paralysis.
The second principle suggests that the court should award
damages in nuisance cases to transfer property rights to those
willing to pay the most for them. This result, however, would
seem more appropriate in a socialist than in a capitalist econ-

omy. It would effectively put the government in charge of setting the prices at which property changes hands.

I wish to point out the obvious: There is a commonsensical way courts avoid both these extreme consequences. This middle path involves a role for public law in private or common-law adjudication. Pollution-control statutes, zoning ordinances, and other legislated rules and regulations give legal force to public values – primarily ethical, cultural, and aesthetic concerns – that matter in nuisance cases like that between the cement company and the farmers. These public values provide the appropriate basis on which courts can choose between awarding damages and providing partial or full injunctive relief.

WHY WON'T THE FARMERS BARGAIN?

In order to explain this proposal, let me ask, first, why the farmers go to court to stop the cement company from dumping its dust, noise, and fumes on their land. Why are they unwilling to sit down with the owners of the cement company and voluntarily negotiate a deal beneficial to both sides?

Commentators who take a strongly economic approach to law assume that, absent transaction costs, those who are injured and those who injure them will always bargain to an efficient agreement; that is, they will reach an agreement that minimizes the losses and maximizes the gains possible in the situation.[10] If we make this assumption, we may then conclude that the farmers refuse to cooperate – they engage in "strategic" behavior – because they are trying to gouge the cement company. They threaten to get an injunction, in other words, to drive the hardest bargain they can. Arguably, this sort of noncooperative or "strategic" behavior could be construed as a transaction cost. A. M. Polinsky writes that although this behavior may not generate out-of-pocket costs for the farmers, it "is like other transaction costs in that it may prevent the parties from reaching an efficient agreement."[11]

In Chapter 4, we saw another example of "strategic" or noncooperative behavior. There, when economic analysts asked respondents to a survey to identify the price at which they would sell "rights" to clean air, a majority rejected "being 'bought off,' either for their own sake or for the sake of the community as a whole."[12] The analysts who ran the survey despaired of ascertaining the "true values" of respondents who entered protest and other "strategic" bids. "If this non-cooperation is not random across individuals," Rowe and Chestnut conclude, "it will bias the valuation process."[13]

In Chapter 4, I suggested a possible interpretation of what may have motivated the respondents' noncooperative response. They may have thought that the question of air quality in national parks and other Class I areas, as determined by the Clear Air Act, has been settled in public statutes that have stood up to many years of debate, deliberation, litigation, amendment, and so on. The idea that a few academics with a theory of value could ignore all this must have troubled the respondents. Levels of visibility in the nation's wilderness areas are matters of ethical and aesthetic concern embodied in legislation; they have little to do with the abstractions professors teach undergraduates in microeconomics. The respondents who entered protest bids may also have been troubled that a survey so out of touch with the moral and legal basis of environmental law received funding from a government agency.

A complex and sophisticated fabric of federal statutory law regulates pollution. Local governments also have enacted zoning, health, safety, and other ordinances that settle in advance of litigation the rights of property owners and the remedies they may look for in court. Laws and ordinances of this sort, which remain extremely popular, seek to eliminate pollution to the extent technologically and economically feasible. In this way, these statutes attempt to protect personal freedoms and rights while maintaining at the same time the viability of the economy. These statutes and ordinances may also set aspirational goals based on the public values of the society – values individuals choose through the political process.

The cement company may violate a zoning ordinance. It may not comply with the Clean Air Act, or it may be a "bad actor" in some other way. The farmers may believe that the company should respect the laws of the land – not simply the laws of profit. They may see their role as that of a private attorney general, as it were, who brings societal expectations to the attention of recalcitrant polluters. In the view of the farmers, it may be the cement company, not themselves, that is uncooperative. That is one reason they may sue for and receive injunctive relief.

Those who take an economic approach to the law of nuisance may respond to this suggestion in either of two ways. A naive response insists on the principle that individuals always bargain to an efficient result in the absence of transaction costs. Laws and ordinances that encourage people to engage in noncooperative or "strategic" behavior, then, may be construed as a sort of transaction cost. As Polinsky writes, noncooperative behavior counts as a transaction cost not necessarily because it involves expenses but because "it may prevent the parties from reaching an efficient agreement."

This response is naive, of course, because it defines as a transaction cost *anything* that keeps parties from bargaining to an efficient outcome. If "transaction costs" are defined in this way, it is hardly informative to say that absent these costs, individuals would bargain to that sort of outcome.

More sophisticated analysts concede that statutes, ordinances, and the like are legitimate factors in nuisance cases and cannot be dismissed as obstacles to bargaining. These analysts may argue, however, that relevant statutes and ordinances should be written to maximize efficiency or social wealth overall, even if they may not do so in specific cases. Property rights can be fairly absolute when the costs of voluntary transactions are low, Richard Posner writes, but "when transaction costs are prohibitive, the recognition of absolute rights is inefficient." In this situation, "alternative mechanisms to property rights must be found – such as liability rules, eminent domain, or zoning."[14]

One must look at the particular statutes and regulations that affect nuisance cases – for example, zoning ordinances in particular localities – to see to what extent they are motivated by efficiency considerations and to what extent aesthetic, cultural, ethical, environmental, and other values may be involved. This is an empirical question (one must read the ordinances to find out), which I shall not consider here. I am concerned, however, with the philosophical thesis that public law is justified, in general, in allocating property rights efficiently in problematical areas like pollution where transaction costs may be high. Later in this chapter, I shall argue that this is an incoherent thesis.

WHO SETS THE PRICE?

Throughout this book, I have argued that the goals of social regulation – clean air and water, workplace safety, public health, and the like – are ethical, not economic. They are attempts, as I have argued, to make society better, not to make the economy more efficient. Many economists, in contrast, believe that the goals of social regulation are primarily economic not ethical. On this view, these problems arise because of the failure of markets to allocate scarce resources in efficient ways.

This economic approach to social regulation rests on an analogy between land, air, and water, on the one hand, and any scarce resource, such as coal or timber, on the other. Society has just so much land, air, or water to allocate among competing uses, so the analogy goes. The job of allocation, in this approach, is best done by free, fair, and informed markets in which all participants seek to maximize profit.

Let us, for the sake of argument, accept the analogy between environmental and other scarce resources and likewise accept the idea that free and fair markets provide the best way to allocate such resources among those who compete for their use. As a first step toward the goal of letting the market decide, the government must establish and enforce property rights in these scarce resources.

What does this entail? It entails that the government must protect the freedom of the owners of these property rights to do as they please with them, as long as they respect the similar freedom of others. And it entails that the government – possibly by enforcing laws relating to assault, theft, and trespass – will try to prevent individuals from taking or usurping those rights without the consent of their owners.

For centuries, common-law courts have protected individuals from injuries of the sort typically caused by pollution. If the wastes from a person's privy percolate through his wall and into his neighbor's cellar, for example, common law will require the polluter to cease and repair the nuisance, because, as an English court found in 1705, he is "bound of common right to keep his wall so as his filth might not damnify his neighbor."[15] Similarly, one might suppose that factories are likewise bound by common right to maintain their walls, scrubbers, filters, liners, drums, or stacks so that their emissions and effluents do not damnify their neighbors. A look at current common-law practice, however, shows that this is not necessarily so.

A frequently discussed American case, *Boomer v. Atlantic Cement Company*, is typical of a host of its kind.[16] There, plaintiffs living near a cement plant sought to enjoin it "from emitting dust and raw materials" that reached their land.[17] This case is structurally similar to the one involving the percolating privy in England. In the English case, the polluters had to stop the nuisance; the neighbors received injunctive relief. Why should comity between neighbors be treated any differently in America than in England?

Richard Posner, as we have seen, suggests that property rights may be treated by the courts as absolute (i.e., successful plaintiffs will receive injunctive relief) in situations in which parties can bargain directly and the costs of bargaining are low. The bargaining costs between neighbors in England, however, are no greater than between neighbors in America. Can we infer, then, that Posner would grant injunctive relief to Mr. Boomer? Would Judge Posner allow a few dirt farmers to close down a billion-dollar cement company? Is this any way to maximize social wealth?

The trial judge in *Boomer* held that Atlantic had "created a nuisance insofar as the lands of the plantiffs [were] concerned," but refused to grant the injunction, noting the "defendant's immense investment in the Hudson River Valley, [and] its contribution to the Capital District's economy."[18] The trial court, in short, found that balancing interests rather than protecting property rights is an appropriate way to resolve nuisance cases. "This said," one commentator notes, "the scales were found to weigh more heavily in favor of the cement plant, contributor to local affluence, than in favor of the several properties inundated by the sound and stench of progress."[19]

Nuisance cases like *Boomer* present us with the fundamental question whether courts should grant injunctive relief in tort or balance interests instead. Should courts require companies like Atlantic to stop polluting (and therefore to close down) if they cannot buy Boomer's consent to suffer their pollution? Should courts instead allow the nuisance as long as it "pays its way," that is, as long as the benefits outweigh the costs?

To understand this question, it is useful to distinguish between two ways property rights may be legally protected. The courts may apply a *property rule* or a *liability rule* in protecting privately held entitlements. There is an important difference.

When the government applies a property rule, the property holder determines the price at which a particular right is exchanged. This kind of exchange happens in an actual market. When a liability rule is in force, the right changes hands at a price the government sets, whether the owner consents to it or not. In this sort of hypothetical market, consent is assumed, not actual; transfers will take place not necessarily because they are agreed upon but because they pass a cost-benefit or interest-balancing test.

If Mr. Boomer, for example, held an entitlement backed

183

by a property rule to enjoy his land free of Atlantic's pollution, the court would have given him the injunction he sought. Atlantic, then, would have to accommodate Boomer, either by not polluting his property or by paying him the amount he demanded. When an entitlement is backed by a property rule, the buyer meets the seller's price. As Guido Calabresi and A. Douglas Melamed explain: "An entitlement is protected by a property rule to the extent that someone who wishes to remove the entitlement from its holder must buy it from him in a voluntary transaction in which the value of the entitlement is agreed upon by the seller."[20]

With an entitlement protected by a liability rule, it is different. "Whenever someone may destroy the entitlement if he is willing to pay an objectively determined value for it, an entitlement is protected by a liability rule."[21] If the rightholder would rather keep his home, bodily safety, or whatever than go without it for a price, he does not have that choice in this kind of a "market." The buyer must pay not the seller's price but a price determined, for example, by an agency of the state.

Let us suppose, first, a legal framework that takes free markets and property rights seriously enough to let polluters and pollutees strike their own bargains, rather than have the government, by applying an interest-balancing or cost-benefit test, impose bargains on them. What would result?

Plaintiffs from coast to coast would refuse to take payment for damage to their person and property; they would go to court and get injunctive relief. We can infer this, first, from "the fact that the great majority of nuisance suits have been in equity, and concerned primarily with the prevention of future damage."[22] Second, environmentalists constitute a strong ideological faction in this country; it is not hard to imagine that they will prefer an injunction to selling out to a polluter at any price.[23]

Third, surveys I described in Chapter 4 suggest that a majority of Americans would refuse "being bought off to permit pollution," and thus they would set a prohibitively high compensation value for their right to be free of other people's wastes. Respondents to these surveys did not want to assume away their right to injunctive relief against polluters; they refused to accept "damages," as it were, instead of compliance with the law.

Finally, the history of urban redevelopment indicates that many people will refuse a money payment when they wish to keep their way of life instead. When a person has to purchase an entitlement, moreover, he or she is limited by his or her budget and therefore may not bid much for it. When a person is asked to sell that entitlement, however, the sky is the limit, since his or her ability to receive money vastly exceeds his or her ability to pay.[24]

These arguments lead us to conclude that if all relevant environmental attributes were fully owned by individuals and freely exchanged in competitive markets, and if these entitlements were backed by a property rule, then polluters would have either to eliminate their effluents entirely or to reduce them to levels so insignificant that they arguably would not violate personal or property rights. To say the same thing in other words: If an efficient allocation is any allocation of resources reached by free, voluntary, and informed exchanges in competitive markets, where property rights are backed by property rules, then no pollution is generally the efficient solution. This is the same outcome, roughly speaking, as that envisioned by the more aspirational of our federal pollution-control laws.

Those who take the economic approach, however, do not generally advocate a policy of protecting property rights with a property rule so that free, competitive markets can function to set the prices at which people actually consent to the harm and risk of harm pollution imposes on them. Instead, we may do better, according to this approach, to determine prices for environmental attributes, personal safety, and the like on some more "rational" or more "objective" basis. This requires us to assume in advance that people consent hypothetically or counterfactually to arrangements that transfer resources to those willing to pay the most for them. Then we may conclude that Mr. Boomer consents hypothetically to an award of damages even though he actually asks for injunctive relief.

Once we have made this assumption, we might then commission an economist to find out how much any resource is "objectively" worth, for example, by determining willingness-to-pay and willingness-to-sell (compensating) prices for it. This approach to valuation does not have to confront the possibility that individuals may refuse to sell easements to their kidneys, livers, houses, and so on. It does not have to confront the possibility that people may wish their political representatives, rather than economic analysts, to make the major decisions regarding social regulation. Respondents who refuse for these reasons to cooperate with the contingent valuation vehicle – who refuse to exchange property for a profit – would simply be noncooperative and would be excluded from the survey. Why should they have property rights?

The cost-benefit approach to the allocation of environmental resources, indeed, does not really have to consider property rights at all; economic analysis of this sort has little if any conceptual relation to free markets in which the buyer meets the seller's price. However rights are distributed – or even if there are no rights and no free markets – decisions would be deemed "efficient" if they passed a cost-benefit test.[25] Arguably, a socialist society, in which technocratic economists are in charge, could allocate its resources far more efficiently than a free market society. This is because, in a centralized or planned economy, the theory of the Economic Man may reign supreme, Kaldor–Hicks efficiency may provide a legal test, and no one need be concerned about property rules and property rights.

WHAT ARE PROPERTY RIGHTS?

So far, I have contrasted two extreme conceptions of property. According to the first conception, deriving from Locke's first principle, a person has a "natural" right to acquire and to transfer property; no one can take what a person owns

186

without his or her consent. The second conception, which derives from Locke's second principle, supposes that property rights should go to those who are willing to pay the highest price for them. Thus, anyone can acquire a property right by paying this price, which would be determined by the government, perhaps on the basis of contingent valuation and other methodologies. The owner's hypothetical consent to the transfer is assumed; actual consent is not necessary.

These two extreme positions, as one would expect, would lead to extreme consequences. If the government always protected property rights with a property rule and therefore required consent for any transfer to take place, it would have to prohibit all pollution. Libertarians correctly draw this conclusion from their conception of the inviolability of property rights. The remedy in cases like *Boomer*, as Murray Rothbard observes, is both radical and crystal clear: "The remedy is simply to enjoin anyone from injecting pollutants into the air, and thereby invading the rights of persons and property."[26] The problem with this remedy is practical: It would bring the economy to a screeching halt.[27]

On the other hand, if we assume that property holders consent hypothetically to any invasion, intrusion, or transfer that is efficient or meets a Kaldor–Hicks compensation test, we should hardly have any notion of a property *right* at all. As Coase has shown, indeed, absent transaction costs, an efficient allocation of resources is independent of the way property rights are initially distributed; from the point of view of the efficiency criterion, these rights are entirely epiphenomenal. What matters is that resources are used most profitably, and this the government can ensure by ordering the necessary transfers, once it has developed methodologies for measuring what these resources are "objectively" worth. Fortunately, academic economists are hard at work on this problem, and it won't be long before they solve the methodological and theoretical difficulties that stand in their way.

As one might expect, neither of these extreme principles by itself provides the appropriate criterion for environmental and land-use policy. There are cases in which the courts should back property rights with a property rule; there are times when they may appropriately apply an interest-balancing test. The question has to do with what other rules, norms, values, and expectations bear upon the situation. These other factors – many of which are determined by common-law practice and by legislation – ultimately determine what property rights consist of and how they are to be enforced.

First, the appellate tribunal, in reviewing *Boomer*, found that the zoning map of the area permitted the manufacture of cement. This is a relevant factor because one way a modern industrial society deals with competing uses of land (which might otherwise flood the courts with cases like *Boomer*) is to zone different parcels for different purposes, for example, industrial and residential. In 1926, the U.S. Supreme Court declared that a zoning ordinance would be constitutional if it were substantially related to "public health, safety, morals, or general welfare."[28] Later, the Court held that land-use regulations may also promote "values [which] are spiritual as well as physical, esthetic as well as monetary."[29]

It is commonly supposed that zoning ordinances constrain property rights because they make illegal certain uses of certain land. One may argue at least as reasonably, however, that zoning creates the rules and expectations that make the use of property possible. Zoning protects property rights that might otherwise come in conflict with one another, as, for example, when a cement factory locates in a residential area. Zoning alleviates or avoids these incompatibilities in advance by defining which area can be used for which purpose. This is a matter not so much of curtailing property rights as of establishing in advance of litigation what those rights are.

Second, the trial court in *Boomer*, in awarding the plaintiffs damages rather than injunctive relief, emphasized that the "company installed at great expense the most efficient devices available to prevent the discharge of dust and polluted air into the environment."[30] The appellate tribunal, upholding the lower court, also observed that the company used the "most modern and efficient devices to prevent offensive emissions and discharges."[31] These references to technology suggest that New York courts may not enjoin pollution from a properly sited plant if it is technologically up to par.

The state of the art in pollution control technology, then, may be one factor that leads courts to decide to enjoin a particular nuisance. The right to enjoy one's person and property free of pollution may be backed by a property rule (and therefore by the threat of injunction), in other words, to the extent that polluters contravene zoning or fail to employ the best technologically and economically achievable means to control their emissions. Along with zoning, technology may in this way define what one may do with what one owns and, in that way, the nature and extent of property rights.

Boomer played in the New York courts from 1967 to 1970, at the time Congress was considering major amendments to the Clean Air Act. Those who testified at congressional hearings looked over their shoulder at the *Boomer* courts and noted the role of pollution control technology in defining property rights. One witness said:

> The [*Boomer* Appeals] Court discussed the state of the art and said they could not foresee any improvement in the future. I think this is a step in the wrong direction. I think the courts and the legislators have to provide inducements to industry to see that there will be improvements in the state of technology and such inducements have to be written into the law.[32]

During the 1960s and 1970s, the public became worried that pollution could reach intolerable levels overall – worried, indeed, that it had already done so – even when industries, under threat of tort action, installed the "most efficient devices available" to control emissions. These devices, in other words, were not acceptable to the public even if they were acceptable to the courts. Accordingly, Congress wrote "technology-forcing" legislation to change the equation by which equities are balanced in common-law courts. Public law for pollution, like zoning law, then, creates rules and expectations judges use to justify decisions to award damages, to grant injunctions, or to declare against plaintiffs in tort cases. The nature and extent of property rights are defined in legal decisions of this sort.

What we can infer from this discussion is that property rights result from a congeries of statutes, ordinances, precedents, reasonable expectations, and social practices that, as a whole, need conform to no general theory and need serve no one purpose. They are to be understood in historical terms, that is, in relation to an evolving social conscience and changing public interests and attitudes. The history of nuisance and zoning law, moreover, shows that a variety of environmental and aesthetic concerns have become increasingly important in the way property rights are defined and enforced in private law and in federal courts.

LAW AND ECONOMICS

A Lockean approach in political theory takes property to be prior to government; it supposes that government serves primarily as a prophylactic on markets to make them equitable and efficient. Property rights, therefore, are supposed to exist before the legal and political decisions that come along to enforce them; these rights are more or less "given" in the nature of things and the uses people can make of them. People have a natural freedom to trade these rights as they see fit; the government functions primarily to provide security, enforce contracts, allocate "public" resources, internalize externalities, and the like. "The great and chief end therefore, of men's uniting into commonwealths, and putting themselves under government, is the preservation of their property."[33]

The fundamental problem with this view is that in a state of nature, as Spinoza tells us, each person has as much right as he or she has power, so that whatever anyone attempts and does that person attempts and does by supreme natural right. "From which it follows that the law and ordinance of nature, under which all men are born, and for the most part live, forbids nothing but what no one wishes or is able to do, and is not opposed to strifes, hatred, anger, treachery, or, in general, anything that appetite suggests."[34] Government does not come along to secure and protect rights that exist beforehand, for there is only one such right, namely, the one might makes. Government exists to replace strife, hatred, anger, and treachery with community and cooperation. It attempts to substitute the rule of law for the rule of force.

What the rule of law requires in various circumstances is a matter of opinion. One of the most important ends of government, then, is to provide open and fair political structures so that people with different opinions can avoid strife and pursue community and cooperation. The structure of a modern democratic state seems to be the best devised for this purpose, since it provides a legislative process in which people can seek to convince one another of their views of the common good without resorting to violence. If they see fit, moreover, people assembled in their legislatures may establish markets and define property rights in limited ways for particular purposes. These sorts of enforceable rights do not exist in nature prior to the formation of government.

What the rule of law means in our society is determined by a host of agencies such as legislatures, regulatory agencies, and courts, which decide, among other things, what sort of pollution control devices a cement company must use, where it may be located, how it must provide for the health and safety of its workers, and what minimum it must pay them. The relevant decisions are contained in a history of statutes, ordinances, opinions, regulations, and the like, which cut property rights from whole cloth.

Does Mr. Boomer have a right to injunctive relief, damages, or neither in a state of nature? The absurdity of the question suggests that property rights are a creature of government, which is to say, of political choice. They do not exist as pre-political rights goverments are instituted to protect.

Thus, it makes little sense to appeal to property rights, competitive markets, and the profit motive, as if these provided a more rational alternative in resource allocation to statutes, such as the Clean Air Act, that allocate environmental resources on primarily ethical rather than economic grounds. Statutes, zoning ordinances, and a panoply of other legal instruments, on the contrary, define what property rights there are, how they are to be enforced, and the conditions under which they may be exchanged. These legal instruments cannot be judged, then, against the allocation of property rights that would have no status or worth apart from them.

The idea that law attempts to allocate property rights efficiently, for example, by minimizing transaction costs, assumes the Lockean principle that the property rights are *there*, already defined, for law to help to allocate in efficient and equitable ways. This principle is incoherent. Without government in place – without a statutory framework, a legal culture, and a well-ordered society under law – there are no property rights. There are no transactions and no transaction costs. There is only strife, hatred, anger, treachery, or, in general, anything that appetite suggests.

Property rights and, therefore, allocatory efficiency, are intelligible only within a particular legal structure that already has rules that distinguish the pig from the parlor in nuisance cases, that is to say, rules that determine which activities may be permitted and which may not be permitted in various locations. These rights do not exist prior to the legal system; rather, it determines whether there are any property rights and what they are.

To understand property rights, free exchange, and markets as something other than Platonic ideals in economic theory, which is to say, to understand them at all, one has to understand the legitimate power of courts, regulatory agencies, zoning boards, and legislatures. These institutions *create* – they do not *correct* – markets.

MARKETS AND THE VALUE OF LAND

At the outset of this chapter, I quoted Julian Simon to the effect that wonderful as a parcel of land may be for growing wheat and soybeans, it may have "greater value to the economy as a shopping center, which is why the mall investors could pay the farmer enough to make it worthwhile for him to sell." This suggests that the price that land (or any other resource) might command on the free market determines or measures the value of the competing uses to which it may be put. This abstract principle or definition hardly applies, however, to the farmer and the mall.

The price of farmland since the Depression has been determined not by a freely functioning market, whatever that might mean, but by political decisions – specifically, by agricultural, fiscal, and monetary policy. During the 1970s, prices soared for farmland that qualified for price support and commodity payments; because the government paid tens of billions of dollars for farmers to refrain from producing wheat and soybeans, farmers bid up the price of land where they could refrain from producing those crops. Fiscal and monetary policy, moreover, kept the dollar reasonably weak, and farmers who did plant could compete in export markets.

Ten years later, the situation completely changed. The Reagan administration threatened to cut back on commodity payments, and it raised the value of the dollar relative to other currencies. The price of farmland, owing to these political decisions, plummeted.[35] If the price of farmland now varies with the value of anything, it does so inversely with the overseas value of the dollar.

The value of the farmers' land to the developers had a lot to do with its location. It also had to do with sewer permits, zoning variances, the cooperation of environmental groups, the status of wildlife in the area, the availability of highway funds, and the like. Political bargaining is far more important than economic bargaining in building a shopping center or buying anything bigger than a private home. To think that building a shopping center consists essentially of a private exchange of property, at free market prices, between a developer and a farmer is to remain aloof from reality. It is to live inside academic theory and to be oblivious of the world.

The developers of the shopping center in our town knew this. Before they approached the farmer who owned the land, they checked to see if they could get the necessary variances from the zoning board. Then they had to be sure the county was willing to develop the necessary highways to service the mall. My friend's land, for example, would have to be condemned (she would not sell it) to make way for the cars. The health department, the sewer commission, and twenty other city and county offices had to agree to the project. A parcel of land the developers needed lay in a soil conservation district; a federal permit, then, might be required. This could necessitate an environmental impact statement.

The developers sat down with the two major environmental groups (one a branch of the Sierra Club; the other, of the Audubon Society) that might, if they did not cooperate, hold up the project for forty years in the courts. The Sierra Club agreed not to sue, in exchange for certain amenities in the project design and a 60-acre "forever wild" zone (except for bicycle paths) between the shopping center and the lake. The Audubon Society secured an endowment for the town's well-known bird sanctuary. Because of these excellent public relations tactics, the developers got all the permits and easements they needed and the mall was speedily built.

I still hope I can lure my friend to the movies at the Pyramid Mall. The pizza is good there. Besides, the project itself was well handled: We do have the "forever wild" zone, and the bird sanctuary is endowed. Things worked out, however, not because markets functioned efficiently but because power was used responsibly. To improve land use and development, we do not need to work out methodological problems in market theory. We need better environmental statutes. And we need to understand better the responsible use of political power.

Chapter 9

Where Ickes went right;
or, Reason and rationality in
environmental law

On January 8, 1939, Irving Brant, an ardent environmentalist, went to see Secretary of the Interior Harold Ickes in an effort to protect a grove of sugar pines about to be cut near Yosemite Park. Ickes agreed to "scrape up a couple of millions" to save the trees. In his diary, he wrote:

> I am very much in favor of doing what I can to save at least part of this grove of magnificent trees. . . . To me a grove of sugar pines is even more impressive than a grove of redwoods. I like the majesty, the symmetry, and the denseness one finds in a grove of sugar pines.[1]

As head of the National Park Service, with its commitment to aesthetic preservation, Ickes emphasized the duty of the nation to protect the magnificent aspects of its natural heritage. Ickes's "nonutilitarian" attitude, particularly his refusal to regard forests simply as crops, however, brought him into conflict with the U.S. Forest Service, headed by Gifford Pinchot, which he then tried unsuccessfully to wrest from the Department of Agriculture. Ickes claimed to have learned conservationist principles from Pinchot, whom he knew briefly during the Bull Moose campaign of 1912.[2] "A quick study," one commentator says, "Ickes was soon trading insults with his old mentor Pinchot."[3]

Since the New Deal, environmental law and policy have evolved as a continuous compromise between the heirs of Ickes and the heirs of Pinchot – between those who approach the protection of public health, safety, and the environment primarily in ethical terms and those who conceive it primarily in economic terms. The first attitude is moral: It regards hazardous pollution and environmental degradation as evils society must eliminate if it is to live up to its ideals and aspirations. The second attitude is prudential or practical. It argues that the benefits of social regulation should be balanced more realistically against the costs.

Successful regulation, as I think, must draw on each of these approaches. The failure to reconcile them – the growing divergence between the two positions – threatens to stall efforts both to improve environmental quality and to minimize risks to public safety and health. My purpose in this last chapter is to propose a conceptual framework in which to reconcile ethical and economic approaches to public policy. I hope to suggest how each may contribute to the reform of environmental law and social regulation.

SAFETY FIRST

The general intent of social legislation as it now stands is easy to state: It is the protection of the safety and health of the individual and the quality of the natural environment. Most of our environmental laws, as they are now written, emphasize ethical over economic considerations, insofar as they aim to protect health, safety, and environmental quality rather than to make markets more efficient or to maximize social benefits over social costs. The legislation we have – however it may need reform – puts the health and safety of the individual and the integrity of the environment first. It attends afterward to the welfare of this generation and the prosperity of generations to come.

In section 112 of the Clean Air Act, for example, Congress requires the administrator of the Environmental Protection Agency (EPA) to list hazardous air pollutants and promulgate emission standards that provide "an ample margin of safety to protect the public health."[4] In putting safety first, the statute rejects an interest-balancing or a cost-benefit test.[5]

In the 1972 Federal Water Pollution Control Act (renamed the Clean Water Act in 1977), Congress declares as a "national goal" that "the discharge of pollutants into the navigable waters be eliminated by 1985."[6] The Resource Conservation and Recovery Act requires that standards regulating hazardous waste be based solely on the protection of public health and the environment.[7] And the Occupational Safety and Health Act directs the secretary of labor to regulate toxic materials by setting standards that most adequately ensure to the extent feasible "that no employee will suffer material impairment of health" even if the employee is regularly exposed to the hazard throughout his or her working life.[8]

Laws protecting public health, safety, and the environment resemble child labor, civil rights, and antidiscrimination statutes insofar as they identify moral evils and seek to minimize or to eliminate them. The moral evil may be that an eight-year-old "hurries" coal in a mine, that a qualified applicant is refused employment because he or she is black, that a worker dies of liver cancer because he or she has been exposed to vinyl chloride, or that a town's drinking water is contaminated because a company's underground storage tanks leak. The wrong may be an aesthetic one: A magnificent wilderness is replaced by a commercial honky-tonk, or a beautiful landscape is strip-mined with no attempt at restoration.

Public laws concerned with preventing these evils express virtues we insist on as a society – our love for our children, our responsibility for one another, our respect for human dignity, our compassion for the unfortunate, our admiration for the environment. Moral judgment is basic to these statutes; there is no deeper or better analysis of their intention than to understand the principles and ideals they express and the evils they seek to prevent.

Laws regulating pollution and protecting public health, safety, and the environment, however, also differ in important respects from other examples of moral legislation. Pollutants and the risks they cause are evils, but unlike child

197

labor and racial discrimination, they are to some extent necessary evils, because they inevitably accompany beneficial activities we are unwilling to do without. What is more, even a single instance of discrimination, voting fraud, or sexual harassment is a crime to which Americans are opposed as a society; the nation recognizes a duty to bring the blessings of justice and liberty to all its citizens. In controlling pollution and other risks, however, a conception of diminishing returns applies: As pollution levels approach zero, further reductions, as a rule, cost more to make but may be less important from a moral point of view.

We also recognize that economic, technological, and scientific factors limit what we can expect to accomplish in environmental protection – although such factors would not influence the way we apply civil rights laws, for example, against segregation. Those who administer environmental laws simply cannot exclude considerations of technical and economic feasibility from regulatory decisions under, say, the Clean Air Act – even if the Supreme Court has found claims based on these considerations to be "wholly foreign" to the spirit and letter of that statute.[9]

These differences have not been lost on the critics of safety and environmental legislation. They forcefully point out that a completely protected environment and a risk-free workplace are chimeras. We cannot entirely eliminate hazards created by people; rather, we must accept some risks that are insignificant, uncertain, or impossible to control; we must accept others because the costs of controlling them still further, *even from an ethical point of view*, are grossly disproportionate to the additional safety we may gain. To close down an electric company if it is unable, in spite of making impressive efforts, to meet air quality standards, for example, may be a Pyrrhic victory for health and safety regulation, because people need electricity as well as clean air to survive.[10] Officials have no choice but to reconcile environmental law with the law of diminishing returns.[11]

These critics also point out that in regulating environmental risks, legislation swallows the camel while straining at the gnat. We do little about the major avoidable causes of illness, injury, and death; for example, we hardly control tobacco, alcohol, or handguns, although we show great concern about – and go to great lengths to avoid – some risks that are quite small.[12] These anomalies can sometimes be explained; however, they are sometimes baffling. An uncompromising insistence on a no-risk society may contribute to tedious litigation and bureaucratic inertia – and many major hazards may go unregulated as a result.[13]

Environmentalists and others who support the language and spirit of the laws are sensitive to these criticisms. They understand regulatory agencies may make progress toward national goals only by taking account of the obstacles – including the costs – that stand in the way. Agencies should respect the intention of statutes that seek to make the air and water clean and not, necessarily, to make the economy efficient. Yet agencies should try to implement this statutory intention in realistic ways.

How may agencies best do this? How shall they take costs into account, if not by balancing them against benefits, as many economists recommend? What criteria may we use to ensure that regulations are reasonable? What concepts may we apply, if not those associated with Kaldor–Hicks efficiency or a cost-benefit test?

There are two ways one may answer. Some environmentalists contend that costs and other obstacles may legitimately affect the timetable by which we accomplish the goals set out in legislation. These environmentalists deny, however, that economic, technological, and similar realities should influence the goals themselves – for these have an ethical, not an economic, justification. In this view, technical, economic, and similar factors enter at the level at which the laws are administered. They should not, however, trammel the moral purity of the statutes.

After explaining this answer, I shall argue for a somewhat different one. I shall argue that we may make more, rather than less, progress toward a safer, more healthful, and more "natural" environment if, in setting standards and targets, we take into account the means available to achieve them. This involves considering not only health but also technical and economic feasibility in interpreting legislative mandates. If we continue to cast social and environmental policy entirely in the optative mood, the perfect society to which we aspire in theory may become a powerful enemy of the good society we can become in fact.

In this final chapter, I shall propose a conceptual framework, different from that of cost-benefit analysis, for bringing our goals into a reasonable relationship with the costs and other difficulties involved in achieving them. I shall suggest how we can take economic, technical, and other constraints seriously and, at the same time, maintain the ethical and, in that sense, the noneconomic nature of our aspirations.

BRINKSMANSHIP

During the heyday of the environmental movement, in the 1970s, legislators and administrators deliberately set pollution control goals they knew industry could not at that time achieve. The 90 percent reduction requirements for automobile emissions under the Clean Air Act, for example, represent what Congress thought necessary to protect public health, not what it believed was technologically or economically feasible.[14] Senator Robert P. Griffin described this aspect of the Clean Air Act as the "concept of brinksmanship."[15] Speaking of automobile emissions, he said: "An industry pivotal to the U.S. economy is to be required by statute to meet standards which the committee itself acknowledges cannot be met with existing technology."[16]

Administrators similarly engaged in brinksmanship in enforcing the new environmental statutes. Here, former EPA Administrator Ruckelshaus, speaking in 1974, recalls his actions during the early days of the agency:

> I started out with a fairly arbitrary stance that must have appeared to be very unreasonable, if not irrational, to a lot of people I was regulating. . . . If some of the things I said struck

them as just a little bit irrational, I thought that would stimulate them more than anything else I could do. So, I would purposely from time to time make statements that went over the edge.[17]

Some statutes explicitly set environmental goals without regard to the costs, benefits, obstacles, or means involved in achieving them. The Clean Air Act, for example, permits EPA to consider economic and technological feasibility in setting new stationary-source[18] and new automobile emissions standards.[19] Economic and technological feasibility, however, are not allowed to affect the overall goals of the act. Feasibility may "affect *when* the goals are met. The Act thus tries to use time to avoid either compromising its ideals or ignoring feasibility."[20]

What is interesting about this kind of brinksmanship, from a philosophical point of view, is its strict separation of means and ends in social regulation.[21] Brinksmanship becomes a possibility when legislation asserts categorical ends, for example, that pollution be controlled so as not to exceed levels at which the most sensitive groups are protected with an adequate margin of safety.[22] The laws may mandate goals that are unrealistic – indeed, utopian – given the technological problems, costs, and other impediments to achieving them.

Congress may deliberately set goals of this sort in order to shake things up and get progress started. In 1970, this may have been a plausible strategy; the space program had great successes, and no one was sure what else technology might do. But it may be a less plausible strategy today, when legislators have more information about the pace of technological development and about the costs of regulation.[23]

When statutes assert utopian and draconian goals, the administrative agencies nevertheless take economic and technological feasibility into account, sometimes on a case-by-case basis, in promulgating standards and rules to enforce those statutes. The agencies then set the timetable – often through a series of postponements – by which industries must comply to the uncompromising objectives of the law. Deadlines are not met, even those mandated by statute; for example, water pollution and the dumping of wastes in the ocean continue long after legislative cutoff dates have passed. The sheer unenforceability of some statutes may attract more scorn than respect to the law. The ends of legislation may then drift farther and farther from the means that are in fact employed to achieve them.

Environmentalists are well aware of the growing incongruity between the aspirational ends of legislation and the practical means agencies use to achieve them. Many environmentalists, however, resist attempts to interpret statutory provisions in ways that bring legislative mandates into line with scientific, technical, and economic realities. Environmentalists may argue that the goals of legislation involve ethical rights and duties that are not to be compromised. If agencies must take costs and other constraints into account, on this view, they should do so only insofar as these may affect the speed with which society reaches its uncompromised objectives.

Sheldon Novick expresses this thought as follows:

When concern for the individual is given first priority, therefore, costs should be weighed, but only as the limit on the speed with which goals can be attained. Any delay in reaching the goal of zero pollution means lives will be lost, yet the government cannot simply leap across the intervening ground. Once the paramount concern for the injured person is acknowledged, other considerations must be consulted. How quickly can EPA achieve that person's protection?[24]

It is not surprising that environmentalists should view pollution control and other social legislation in terms of a robust distinction between ethical ends and practical means. First, this view generally conforms with legislative history.[25] Second, it provides an apparently strong – or, at least, an initially uncompromised – legal position for corporations to reckon with. If the statutes are interpreted narrowly, for example, to insist on draconian safety standards, zero-level risks, and the like, environmental groups, moreover, can use litigation to prod agencies to be tough with polluters.

Third, environmentalists may fear what might become of pollution control legislation if minimum health and safety requirements are made explicitly sensitive to costs. It is simple enough to write laws that instruct agencies to consider "technological feasibility and economic practicality" in setting targets and standards.[26] The problem is that agencies and even the courts might interpret this vague language as permitting or even mandating cost-benefit analysis. Thus, the non-normative goal of efficiency in the allocation of resources may replace the important ethical purposes of regulation.[27]

By distinguishing sharply between ethical ends and economic and technological means, environmentalists bring home the truth that Congress sets goals that have less to do with maximizing social welfare than with honoring cultural commitments and moral obligations. Environmentalists may then emphasize the obvious difference between balancing costs and benefits, on the one hand, and pursuing ethical, cultural, or political objectives on the other. A sharp distinction between means and ends keeps the nose of the cost-benefit camel from nuzzling under the policy tent.

The principal reason that environmentalists may distinguish sharply between the ethical concerns involved in setting goals and the economic and other constraints involved in implementing them, however, may be this: To think of the legislature as engaging in principled moral deliberation and, therefore, as setting the virtual elimination of pollution as a national goal is to recognize that Congress is not restricted to simply balancing interests but may consider moral, cultural, and other values on their merits and in their own terms. By differentiating legislative and administrative activities in this way, environmentalists connect public values with public policy and make unambiguous the rights and principles upon which social and environmental regulation is ultimately based.[28]

The sharp dichotomy between moral ends and prudential or expedient means, however, has an unfortunate result. It permits greater and greater distances to develop between legislated goals and the policies promulgated to implement them.[29] As these distances becomes more and more obvious – because inadequate implementation plans are approved, deadlines are allowed to slip, violations are left unmonitored, compromising consent decrees are signed, harmful pollutants are not listed, standards are based more and more on economic grounds, scientific evidence is scanty and uncertain, and everything is held up indefinitely in litigation – the law itself, for all its aspirational language, begins to lose touch with reality. Articles appears accurately describing the "deflation,"[30] "relaxation,"[31] and "erosion"[32] of the Clean Air Act and "back-door cost-benefit analysis" in safety-first legislation.[33] Any connection between ends and means becomes harder and harder to find.[34]

Consent decrees worked out by EPA and industry reveal this general problem. These decrees typically contain two sections: the "Whereas" section, which refers to statutory requirements and the nature of the alleged violation, and the "Therefore" section, which lists steps an emitter agrees to take to reduce or control its emissions. Anyone who reads a number of these documents may come away with the impression that the steps described in the second section are so tenuously related to the goals stated in the first that the word "Therefore," traditional in these decrees, should be changed routinely to "Nevertheless." These decrees sometimes represent on a case-by-case basis, however, the best progress that can be expected at a particular time, given the difficulties of enforcing deadlines, determining compliance, and litigating agency actions.

The problem may come down to this: When the ends of legislation are determined independently of the means involved in achieving them, they recede from attention and all interest centers on specific administrative actions. As then EPA Administrator Costle remarked in 1980, "the system is so cumbersome and problematical that it almost literally forces us to focus on the trees instead of the forest."[35] George Eads goes farther. Because the way a statute is implemented may so thoroughly accommodate the economic and technological factors that are excluded from its purposes, the statute itself, according to Eads, "thus becomes what I would term a 'policy fiction,' and arguments, intense though they may be, about changing the structure of the act to reflect these accommodations become arguments, at least in part, over the value of maintaining this policy fiction."[36]

The question has to arise whether we might not make more progress toward reducing risk and cleaning up the environment if in the goals set by legislation themselves economic and related factors were taken into account. Choosing a closer point of aim might allow the regulatory arrow to fly farther in the intended direction. In the next section, I consider this question.

BUBBLES AND BANKING

During the 1960s, some economists recommended that the government set pollution standards on political grounds, much as it sets targets for inflation and unemployment, and then use an effluent tax, an auction of rights to pollute, or some such market mechanism to reach those levels.[37] They believed that even if an effluent tax might not be able to determine "optimal" levels of pollution, it could provide a cost-effective way of reaching the statutory targets.

Economists were not all in favor of this idea.[38] Critics pointed out that effluents have different effects per unit even within a region; the emissions from some industries, which may be near residential or wilderness areas or the like, may be far more obnoxious than the same discharges from other industries located farther away, for example, or in the path of different wind currents. An effluent tax, however, encourages industries that can do so most cheaply – not those that cause the most harm – to make marginal investments in controlling pollution. Thus, the tax idea, though interesting, seemed too complicated and difficult to provide a cost-effective way of making progress toward the goals set by legislation.

After 1979, discussion of market incentives for abating pollution centered on EPA's Bubble Policy, which has many of the advantages without the drawbacks of an effluent tax.[39] A "bubble" imagines an entire plant or even region to be surrounded by a hypothetical dome and, therefore, to have but one stack. The plant, under this legal fiction, may reduce emissions from some sources in compensation for emissions that would be more expensive to reduce from other sources – as long as a mandated overall reduction is achieved. Thus, in an area as small as a single plant, where emissions are not likely to have differential effects owing to location, EPA has allowed industries to treat different sources differently and thus to control pollution in cost-saving ways.

Under the 1982 Emissions Trading Policy,[40] establishing an "emission reduction credit," EPA has experimented with offsets, nets, and emissions banks. Offsets enable new factories to enter dirty-air areas as long as they contribute no more new effluents than they offset by securing reductions from existing sources. Netting allows a factory to escape some regulatory review of new technology as long as net emissions do not increase. Finally, under emissions banking, firms can store for future use or even offer for sale credits for "extra" or nonmandated reductions.

These market-based approaches to pollution control policy have been controversial, but among the many criticisms discussed in the literature, the most interesting seems to be this: The applicable pollution control statute, let us suppose, requires plants to use the best available control technology, and it bases permissible levels on what that technology can achieve. By "reducing emissions more than required by law in order to gain emission reduction credits, plants could alert control authorities to the fact that additional control was possible."[41] These authorities, acting under the statute, should then make this better technology mandatory throughout the industry, not issue plants a "credit" to offset pollution elsewhere.

In a legal regime that allows emissions "trading," even if enforcement officials discount trading credits at, let us say, 20 percent, they will at best achieve a 20 percent incremental improvement over some baseline at which trading (or off-setting, or bubbling) is supposed to begin. The 20 percent improvement over a "given" baseline may not be as good as what *might* be achieved in the absence of trading schemes; it is certainly not all that the Clean Air Act literally requires. Those who defend bubbles, offsets, and so on may reply, however, that even if trading schemes relax the draconian demands of the law, they will enhance progress toward a cleaner and safer environment.

Emission trading, in theory, has two principal advantages. First, it gives polluters incentives to make all the reductions they can at the least cost, thereby saving them, consumers, and society money. Indeed, polluters can even make money by polluting less and selling the credit to neighboring industries. Second, by building in a discount or "vigorish" to reduce total pollution by a given percentage, EPA ensures that aggregate pollution will be abated by that much over what would have been achieved had polluters simply met "best available technology" requirements then in place.

Critics point out, however, that under a trading scheme, a firm may claim credits for reductions it would have made anyway – for example, because it has installed hoods that happen to exceed requirements, or introduced a cleaner way of coking – but for reasons that have nothing to do with controlling pollution. EPA cannot assess all the motivational, economic, and technological factors behind each claim; consequently it must grant credits for many if not most of these fortuitous reductions.

The Clean Air Act, however, leaves little room either in its language or in the way the courts have interpreted it for the idea of an "extra" or a "surplus" reduction in emissions. On the contrary, the law recognizes no resting point; it requires, for example, that new sources install the "best system of emission reduction which . . . has been adequately demonstrated." This suggests that if a firm develops a new technology that does better than a previous "best," it should not be granted credit it can use to do worse than it might elsewhere. Rather, that new technology, if it works out, should become the new "best," and EPA should require it throughout the industry.

Those who defend reduction credits reply, "Beneath such arguments lies the view that more emissions reduction is always better, that each possible increment of progress must be seized because there is no 'stopping point' at which individual or cumulative reductions are truly sufficient."[42] Advocates of emission trading urge that *even if this view is correct* – that is, even if more reduction is always better – this "better" has become a formidable enemy of the good, and it is preventing agencies and industries from doing all they can to abate pollution.

It is important to see the force of this reply. Those who offer it do not assume that there is some "optimal" level of pollution at which reductions are sufficient, for example, because the benefits of further reductions would not be worth the costs. Theirs is not that kind of argument. They may, in contrast, accept the idea that pollution is an evil that should be eliminated, not an "externality" to be priced by markets. They contend, however, that the one sure way to prevent industries from improving their performance beyond minimum requirements is to convert every additional reduction into a new minimum requirement.

If we are serious about encouraging improvements, we must recognize some as supererogatory, that is, as better than good enough, at least temporarily, and acknowledge them as such. This implies that we accept some level of accomplishment as "good enough," not on cost-benefit grounds but because we need to recognize plateaus or resting points to reward and thereby to encourage further progress.

Those who offer this reply contend, moreover, that emission-trading systems will in fact provide greater reductions than would be achieved without them, even if some reductions are credited that would have happened anyway. To suppose otherwise, according to this reply, is to commit the fallacy of disparate comparison.[43] This is the fallacy one commits when one compares a fabulous torte shown, with a complicated recipe, in a gourmet magazine and a fairly good, but not great, cake actually baked and on the table.

The Clean Air Act, according to these critics, provides a fantastically complex recipe along with a beautiful picture of pollution-free air. The recipe has not worked so far to produce anything like what is shown in the picture, and there are few who think that it will. Meanwhile, the results of emission trading, while not as attractive as the cake in the illustration, are still better than any we have baked – and may hope to bake – following literally the recipe provided in the Clean Air Act.

The principal environmentalist objection to "bubbles" and related methods for controlling pollution is that they assume a level of pollution that is allowed and trade within it. A market for pollution "rights," for example, may imply that certain amounts of pollution are socially acceptable at a given time, even though further reductions are technologically and economically possible. An environmentalist may prefer conventional "command and control" techniques of regulation, since they embody the uncompromising principle that "can" implies "ought" – that polluters ought to do anything they possibly can to reduce emissions. Environmentalists may argue that industry ought to make any reductions it can, in view of the mandate of the laws.

I think that this response is mistaken. It is a commonplace of ethics that "ought" implies "can": No one has a duty to do what he or she is not able to accomplish. The converse, however, does not follow: It is not true that a person has a duty to do anything he or she can, even in a noble cause. There is some level of effort at which further attempts may become supererogatory, that is, may remain morally praiseworthy but go beyond the call of duty. I believe that environmentalists are correct in recognizing pollution as an ethical rather than primarily an economic problem. They cannot conclude from this, however, that polluters have a duty to do whatever they can to reduce their emissions.

Trading policies are most interesting, perhaps, because they highlight the line at which ethical and economic considerations meet – the line that divides what we aspire to from what we can accomplish within our means. Markets in pollution "rights," offsets, and similar schemes do not necessarily replace ethical thinking with economic thinking, moral norms with economic principles. Rather, they may help us build toward our ethical objectives from the means available to accomplish them, and this way of appraising ends and means together, to which economic theory has contributed a great deal, may be important in determining what we can do and therefore what we ought to do. At some point, we must recognize that the commitment, effort, and expense we undertake is *morally* sufficient and that further commitment goes beyond the call of duty. This does not alter the ethical nature of our commitment. It simply distinguishes it from fanaticism.

The problem of resolving the conflict between morals and markets or between ethical and economic perspectives on environmental law is essentially the problem of adjusting our ideals to reality and adjusting the ends we seek to the means available to implement them. The problem to think about – the interesting theoretical problem in that sense – lies in distingishing what duty requires from what might count as supererogatory, given the difficulties of achieving it. I shall now discuss this problem.

MEANS AND ENDS IN SOCIAL REGULATION

Cleaning up our country – like building the transcontinental railway and going to the moon – is a national effort. It is a project that involves citizens as citizens, not simply as individuals. The environment concerns us collectively, and in protecting it we protect part of our history, part of our identity, and part of our idea of ourselves as a nation.

There is, however, an important difference between social regulation and many other aspirational activities, such as landing a person on the moon. Americans had a rough idea of what would be necessary to beat the Russians to the moon. The costs were reasonable; the technology available; the political forces, in place. When the United States declared a "war against pollution" in the 1960s, however, no one knew exactly what would be required to win. It was a moral crusade in which partisans were not always aware of the political, technological, and economic forces they were up against.

Twenty years ago, it was impossible to calibrate the goals of social regulation with the obstacles that stood in the way of achieving them. When Congress passed the Clean Air Act, it probably knew that no one could determine "safe" threshold levels for many dangerous pollutants.[44] It required an "ample margin of safety" anyway, leaving it to others to make that language operational. Likewise, Congress wrote laws forcing the development of pollution control technology. It had little idea whether technology, when forced, could bring pollution within hoped-for "safe" thresholds. The mood then was to experiment and see how far the environmental "revolution" would extend.

Regulators soon confronted an array of problems in implementing the goals Congress had set. These difficulties include pervasive scientific uncertainty concerning the health effects of many pollutants, especially those acting synergistically; the prohibitive costs involved in monitoring; the limited ability of technology to control, measure, trace, and otherwise deal with emissions; and the expensive and time-consuming legal hurdles involved in enforcing the law. These difficulties and many others intrude between the legislative cup and the policy lip.

There appear to be three ways to bring the cup and the lip together, that is, three ways to adjust legislated ends to the means available to accomplish them. First, we may interpret the laws narrowly to restrict pollution to thresholds that provide an ample margin of safety even for the most sensitive groups. If this entails a no-risk society, so be it;

industry will have to comply. To be sure, quick compliance may bring the economy to a halt; accordingly, the agencies may stretch out the timetable for eliminating effluents. Environmental groups, however, could control the pace of progress through litigation. They could contend, successfully, that statutes like the Clean Air Act insist on absolute purity, without regard to technical constraints or economic costs.

Although this approach might look good to environmental organizations at first, it would not serve their interests in the long run. For one thing, it would put them in an adversarial role with respect to EPA and other agencies, which must also respond to industry and political pressures. If environmental lobbies alienate the bureaucrats, they may achieve nothing except after long and expensive legal battles. EPA could retaliate, moreover, by "going by the book," that is, by insisting that all polluting activities stop forthwith. This would force Congress to rewrite the laws, possibly substituting economic goals for ethical and environmental ones.[45]

Second, the agencies themselves could substitute economic goals, for example, allocatory efficiency, for ethical and environmental ones by attempting to "price" the benefits of environmental quality, health, and safety and "balance" these against the costs. If the agencies in this way made efficiency in the allocation of resources their target, however, they would come to a curious result. It is likely that an honest cost-benefit account – one that established a "value" for life, for example, in terms of unregulated markets – would show that we have far less pollution than is economically optimal; indeed, an "unfudged" analysis might establish that pre–1970 levels were already too strict to be cost-beneficial.

To interpret the Clean Air Act, therefore, as permitting a cost-benefit test is to suggest at least the possibility that the statute may "really" call for more rather than less air pollution. Since this is not even a possibility, we cannot admit this interpretation.

Third, we might permit an agency to take technological and economic factors into account, on a case-by-case basis, as long as it acts in good faith to make progress toward reducing and, we hope, eventually eliminating damage to the environment and risks to human safety and health. Although there is no methodology, of course, for deciding what is reasonable in this regard, this approach may encourage cooperation between the agencies, industry, and consumer and environmental groups in understanding the technical, scientific, and economic details that in fact determine the outcomes of regulatory decisions. The ends of regulation, then, would remain ethically motivated, but they would also conform to the means available to achieve them.

In a series of important decisions, the courts have interpreted social legislation in a way that encourages this third approach.[46] In *International Harvester Co. v. Ruckelshaus*,[47] for example, Judge Harold Leventhal remanded to EPA stringent emissions standards because the agency had not adequately assessed the risks the emissions imposed, the feasibility and practicality of the technology it required, or the costs the automobile industry would have to pay to comply. The standards appeared arbitrary and capricious, then, not because they were inconsistent with the language of the Clean Air Act but because they were not justified by an appropriate analysis of scientific and technological considerations. Judge Leventhal wrote, "The court was convinced by its examination that EPA had not established the reliability of the methodological approach on which it relied."[48]

In complementary cases, the District of Columbia Circuit Court of Appeals interpreted a relevant section of the Clean Air Act as permitting EPA to consider costs but not to impose a cost-benefit test.[49] The court instructed the agency to adopt the system "which can reasonably be expected to serve the interests of pollution control without becoming exorbitantly costly."[50] One commentator notes that although EPA can consider costs under this section of the Clean Air Act, this consideration is *"not* of the cost-benefit type."[51]

In the *Benzene* decision,[52] moreover, a plurality of justices found that "safe" does not entail "risk free." Justice Stevens argued that OSHA could not regulate a chemical simply because it posed *some* risk; the agency would also have to show

the risk was "significant" and thus reasonably warranted
regulation. The Supreme Court quickly supplemented this
decision with one involving levels of cotton dust that did
impose significant risks to workers in textile plants.[53] The
Court found that when Congress intends cost-benefits analysis to be used, it explicitly says so. Because the OSHA statute
mandates safety, not efficiency, it explicitly prohibits a cost-
benefit test.

Finally, in 1986, a tribunal for the D.C. Circuit reviewed a
decision by EPA setting a standard for vinyl chloride emissions at levels less strict than industry might achieve at great
effort and expense.[54] In approving the action, Judge Robert
Bork, writing for the majority, found that when EPA cannot
determine a "safe" threshold for a pollutant, it may take not
only health but also technological and economic factors into
account to establish emission standards industry can achieve
without paying costs "grossly disproportionate" to the
amount of safety thereby attained.

In a ringing dissent, Judge Wright argued that EPA had
not – as the majority claimed – "evaluated economic and
technological feasibility in this case only as a last resort, when
faced with chronic scientific uncertainty as to the extent of
harmful effects of a particular hazardous pollutant."[55] Instead, the agency had engaged in cost-benefit analysis on
the slim excuse that the other extreme – the total elimination
of risk – would destroy the industry. Judge Wright properly
reminded EPA that the Clean Air Act, like OSHA and other
statutes, "is . . . devoid of ambiguity on the permissibility of
cost-benefit analysis."[56] Wright noted that neither the courts
nor agencies have the "power to apply 'laws' of efficiency
and cost-benefit optimality to legislative schemes if the structure and history of those schemes indicate that Congress
intended otherwise."[57]

The D.C. Circuit Court reheard the vinyl chloride case in
the spring of 1987 and, in a unanimous opinion issued the
following summer, overturned the tribunal's decision and
disapproved EPA's action. Judge Bork, who wrote this opinion as well, reversed his position and agreed with Judge

Wright that "the Administrator cannot consider cost and technological feasibility in determining what is 'safe.'"[58] Bork, who at that time was awaiting congressional hearings on his nomination to the Supreme Court, found deference to the will of Congress, rather than to the "laws" of efficiency, to be more important than he had originally supposed, and he chided EPA for using economic and technological considerations in defining emission levels that are "safe."[59] When the risk is uncertain, for example, when scientific data are utterly inadequate, EPA might rely on considerations other than safety in setting standards; however, these economic and technical considerations cannot replace, but can only help the agency achieve, the safety goals mandated by Congress. Bork sensibly argued that EPA may "set the emission standard at the lowest level that is technologically feasible" – in other words, it may consider the means, including the costs of regulation – only when it also determines that the standard will protect public safety and health.[60]

These cases and many others suggest that the courts wish to steer a middle course between the extremes of "no risk" regulation, on the one hand, and cost-benefit analysis, on the other. They may best do this, as William Pederson suggests, if they "combine a view that environmental protection is of great – even crucial – importance . . . with a skepticism about the means and methods often chosen."[61] The important thing is for administrative actions to bear a reasonable relationship with statutory values in the context of all the "realities" that make the assessment and control of risk so difficult. There is no general theoretical path to achieve this kind of relationship; it depends on the minute particulars of each case.

Agencies do not depart from ethical deliberation when they calibrate the ends they seek to the means and conditions by which they may attain them. For what is deliberation, after all, except the appraisal of ends in relation to the means that will lead to the outcomes actually produced? "There can be no control of the operation of foreseeing consequences (and hence of forming ends-in-view) save in terms of the conditions that operate as the causal conditions of their attainment."[62]

To will the end, we must also will the means, and therefore we should make some effort to assess goals in relation to the obstacles, constraints, and costs that make them difficult to achieve. The difference between reasonable and unreasonable purposes and goals, as John Dewey writes, is precisely the difference between those formed without "consideration of the conditions that will actually decide the outcome and those which are formed on the basis of existing liabilities and potential resources."[63]

The problem with values conceived of as intrinsically right or good is that, like all other interests and desires, they are subject to failure and defeat. Saying "We shall not lose" will not alter the fact that we may very well lose; in fact, we often do lose in the battle to abate pollution. This may have nothing to do with the moral righteousness of the cause to which we are committed. We lose because we fail to adjust our goals to the means and resources available to attain them.

In the environmental arena, the means or resources available to us are largely technical. They may include landfill liners, scrubbers, hoods, filters, and hundreds of other devices for controlling and disposing of effluents and emissions. All these technologies are prone to failure, some more catastrophically than others; all must be maintained; some are difficult to operate; others may be easy to operate but are unlikely to meet specifications. What is more, some pollutants are more dangerous or offensive than others; they act synergistically in ways hard, if not impossible, to predict; some may produce reversible, others irreversible, environmental damage. The organization of all these details into a practicable policy, which is what agency bureaucrats do and often do very well, is the only effective means by which we may make progress toward our aspirations. One may defeat this kind of progress, however, by insisting on perfection.

Economic analysis has much to contribute not only in discovering the least costly methods to accomplish social goals but also in determining what these goals should be. This is because economic analysis may appear within ethical deliberation to adjust ends to means and thus help us define what we ought to do in relation to what we can achieve. Moreover, economic theory proposes useful techniques, such as emission-trading schemes, which may lead us to accomplish more than we otherwise could and thus help define our purposes in terms of the means we may effectively employ to achieve them.

In the past, economists have too often proposed that society pursue efficiency in the allocation of resources rather than the ethical and cultural goals stated in public law. In previous chapters, I argued that a more efficient allocation of resources, all else being equal, is no better than a less efficient one; efficiency has no normative or ethical worth. By insisting on this worthless concept and by pursuing the many methodological and theoretical questions its application would raise, these analysts have limited the contribution economic theory might have made to policy analysis and social regulation.

Many other economists, on the other hand, have shown regulators not only how to achieve legislated goals more effectively but also how to adjust these goals to the obstacles that might otherwise reduce statutes to policy fictions. The role of good policy analysis and economic assessment is not to determine the goals of society in advance on a priori grounds on the basis of an academic theory. It is rather to inform the political process by which society chooses its own objectives. It may do this by appraising the goals of public policy in relation to the means, for example, the costs, actions, and materials, that society must employ to accomplish them.

By focusing societal attention on means together with ends, economic and policy analysts can help to turn brinksmanship into statesmanship. Economic analysis may help us define the line at which obligatory effort shades into supererogation.

SUPEREROGATION

Our efforts to achieve a cleaner, safer, more beautiful environment are constrained, of course, by economic costs; "ought" implies "can." What we "can" do – or can afford to do – is a relative matter, however, depending in part on the importance of the ethical duty or principle at stake. How important, morally speaking, are duties and principles involved in reducing risks and protecting the environment? How much must we do – how far do we have to go in controlling pollution – to remain consistent with those duties and principles?

This question arises in familiar decisions we make both as individuals and as a society. How much shall we give to charity, say, to relieve hunger in Africa? Economic factors are important. We need to know how much we can afford; one may be expected to give only "until it hurts." We might try to assess our "fair share," given the ability of others also to help. And it is useful to know which organizations direct contributions most effectively in providing famine relief.

Now, someone might argue that since charity is a virtue, we have a duty to give all we have to those less fortunate than ourselves. Such an argument would be preposterous. There are some duties that are absolute: for example, the duty not to murder or enslave others. We must respect the duty not to murder even if we forego a fortune as a result. Yet we are not required to observe the duty of charity to the point of self-impoverishment.

The distinction in ethical theory involved here, which is a very old one, is usually drawn between "perfect" and "imperfect" duties.[64] A perfect duty, such as the duty not to take an innocent life, does not admit of exceptions in order to accommodate wants, interests, or inclinations. An imperfect duty, such as the duty to rescue a stranger, on the contrary, may be overridden by conditions or constraints, for example, one's own ability to swim. Kant correctly points out that imperfect duties, such as acts of benevolence, are duties of virtue rather than of moral obligation or requirement. Actions in accordance with these duties are meritorious; actions not in accord with them are not impermissible even though they lack moral worth.[65]

Now, the question arises whether the duties expressed in our environmental and social legislation involve perfect or imperfect obligations. Do they state goals we must achieve regardless of costs? Do they also involve "imperfect duties" and therefore allow us to consider some progress at some times as supererogatory?

Plainly, polluters have a perfect obligation not to kill; we are horrified to hear reports that a corporation negligently or even willfully vented toxic substances that killed identifiable individuals. When deaths due to vinyl chloride were discovered, for example, EPA moved swiftly to reduce exposure to that pollutant. Where identifiable deaths can be attributed to particular exposures, society must honor the right of innocent individuals not to be killed. The government has an obligation to prohibit this sort of serious incident through statutory and tort law.

With respect to background hazards and risks, however, it is different. No one has a right to a completely risk-free environment or to be protected from *de minimis* hazards even when they are caused by man. The highways, for example, can hardly be perfectly safe, and although each of us has a perfect obligation not to drive recklessly, we are not bound, therefore, to drive at ten miles per hour, even if that would reduce traffic fatalities by many thousands. No, there is a point at which a duty of obligation shades into a duty of virtue; at that point, providing safety may remain morally praiseworthy without being an ethical requirement.

A perfectly unpolluted environment, of course, is meritorious from a moral point of view, and a society acts virtuously in attempting to eliminate pollution, just as it acts virtuously in attempting to eliminate poverty. Yet a society that stops short of committing enormous resources to efforts of this kind does not necessarily violate moral obligations. A virtuous society, of course, makes it a policy to go the "extra mile" to eliminate the causes of poverty, pollution, and other evils. But we are permitted, at some point, to take economic costs and technical feasibility into account.

Thus, with respect to standards for vinyl chloride emissions, for example, EPA has a perfect duty to protect individuals (e.g., those living near vinyl chloride plants) from significant risks. This is a duty, in part, to prevent identifiable injuries and deaths that would otherwise be punished in criminal law or compensated in tort. On the other hand, where the risks are slight and diffuse and the costs and other difficulties of controlling them are great, EPA can argue from an ethical point of view that further controls are supererogatory and that it has no moral duty to require them. The agency need not appeal to non-normative notions of efficiency to conclude that the costs of a very strict standard are grossly disproportionate to the additional safety that such a standard provides. It may argue instead that a reduction below reasonably safe levels counts as supererogatory given the technical, economic, and scientific factors bearing on a particular case.

The problem for social regulation today, as I have argued, is not to determine what is efficient from an economic point of view; it is to weigh ends and means together in order to set targets and standards that are reasonable in relation to the efforts necessary to achieve them. It is to make this appraisal, insofar as possible, to begin with, rather than to make compromises afterward, at the level of enforcement. We may do more, in this way, to achieve goals appropriate to a caring, compassionate nation that respects its natural environment.

REGULATION AND RATIONALITY

When Harold Ickes committed $2 million from the public treasury to save a large grove of sugar pines from being logged, he made a rational decision. His decision was "rational" in the sense that it was reasonable; that is, it was based on good reasons. In his diary, Ickes explains what some of these reasons were: for example, the beauty, age, and stature of the pines, their expressive qualities, their proximity to a national park, their relative rarity, the importance such environmentalists as Irving Brant ascribed to them. Later, Ickes would balance values such as these with the importance of resources for the war effort, but this was not an issue in 1937.[66]

Ickes also took the costs of preservation seriously; he therefore decided to purchase only half the trees and allow the other half to be cut. In "halving the difference," literally, between the environmentalists and the lumber companies, Ickes genially pointed out that $2 million was all he could "scrape up" from the Interior Department budget.

Although Ickes called himself a "curmudgeon,"[67] he showed a tolerance for, and an interest in, ideas; a respect for the opinions of others; a willingness to consider alternatives; and a preference for using the powers of persuasion rather than the powers of office. He recognized the possibility that he could be wrong. Ickes, in short, was "rational" in the sense that he was civilized, open-minded, and intelligent. He was loyal to the community of political leaders in which he included even his opponents, and his loyalty, as well as his self-acknowledged bulldog image, allowed him to do much good whether in reforming the government of Chicago or in preserving natural heritage.

Those who involve themselves in the arts and humanities pursue an ideal of rationality that is defined by these same virtues, that is, tolerance for new ideas, respect for opposing views and opinions, an insistence on noncoercive means of persuasion, and so on. In any of the humanities – in the writing of history, for example – debate goes on publicly in the journals, and one's views are or should be judged on the quality of the arguments and evidence one adduces for them. One seeks the agreement of colleagues, and even if some will not be convinced (one might worry if *everyone* agreed and there were no dissenting voices), knowledge advances and with it the good of the community to which one belongs.

What seems to be emerging from the philosophical literature, moreover, is the idea that the natural sciences, like the humanities, rely on a conception of rationality that is akin to concepts like "reasonable," "civilized," and "intelligent," rather than "methodical" or "deduced from a priori principles laid down in advance." According to this view, scientists have achieved great advances and paradigm shifts because they have been open-minded, flexible, and unafraid to look at the world in new ways. On this view, scientific advance does not depend on methodologies or on criteria for success determined on the basis of metaphysical truths or epistemological foundations.[68]

In the Introduction to this book, I quoted a pragmatist philosopher, Richard Rorty, to the effect that scientists solve problems rationally, that is, in intelligent and perceptive ways, without depending on methodologies, criteria, or first principles laid down in advance. According to Rorty, pragmatists think

> . . . that the habits of relying on persuasion rather than force, of respect for the opinions of colleagues, of curiosity and eagerness for new data and ideas, are the *only* virtues scientists *qua* scientists have. They do not think that there is an intellectual virtue called "rationality" over and above these moral virtues.[69]

Throughout this book, I have contrasted this ethical notion of rationality with a very different conception, which may be found in any primer of policy science, introduction to cost-benefit analysis, or study of applied welfare economics.[70] If public policy is to be "rational" in this second sense, it must result from the application of a methodology or satisfy criteria, preferably quantified, laid down in advance. To be "rational" in this second sense, one would not rely on virtues like open-mindedness and a willingness to consider ideas on their merits. Rather, policymaking would depend on the use of rules, algorithms, and other means to quantify exogenous variables (e.g., "preferences") and then to optimize, maximize, or otherwise proceed along some mathematical dimension or parameter within the decision matrix.

If Ickes were alive today, he could have applied this second idea of rational decision making to the question of protecting the sugar pines. He might then use a methodology to take Irving Brant's views into account, not, of course, by listening to those views and weighing them sympathetically (for which there is no method) but by asking how much environmentalists like Brant are willing to pay for the grove to be preserved. If Congress had given wilderness status to the pines, Ickes might have asked for Brant's willingness-to-accept or willingness-to-sell price, although the environmentalist might not cooperate in this hypothetical bargaining. This "contingent valuation" approach, as I argued in earlier chapters, is rational only in the sense that it is methodical and follows from theoretical principles popular in academic circles at this time. I imagine someone like Ickes would not use it, however, because it is not "rational" in the sense of "civilized," "reasonable," or "sane."

I believe that social regulation must involve choosing between these two conceptions of rationalty, that is, between method and morality. I have argued that we can base regulatory policies on moral, aesthetic, and other substantive concerns and judgments – that we do not have to quantify our political values and cultural identity as if these were exogenous variables that must be brought into contingent markets. For those who insist, nevertheless, on using "neutral" and "rational" methodologies to make policy scientific, I offer this advice from John Barth's *End of the Road*.

> If the alternatives are side by side, choose the one on the left; if they are consecutive in time, choose the earlier. If neither of these applies, choose the alternative whose name begins with the earlier letter of the alphabet. These are the principles of Sinistrality, Antecedence, and Alphabetical Priority – there are others and they're arbitrary but useful.[71]

In this book, I have given my reasons for believing that the principles of efficiency, welfare maximization, and cost-benefit balancing, insofar as they are proposed as methods to be applied in regulatory policymaking, are as arbitrary as the "principles of Sinistrality, Antecedence, and Alphabetical Priority." I have argued that, all else being equal, an efficient allocation is no better than a less efficient one – that the term "better" would have no plausible meaning in this context. I have also suggested that preoccupation with theoretical and other problems in measuring efficiency, "pricing" benefits, and the like prevents economists from making as strong a contribution as they might to the implementation of social and environmental legislation.

The laws require Americans to make progress toward normative goals to which they aspire as a nation, such as a safer society and a cleaner environment, not to allocate resources efficiently or maximize consumer surpluses by balancing benefits and costs. These laws express Americans' perception of themselves as a nation, called upon, to an extent, to appreciate and preserve a fabulous natural heritage and to pass it on reasonably undisturbed to future generations. This is not a question of what Americans *want*; it is not just a question of what they *believe in*; it is a statement of what they *are*. America is not a nation of consumers; its people are not bundles of preferences in search of a perfect market. Rather, they are citizens who contribute to, and insist on, a more edifying and a more democratic conception of their commitment and their nation's destiny.

After spending a day in Yosemite Park, Ickes wrote in his diary, "To contemplate nature, magnificently garbed as it is in this country, is to restore peace to the mind, even if it does make one realize how small and petty and futile the human individual is."[72] However small, petty, and futile we may feel ourselves to be, we can pursue important purposes together, and we can achieve goals (as Ickes and other social reformers and environmentalists have done) that will be recognized by history. But to speak of shared aspirations and common purposes – rather than of individual wants and utilities – may be to speak as with a voice from the wilderness. And when wilderness disappears, voices from it disappear as well.

Notes

1. INTRODUCTION

1 *Munn v. Illinois,* 94 U.S. 113, 126 (1877). In *Nebba v. New York,* 291 U.S. 502 (1934), the Supreme Court went further and held (at 534) "that if one embarks in a business which the public demands shall be regulated, he must know that regulation will ensue."

2 For further analysis of the distinction between economic and social regulation, see George Eads and Michael Fix, *Relief or Reform?: Reagan's Regulatory Dilemma* (Washington, D.C.: The Urban Institute, 1984), pp. 12–15. See also Murray Weidenbaum, *Business, Government, and the Public,* 2d ed. (Englewood Cliffs, N.J.: Prentice-Hall, 1981), chap. 2.

3 *American Textile Manufacturers v. Donovan* 452 U.S. 490 (1981). In this case, the Supreme Court found that the OSHA statute authorized the agency to set standards to make working conditions significantly safer even if those standards may fail to maximize overall social efficiency or to meet a cost-benefit test.

4 See, for example, Arthur M. Okun, *Equality and Efficiency: The Big Tradeoff* (Washington, D.C.: Brookings Institution, 1975).

5 Richard Musgrave argues that three goals justify regulation: the government may redistribute wealth, even out business cycles, and correct market failures in order to increase efficiency in the allocation of resources. Richard A. Musgrave, *The Theory of Public Finance* (New York: McGraw-Hill, 1959), p. 5.

6 Dr. Kneese provides a fuller account of the arguments I ascribe to him in "Environmental Policy," in Peter Duignan and Alvin Rabushka, eds., *The United States in the 1980s* (Stanford, Calif.: Hoover Institution Press, 1980), pp. 253–84.

7 Prepared statement of Dr. Allen V. Kneese, *The Environmental Decade: Hearings Before a Subcommittee of the Committee on Government Operations*, House of Representatives, 91st Cong., 2d sess., 1970, p. 191.

8 Ibid., p. 190.

9 Ibid., p. 187. On page 190, Kneese says "poverty of understanding."

10 Ibid., p. 191.

11 Ibid., p. 192.

12 For a useful bibliography, see Anthony Fisher and Frederick Peterson, "The Environment in Economics: A Survey," *Journal of Economic Literature* 14(1976): 1–33.

13 Eads and Fix, *Relief or Reform?*, p. 14.

14 An enormous theoretical literature elaborates on issues involved in the "prisoners' dilemma" and other paradoxes of rationality. For a useful introduction, see Thomas C. Schelling, *Micromotives and Macrobehavior* (New York: Norton, 1978). Much of the theory has been applied in the literature of environmental ethics. I do not comment on these issues in this book. I attempt to explore a different but, I think, equally important conflict between citizen- and consumer preference maps that vie within the same rational individual.

15 Gary Watson, "Free Agency," *Journal of Philosophy* 72(1975): 205–20.

16 Ibid., p. 215. Watson argues plausibly that a person is free insofar as his valuational and motivational systems coincide: "The free agent has the capacity to translate his values into action; his actions flow from his evaluative system" (p. 216).

17 Cass Sunstein, "Interest Groups in American Public Law," *Stanford Law Review* 38(1985): 29–87; quotation on p. 31.

18 Ibid., p. 32.

19 See Jean-Jacques Rousseau, *The Social Contract and Discourses*, trans. G. D. H. Cole (New York: E. P. Dutton, 1927), Book 4, chap. 2. ("When in the popular assembly a law is proposed, what the people is asked is not exactly whether it approves or rejects the proposal, but whether it is in conformity with the general will, which is their will. Each man, in giving his vote, states his opinion on that point; and the general will is found by counting votes.")

20 Cass Sunstein, "Deregulation and the Courts," *Journal of Policy Analysis and Management* 5(1986): 517–34; quotation on p. 524.

21 Richard Rorty, "Science as Solidarity," manuscript, 1984, p. 3.

22 Ibid.

23 The procedural safeguards in policymaking, e.g., [ings, rules against *ex parte* contracts, and the like, h the political process honest. These procedures ar confused with methodologies but in fact allow so without them.

24 Rorty, *"Science as Solidarity,"* p. 2.

25 Thomas C. Schelling, "Preface," in T. C. Schelling, *tives for Environmental Protection* (Cambridge, Mass.: 1983), p. x.

26 Page 187 of testimony cited in note 7.

27 Paternalistic regulations are pervasive in statutor common law, i.e., in implied warranties and unwai antees. For a good description of the extent of pat private law, see Duncan Kennedy, "Distributive nalistic Motives in Contract and Tort Law, with S erences to Compulsory Terms and Unequal Power," *Maryland Law Review* 41(1982): 563–649.

28 For an argument to this effect, see ibid.

29 See, for example, Tibor Machan, "Pollution and Pc ory," in Tom Regan, ed., *Earthbound: New Introduc in Environmental Ethics* (New York: Random Hot pp. 74–106. Machan argues that a capitalist system approves, "requires that pollution be punished as fense that violates individual rights" (p. 97, italics A welfare state, in contrast, "must rely mostly c regulation and some version of a utilitarian cost-l proach" (p. 93).

30 Ellis Hawley, *The New Deal and the Problem of Monopc* ton, N.J.: Princeton University Press, 1966), p. 47.

31 Arthur M. Schlesinger, Jr., *The Crisis of the Old O1 1933* (Boston: Houghton Mifflin, 1957), p. 33.

32 Hawley, *The New Deal*, p. 52.

33 George Stigler, *The Citizen and the State: Essays on* (Chicago: University of Chicago Press, 1975).

34 See Eads and Fix, *Relief or Reform?*, chap. 4.

35 David Stockman, "Avoiding a GOP Economic Dunk eograph, December 1980, p. 15. Quoted in Eads anc *or Reform?*, pp. 1–2.

36 Murray L. Weidenbaum, "Economic Policy for 1982," quoted in Eads and Fix, *Relief or Reform?*, p. 2.
37 Robert J. Samuelson, "The Real Reagan Revolution," *Washington Post*, February 13, 1985, F1.
38 Executive Order 12,291, issued February 17, 1981, 46 *Fed. Reg.* 13,193 (1981). This order was considerably strengthened by another (50 *Fed. Reg.* 1,036, Jan. 8, 1985), requiring draft regulatory programs to undergo cost-benefit review at the OMB.
39 I paraphrase G. W. F. Hegel, Preface to T. M. Knox, ed., *The Philosophy of Right* (Oxford: Clarendon Press, 1962), p. 13.

2. AT THE SHRINE OF OUR LADY OF FATIMA

1 Henry Adams, *The Education of Henry Adams*, 2d ed. (Boston: Houghton Mifflin, 1970), p. 380.
2 Ibid.
3 Ibid., p. 388.
4 For an account, see Joseph A. Pelletier, *The Sun Danced at Fatima* (Worcester, Mass: Washington Press, 1951).
5 *New Catholic Encyclopedia* (New York: McGraw-Hill, 1967), p. 856.
6 William Baxter, *People or Penguins: The Case for Optimal Pollution* (New York: Columbia University Press, 1974), p. 15. Baxter adds (p. 17), "The question how one organizes society so as to obtain reasonable assurance that resources are deployed effectively, that is, deployed continuously over time so as to yield the maximum aggregate of human satisfactions, is of course the classic and central question to which the science of economics is addressed."
7 Ibid., p. 17.
8 Arthur M. Okun, *Equality and Efficiency: The Big Tradeoff* (Washington, D.C.: Brookings Institution, 1975), p. 2.
9 Joseph Seneca and Michael Taussig, *Environmental Economics*, 2d ed. (Englewood Cliffs, N.J.: Prentice-Hall, 1979), p. 6. The passage reads: "*Efficiency* is defined as maximum consumption of goods and services given the available amount of resources or, what is logically equivalent, the use of a minimum amount of resources to produce or make available for consumption a given amount of goods and services. *Equity* refers to a just distribution of total goods and services among all consumer units."
10 Ibid.

11 "The only kind of preference that counts in a system of wealth-maximization, is . . . one that is backed up by money – in other words, that is registered in a market." Richard Posner, "Utilitarianism, Economics, and Legal Theory," *Journal of Legal Studies* 8(1979): 119.

12 A. Myrick Freeman III, Robert H. Haveman, and Allen V. Kneese, *The Economics of Environmental Policy* (New York: Wiley, 1973), p. 23.

13 For discussion, see Charles Fried, *Right and Wrong* (Cambridge, Mass.: Harvard University Press, 1978), esp. chap. 1.

14 Frank Michelman, "Political Markets and Community Self-determination: Competing Judicial Models of Government Legitimacy," *Indiana Law Journal* 53(1977–78): 147–206, quotation on p. 149. Michelman quotes Kenneth Arrow as follows: "The case for democracy rests on the argument that free discussion and expression of opinion are the most suitable techniques of arriving at the moral imperative implicitly common to all. Voting, from this point of view, is not a device whereby each individual expresses his personal interests, but rather where each individual gives his opinion of the general will." Kenneth Arrow, *Social Choice and Individual Values* (New Haven, Conn.: Yale University Press, 1963), p. 85.

15 Richard N. L. Andrews, "Cost-Benefit Analysis and Regulatory Reform," in Daniel Swartzman, Richard Liroff, and Kevin Croke, eds., *Cost-Benefit Analysis and Environmental Regulations: Politics, Ethics, and Methods* (Washington, D.C.: The Conservation Foundation, 1982), pp. 107–35, quotation on p. 112.

16 Ibid., p. 111.

17 This is Kneese's second condition; the first is that markets are competitive, e.g., nonmonopolistic. Allen V. Kneese, "Environmental Policy," in Peter Duignan and Alvin Rabushka, eds., *The United States in the 1980s* (Stanford, Calif.: Hoover Institution Press, 1980), pp. 253–83, quotation on p. 256. Kneese has stated essentially the same argument in Allen Kneese and Blair Bower, *Environmental Quality and Residuals Management* (Baltimore: John Hopkins University Press, 1979), pp. 4–5.

18 Kneese, "Environmental Policy," p. 256.

19 Ibid.

20 Kneese and Bower, *Environmental Quality and Residuals Management*, pp. 4–5.

21 Ibid.

22 Ibid., p. 259.

23 David William Pearce, *Environmental Economics* (London: Longmans, 1976), p. 1.

24 John Krutilla and Anthony Fisher, *The Economics of Natural Environments: Studies in the Valuation of Commodity and Amenity Resources*, rev. ed. (Washington, D.C.: Resources for the Future, 1985), p. 28.

25 Ibid., pp. 28–29.

26 R. H. Coase, "The Problem of Social Cost," *Journal of Law and Economics* 3(October 1960).

27 Andrews, "Cost-Benefit Analysis as Regulatory Reform," p. 108. Andrews cites Lester Lave for this definition.

28 H. P. Green, "Cost-Benefit Assessment and the Law," *George Washington Law Review* 45(5)(August 1977): 904–5; see also E. J. Mishan, *Cost-Benefit Analysis* (New York: Praeger, 1976), pp. 160–61.

29 For an introduction to and discussion of this approach to the Coase theorem, see Duncan Kennedy, "Cost-Benefit Analysis of Entitlement Problems: A Critique," *Stanford Law Review* 33(1981): 387–445.

30 Burton Weisbrod, "Income Redistribution Effects and Cost-Benefit Analysis," in Samuel B. Chase, ed., *Problems in Public Expenditure Analysis* (Washington, D.C.: Brookings Institution, 1968), pp. 177–222.

31 See, for example, Martin Krieger, "Six Propositions on the Poor and Pollution," *Policy Sciences* 1(1970): 311–24. See also William J. Baumol, "Environmental Protection and Income Distribution," in Harold M. Hoichman and George Persons, eds., *Redistribution Through Public Choice* (New York: Columbia University Press, 1974), pp. 93–114.

32 George J. Stigler, "Director's Law of Public Income Redistribution," *Journal of Law and Economics* 13(1970): 1–10.

33 Carl Rogers, "A Theory of Therapy, Personality, and Interpersonal Relationships, as Developed in the Client Centered Framework," in S. Koch, ed., *Psychology: A Study of a Science* (New York: McGraw-Hill, 1959), vol. 3, p. 210.

34 Ibid., p. 208.

35 Carl Rogers, *Client Centered Therapy* (Boston: Houghton Mifflin, 1965), p. 150.

36 Ibid.

37 Ibid.

38 Rogers, "A Theory of Therapy," p. 208.

39 Ibid., pp. 523–24.

40 James Buchanan, "Positive Economics, Welfare Economics, and Political Economy," *Journal of Law and Economics* 2:127 (1959).

41 For a discussion of social orderings and preference relations, see A. K. Sen, *Collective Choice and Social Welfare* (San Francisco: Holden-Day, 1970), and K. J. Arrow, *Social Choice and Individual Values*, 2d ed. (New York: Wiley, 1983), chap. 2.

42 Immanuel Kant, *Foundations of the Metaphysics of Morals*, ed. R. Wolff, trans. L. Beck (Indianapolis, Ind.: Bobbs-Merrill, 1969). I follow the interpretation of Kantian ethics of W. Sellars, *Science and Metaphysics* (New York: Humanities Press, 1968), chap. 7, and Sellars, "On Reasoning About Values," *American Philosophical Quarterly* 17(1979): 81–101.

43 See Alasdair MacIntyre, *After Virtue* (Notre Dame, Ind.: University of Notre Dame Press, 1981).

44 For the suggestion that property rights to have an abortion be traded in markets as a solution to the political controversy, see Hugh H. Macauley and Bruce Yandle, *Environmental Use and the Market* (Lexington, Mass.: Lexington Books, 1977). These authors write (pp. 120–21): "There is an optimal number of abortions, just as there is an optimal level of pollution, or purity. . . . Those who oppose abortion could eliminate it entirely, if their intensity of feeling were so strong as to lead to payments that were greater at the margin than the price anyone would pay to have an abortion."

45 For this suggestion, see: Charles J. Cicchetti, A. Myrick Freeman III, Robert H. Haveman, and Jack L. Knetsch, "On the Economics of Mass Demonstrations: A Case Study of the November 1969 March on Washington," *American Economic Review* 61(1971): 179–723. The authors use the Clawson–Knetsch–Hotelling travel-cost method to measure political opposition to the Vietnam War. Had they the data, they would also factor in the cost of postage on letters to Congress.

46 William Simon, "Homo Psychologious: Notes on a New Legal Formalism," *Stanford Law Review* 32(1980): 495.

47 Ibid.

48 Philip Rieff, *The Triumph of the Therapeutic* (New York: Harper & Row, 1966), p. 52.

49 MacIntyre, *After Virtue*, p. 22. The idea here is that some theories of political economy take ruler–subject relations seriously, and some do not, except insofar as these relations may
be revealed in a market. For this distinction, see Edward Nell,
"The Revival of Political Economy," *Social Research* 39(1972):
32–53, and John Gurley, "The State of Political Economics,"
American Economic Review 61(1971): 53–63. Gurley writes
(pp. 54–55): "Political economics ... studies economic problems by systematically taking into account, in a historical context, the pervasiveness of ruler-subject relations in society. ...
It is these pervasive relations of power and authority that lead
to conflict, disharmony and disruptive change." Conventional
welfare economics of the sort I criticize here seeks to understand and arbitrate conflict without understanding it in this
context.

50 I lift this idea from Gunnar Myrdal, *The Political Element in the
Development of Economic Theory*, trans. Paul Streeter (London:
Routledge & Kegan Paul, 1953), esp. p. 54. For discussion, see
Hannah Arendt, *The Human Condition* (Chicago: University of
Chicago Press, 1958), sect. 6.

51 Adams, *Education*, p. 476.

3. THE ALLOCATION AND DISTRIBUTION OF RESOURCES

1 405 *U.S.* 727 (1972).

2 Ibid., p. 729.

3 The Council on Environmental Quality wrote: "Mineral King
well illustrates the issue of recreational development for the
pleasure of tens of thousands of people every year versus the
value of an undisturbed naturalness for fewer visitors." *Sixth
Annual Report* 2(1975): 242. For details relating to the Disney
project and its market, see John Harte and Robert Socolow,
Patient Earth (New York: Holt, Rinehart and Winston, 1971),
pp. 168–70; Commentary, "Mineral King Goes Downhill,"
Ecology Law Quarterly 5(1976): 555.

4 See Arnold Hano, "Protectionists vs. Recreationists – The Battle of Mineral King," *New York Times Magazine*, August 17,
1969, p. 24; Peter Browning, "Mickey Mouse in the Mountain," *Harper's*, March 1972, pp. 65–71; "Thar's Gold in Those
Hills," *Nation* 206(1968): 260.

5 National Parks and Recreation Act of 1978, Pub. L. No. 95–625, sec. 314, 92 Stat. 3467 (codified at 16 U.S.C. sec. 45F [supp. III 1979]).

6 Richard A. Musgrave, *The Theory of Public Finance* (New York: McGraw-Hill, 1959), pp. 87–88.

7 Stephen Marglin, "The Social Rate of Discount and the Optimal Rate of Investment," *Quarterly Journal of Economics* 77(1963): 98.

8 Gordon Tullock, *Toward a Mathematics of Politics* (Ann Arbor: University of Michigan Press, 1967), p. 3. Cf. p. 1: "In modern economics and in the political theory which is now developing out of economics, the preference schedule has substituted for the man."

9 A. K. Sen, "Rational Fools: A Critique of the Behavioral Foundations of Economic Theory," *Philosophy and Public Affairs* 6(1977): 317–44. Sen writes (pp. 335–36): "A person is given *one* preference ordering, and as and when the need arises this is supposed to reflect his interest, represent his welfare, summarize his idea of what should be done, and describe his actual choices and behavior. Can one preference ordering do all these things? A person thus described may be 'rational' in the limited sense of revealing no inconsistencies in his behavior, but if he has no use for these distinctions . . . , he must be a bit of a fool. The *purely* economic man is close to being a social moron. Economic theory has been much preoccupied with this rational fool decked in the glory of his *one* all-purpose preference ordering."

10 See Martin H. Krieger, "Six Propositions on the Poor and Pollution," *Policy Sciences* 1(1970): 311–24; and Henry Peskin, "Environmental Policy and the Distribution of Benefits and Costs," in Paul R. Portney, ed., *Current Issues in U.S. Environmental Policy* (Baltimore: Resources for the Future, 1978), pp. 144–63.

11 This distinction has been drawn in a somewhat different form by Henry M. Peskin and Eugene Seskin, "Introduction and Overview," in Peskin and Seskin, eds., *Cost Benefit Analysis and Water Pollution Policy* (Washington, D.C., The Urban Institute, 1975), pp. 4–5. These authors use "allocation" to mean the total amount of a resource which should be produced or otherwise made available; they use distribution the way I use the allocation–distribution distinction to mark the difference between resource management and its consequences on in-

come. For a similar treatment, see Burton Weisbrod, "Income Redistribution Effects and Benefit-Cost Analysis," in Samuel B. Chase, ed., *Problems in Public Expenditure Analysis* (Washington, D.C.: Brookings Institution, 1968), pp. 177, 178. For the same distinction made in somewhat different language, see Otto Eckstein, *Water-Resource Development* (Cambridge, Mass.: Harvard University Press, 1958), p. 17.

12 "Allocation programs include measures to affect relative prices and/or the allocation of resources in an economy, motivated by considerations of economic efficiency. Distribution programs consist of efforts to alter the distribution of incomes in society, motivated by considerations of distributive equity." Edward M. Gramlich, *Benefit-Cost Analysis of Government Programs* (Englewood Cliffs, N.J.: Prentice-Hall, 1981), p. 13.

13 See, e.g., Thomas C. Schelling, "Economic Reasoning and the Ethics of Policy," *Public Interest* 63(1981): 37.

14 For an argument to the effect that the priority of the right to the good is trivial when the good is conceived in terms of preference satisfaction, see Michael J. Sandel, *Liberalism and the Limits of Justice* (Cambridge: Cambridge University Press, 1982). I have reviewed Sandel's arguments in "The Limits of Justice," *Yale Law Journal* 92(6) (1983): 1065–81.

15 Ronald Dworkin, "Liberalism," in Stuart Hampshire, ed., *Public and Private Morality* (Cambridge: Cambridge University Press, 1978), pp. 112–43.

16 Some critics of liberalism, like Sandel (see note 14), believe that liberals are doomed to carry on this empty debate. I do not believe that the efficiency-or-equality issue is *necessarily* central to the discussion of public policy within liberalism, and I argue this in Chapter 7.

17 Leading examples of this literature include Ronald Dworkin, *Taking Rights Seriously* (Cambridge, Mass: Harvard University Press, 1977), and Richard Posner, *The Economics of Justice* (Cambridge, Mass: Harvard University Press, 1985).

18 There are some court cases, for example, those involving affirmative action, to which debates of this sort are quite relevant. See, for example, Ronald Dworkin, "Reverse Discrimination," in *Taking Rights Seriously*, pp. 223–39.

19 For discussion relating the social discount rate to environmental ethics, see J. A. Doeleman, "On the Social Rate of

Discount: The Case for Macroenvironmental Policy," *Environmental Ethics* 2(1980): 45, and sources cited therein.

20 Derek Parfit, "Energy Policy and the Further Future" working paper, Center for Philosophy and Public Policy, University of Maryland, February 23, 1981. A slightly different version of the passage cited appears in Parfit, "Energy Policy and the Further Future: The Identity Problem," in Douglas MacLean and Peter F. Brown, eds., *Energy and the Future* (Totowa, N.J.: Rowman & Littlefield, 1983), pp. 167–79, esp. p. 17.

21 William Blackstone summarizes well my view on this point. See Blackstone, "The Search for an Environmental Ethic," in Tom Regan, ed., *Matters of Life and Death* (Philadelphia: Temple University Press, 1980), p. 331.

22 Immanuel Kant, *Critique of Judgment*, trans. H. Bernard (New York: Hafner, 1951), sec. 59.

23 Mill argues in several passages that one may be legitimately compelled under certain circumstances to be a "good Samaritan." See "On Liberty," in *Collected Works*, vol. 18 (Toronto: University of Toronto Press, 1977) p. 224.

24 I have argued this position more fully in "Liberalism and Law," in Douglas MacLean and Claudia Mills, eds. *Liberalism Reconsidered*, (Totowa, N.J.: Rowman & Littlefield, 1983), pp. 12–24.

25 See Council on Environmental Quality, *Public Opinion on Environmental Issues* (1980).

26 Ibid., pp. 4, 11. For more evidence, see John M. Gilroy and Robert Y. Shapiro, "The Polls: Environmental Protection," *Public Opinion Quarterly* 50(1986): 270–79. This excellent survey describes and summarizes many polls.

27 Pascal's wager seems to follow along these lines. "Let us weigh the gain and loss in wagering that God is. Let us estimate the two chances. If you gain, you gain all; if you lose, you lose nothing. Wager, then, without hesitation that He is." B. Pascal, *Pensées*, trans. W. Trotter (1952), sec. 233.

28 Robert Goodin extends this analysis to many goods besides environmental ones. See Goodin, *Political Theory and Public Policy* (Chicago: University of Chicago Press, 1982), chap. 6.

29 "That which is related to general human inclination and needs has a *market price*. . . . But that which constitutes the condition under which alone something can be an end in itself does not

have a mere relative worth, *i.e.*, a price, but an intrinsic worth, *i.e.*, *dignity*." Immanuel Kant, *Foundations of the Metaphysics of Morals*, ed. R. Wolff, trans. L. Beck (Indianapolis, Ind., Bobbs-Merrill, 1959), p. 53 (emphasis in original).

30 For a general discussion of the distinction between "positive" and "negative" freedom, see Isaiah Berlin, *Four Essays on Liberty* (London: Oxford University Press, 1969), esp. the third essay and pp. xxxvii–lxiii of the Introduction; and Gerald MacCallum, "Negative and Positive Freedom," *Philosophical Review* 76(1967): 312–21.

31 David W. Minar, *Ideas and Politics: The American Experience* (Homewood, Ill.: Dorsey Press, 1964), p. 416.

32 Quoted in this context by William Ruckelshaus in "Risk, Science, and Society," *Issues in Science and Technology* 3(Spring 1985): 24.

33 I paraphrase Ruckelshaus, ibid., p. 30.

4. FRAGILE PRICES AND SHADOW VALUES

1 Robert D. Rowe, Ralph C. D'Arge, and David Brookshire, "An Experiment on the Economic Value of Visibility," *Journal of Environmental Economics and Management* 7(1980): 1. For a similar study and useful bibliography, see John Balling and John Falk, "Development of Visual Preference for Natural Environments," *Environmental Behavior* 14(1)(1982): 5–28.

2 Ibid., p. 2.

3 The Clean Air Act as amended August 1977, Pub. L. No. 95–11, sec. 160 (3).

4 Rowe et al., "An Experiment," p. 2.

5 The Sixth Circuit Court in *TVA v. Hill* described the statute as an expression of the "public conscience" (549 F.2d 1064, 1074 [6th Cir. 1976], *aff'd*, 437 U.S. 153 [1978]).

6 16 U.S.C. sec. 1536 (1976).

7 437 U.S. 153, 173 (1978).

8 The 1978 amendments to the Endangered Species Act created a high-level Endangered Species Committee to deal in a juridicial way with "irresolvable conflicts." The committee unanimously voted to deny an exemption in the Tellicio Dam case. It permitted the Grayrocks reservoir to continue, after conditions were met to mitigate its effect on the habitat of the whooping crane.

9 I have discussed the legislative and judicial history of the Endangered Species Act in "On the Preservation of Species," *Columbia Journal of Environmental Law* 7(1)(1980): 33–67.

10 Judith Bentkover, "The Role of Benefits Assessment in Public Policy Development," in Judith Bentkover, Vincent Covello, and Jeryl Mumpower, *Benefits Assessments: The State of the Art* (Boston: D. Reidel, 1986), p. 10.

11 Ibid., p. 11.

12 For major surveys, discussions, and bibliographies, see Bentkover, Covello, and Mumpower, *Benefits Assessments*, and George L. Peterson and Alan Randall, eds., *Valuation of Resource Benefits* (Boulder, Colo.: Westview, 1984).

13 For a sample of this literature, see Marion Clawson and Jack Knetsch, *Economics of Outdoor Recreation* (Baltimore: Resources for the Future, 1966).

14 For discussion of "existence value," see J. V. Krutilla, "Conservation Reconsidered," *American Economic Review* 57(4) (September 1967): 777–86. For discussion of "option value," see Burton Weisbrod, "Collective-Consumption Services of Individual Consumption Goods," *Quarterly Journal of Economics* 78(1967).

15 William Schulze et al., "The Economic Benefits of Preserving Visibility in the National Parklands of the Southwest," *Natural Resources Journal* 23(January 1983): 149–73, quotation on p. 154.

16 For a definition of public goods, see Paul Samuelson, *Economics*, 10th ed. (New York: McGraw-Hill, 1976), pp. 159–60.

17 Robert D. Rowe and Lauraine G. Chesnut, *The Value of Visibility: Economic Theory and Applications for Air Pollution Control* (Cambridge, Mass.: Abt, 1982), p. 10.

18 Congress intended clean and safe air – not allocatory efficiency – to be the goal of the Clean Air Act. Thus, the statute precludes the kind of cost-benefit balancing envisioned by the Wyoming economists. See *American Textile Manufacturers Institute v. Donovan*, 452 U.S. 490, 510 (1981), which states: "When Congress has intended that an agency engage in cost-benefit analysis, it has clearly indicated such intent on the face of the statute." The D.C. Circuit, in permitting EPA to consider costs in regulating vinyl chloride emissions, distinguishes taking costs into account from cost-benefit analysis. See *National Resources Defense Council v. EPA*, 804 F.2d 710 (D.C. Cir. 1986), *vacated, rehearing granted en banc*, 810 F.2d 270 (1987).

19 Thus, it seems to be EPA policy that, in the presence of scientific uncertainty concerning risk, the cost of regulations
should not be "grossly disproportionate" to health benefits.
See the Vinyl Chloride case cited in note 18, above.

20 See Balling and Falk, "Development of Visual Preference for
Natural Environments."

21 See Immanuel Kant, *Critique of Judgment*, trans. J. H. Bernard,
(New York: Hafner, 1951), p. 145. For discussion of repro-
ductions of natural objects, see Martin Krieger, "What's Wrong
with Plastic Trees?," *Science* 179(1973): 446–555; Laurence
Tribe, "Ways Not to Think About Plastic Trees: New Foundations for Environmental Law," *Yale Law Journal* 83(1974):
1315–48. Mark Sagoff, "On Preserving the Natural Environment," *Yale Law Journal* 84(1974): 205–67; and Mark Sagoff, "On
Restoring and Reproducing Art," *Journal of Philosophy*
75(9)(1978): 453–71.

22 Rowe et al., "An Experiment," p. 9.

23 *American Textile Manufacturers v. Donovan* (cotton dust) 452 U.S.
490 (1981).

24 For discussion, see Steven Kelman, *What Price Incentives? Economists and the Environment* (Boston: Auburn House, 1981).

25 Stanley Milgram, "Behavioral Study of Obedience," *Journal of
Abnormal and Social Psychology* 67(1963): 371–78, and "Issues in
the Study of Obedience," *American Psychologist* 19(1964): 848–
52.

26 Karl Samples, John Dixon, and Marcia Gowen, "Information
Disclosure and Endangered Species Evaluation," *Land Economics* 62(1986): 306–12; quotation on p. 306.

27 Ibid., p. 310.

28 Ibid., p. 311.

29 Ibid., p. 312.

30 Ibid.

31 Rowe and Chestnut, *The Value of Visibility*, pp. 80–1 (citations
omitted, italics added). These authors cite three studies that
encountered a 50 percent protest or rejection rate.

32 For a review of Tarasovsky and other work in this context, see
A. J. Cuyler, "The Quality of Life and the Limits of Cost-
Benefit Analysis," in L. Wingo and A. Evans, eds., *Public Economics and the Quality of Life* (Baltimore: Johns Hopkins University Press, 1977), pp. 141–53.

33 Thomas C. Heller, "The Importance of Normative Decision-

making: The Limitations of Legal Economics as a Basis for a Liberal Jurisprudence – As Illustrated by the Regulation of Vacation Home Development," *Wisconsin Law Review* 1976: 405.

34 Ibid.
35 Ibid., pp. 405–6.
36 Ibid., p. 399.
37 Ibid., p. 404.
38 Ibid., p. 408.
39 Ibid.
40 Guido Calabresi and A. Douglas Melamed, "Property Rules, Liability Rules, and Inalienability: One View of the Cathedral," *Harvard Law Review* 85(1972): 1089–1128.
41 "To the extent that those members of society who approve of the distributive impact of housing code enforcement value this impact more than its opponents disvalue it, its allocative efficiency will be increased by the net equivalent dollar gain it generates for such 'non-involved' parties." Richard Markovits, "The Distributive Impact, Allocative Efficiency, and Overall Desirability of Ideal Housing Codes: Some Theoretical Clarifications," *Harvard Law Review* 89(1976): 1833.
42 Burton Weisbrod argues that distributive justice, rather than being a condition under which markets can be desirable institutions, is itself good to be marketed. Weisbrod, "Income Redistribution Effects and Cost-Benefit Analysis," in Samuel B. Chase, ed., *Problems in Public Expenditure Analysis* (Washington, D.C.: Brookings Institution, 1968), pp. 177–222.
43 Calabresi and Melamed, "Property Rules," p. 1111–12.
44 Duncan Kennedy, "Cost-Benefit Analysis of Entitlement Problems: A Critique," *Stanford Law Review* 33(1981), p. 387.
45 For a technical explanation of the concept of a category mistake, see Gilbert Ryle, "Categories," in Anthony Flew, ed., *Logic and Language*, 2d ser. (Oxford: Blackwell, 1953; New York: Doubleday, Anchor Books, 1965), p. 68. For a less technical treatment see Gilbert Ryle, *The Concept of Mind* (London: Hutchinson, 1949), p. 11.
46 For discussion of the extent to which markets permit a "voice" option, see A. O. Hirschmann, *Exit, Voice and Loyalty* (Cambridge, Mass.: Harvard University Press, 1973).
47 W. B. Yeats, "The Second Coming," in *The Collected Poems of W. B. Yeats* (New York: Macmillan, 1956), p. 185.

48 See Jon Elster, "Sour Grapes: Utilitarianism and the Genesis of Wants," in Amartya Sen and Bernard Williams, eds., *Utilitarianism and Beyond* (Cambridge: Cambridge University Press, 1982).

49 Robert Goodin, "Laundering Preferences," in J. Elster and A. Hylland, eds. *Foundations of Social Choice Theory* (Cambridge: Cambridge University Press, 1983).

50 Elmer Eric Schattschneider, *The Semisovereign People* (Hinsdale, Ill.: Dryden Press, 1960), chap. 2.

51 Aaron Wildavsky, *Speaking Truth to Power: The Art and Craft of Policy Making* (New York: Macmillan, 1979), p. 202.

5. VALUES AND PREFERENCES

1 Edith Stokey and Richard Zeckhauser, *A Primer for Policy Analysis* (New York: Norton, 1978), p. 262.

2 Ibid., p. 263.

3 Wilfrid Sellars, *Science and Metaphysics* (New York: Humanities Press, 1968), p. 225.

4 For discussion, see Jon Elster, "Sour Grapes: Utilitarianism and the Genesis of Wants," in Amartya Sen and Bernard Williams, eds., *Utilitarianism and Beyond* (Cambridge: Cambridge University Press, 1982), pp. 219–37.

5 For results of relevant polls, see U.S. Council on Environmental Quality, *Public Opinion on Environmental Issues* (Washington, D.C.: Government Printing Office, 1980).

6 J. A. Mirrlees writes: For any individual, "the sum of his utilities describes his considered preferences regarding the lives of his alternatives selves." Mirrlees, "The Economic Uses of Utilitarianism," in Sen and Williams, eds., *Utilitarianism and Beyond*, p. 70. The problem is that no one, no matter how reflective, knows how to predict and thus to evaluate the lives of his "alternative selves."

7 The quotation is from Tennyson's "Ulysses": "I am a part of all that I have met; / Yet all experience is an arch where through / Gleams the untraveled world, whose margin fades / Forever and forever when I move" (lines 19–22).

8 John Stuart Mill, "What Utilitarianism Is," in *The Utilitarians* (Garden City, N.Y.: Doubleday, 1961), p. 410.

9 F. H. Knight, *The Ethics of Competition and Other Essays* (New York: Harper Bros., 1935), pp. 22–23.

10   For an introduction to these objections, see Bernard Williams, *Morality: An Introduction to Ethics* (New York: Harper Torchbooks, 1972), pp. 90–107.

11   For a survey of the literature, see A. Campbell, P. E. Coverse, and W. Rodgers, *The Quality of American Life: Perceptions, Evaluations, and Satisfactions* (New York: Russell Sage Foundation, 1976). Also Hazel Erskine, "The Polls: Some Thoughts About Life and People," *Public Opinion Quarterly* 28(Fall 1964), and Gerald Gurin, *Americans View Their Mental Health* (New York: Basic Books, 1960).

12   See W. W. Jacobs, "The Monkey's Paw," J. Keats, "Ode to a Grecian Urn," and Tibor Scitovsky, *The Joyless Economy* (New York: Oxford University Press, 1976).

13   N. Rescher, *Unpopular Essays on Technological Progress* (Pittsburgh: University of Pittsburgh Press, 1980), p. 19.

14   Alan Randall and George Peterson, "The Valuation of Wildland Benefits," in Peterson and Randall, eds., *Valuation of Wildland Benefits* (Boulder, Colo.: Westview, 1984), pp. 3–4.

15   This is one condition of a perfectly competitive market quoted from Kneese in Chapter 1.

16   Richard Posner, *The Economics of Justice* (Cambridge, Mass.: Harvard University Press, 1981), p. 60.

17   A. O. Hirschman, *Shifting Involvements: Private Interest and Public Action* (Princeton, N.J.: Princeton University Press, 1982), p. 10.

18   Fred Hirsch, *Social Limits to Growth* (Cambridge, Mass.: Harvard University Press, 1976).

19   There would be some virtue in having more races, or cultural spheres, in which people can compete.

20   Hirsch, *Social Limits to Growth*, p. 1.

21   Mary Douglas and Baron Isherwood, *The World of Goods* (New York: Basic, 1979), esp. chap. 1, "Why People Want Goods."

22   Hirsch, *Social Limits to Growth*, p. 5.

23   Ronald Dworkin takes a similar position in "Liberalism," in Stuart Hampshire, ed., *Public and Private Morality* (Cambridge: Cambridge University Press, 1978), p. 136.

24   Stokey and Zeckhauser, *A Primer for Policy Analysis*, p. 257.

25   Gunnar Myrdal, *The Political Element in the Development of Economic Theory*, trans. Paul Streeter (London: Routledge & Kegan Paul, 1953), p. 54.

26   Ibid., pp. 194–95.

27 Richard Posner, "The Ethical and Political Basis of the Efficiency Norm in Common Law Adjudication," *Hofstra Law Review* 8(1980): 488.

28 Herman Leonard and Richard Zeckhauser, "Cost-Benefit
Analysis Applied to Risks: Its Philosophy and Legitimacy," in
Douglas MacLean, ed., *Values at Risk* (Totowa, N.J.: Rowman
& Littlefield, 1986), p. 33.

29 *TVA v. Hill* 437 U.S. 153, 187–88 (1978) (snail darter); *American
Textile Manufacturers Institute v. Donovan* 452 U.S. 490 (1981)
(cotton dust). Kip Viscusi comments: "The Supreme Court,
for instance, has explicitly prohibited the use of a benefit-cost
test for OSHA standards pertaining to toxic substances and
hazardous physical agents. Since the statutory mandates in
most risk-reducing legislation are written narrowly, court decisions of that kind could prove quite common." Viscusi,
"Presidential Oversight: Controlling the Regulators," *Journal
of Policy Analysis and Management* 2(2)(1983): 162.

30 Thomas C. Schelling, ed., *Incentives for Environmental Protection*
(Cambridge, Mass.: MIT Press, 1983), p. ix. ("There is a discrepancy between the approach of economists to environmental protection and the approach of nearly everybody else.")

31 Leonard and Zeckhauser, "Cost-Benefit Analysis," p. 3. Posner in "The Ethical and Political Basis" argues that by consenting to a market transaction, an individual consents *ex ante*
to the effects or consequences of that transaction. As well argue
that you consent to being mugged or hit by a drunk driver
when you voluntarily cross a street or drive your car, knowing
the risks. For this reply to Posner, see Ronald Dworkin, "Why
Efficiency?," *Hofstra Law Review* 8(1980): 563–90.

32 Leonard and Zeckhauser, "Cost-Benefit Analysis," p. 36.
Richard Posner takes the same position. He asks, How are we
to elicit consent "not so much to individual market transactions
. . . as to institutions, such as . . . the market itself?" He answers
that "we should look for implied consent, as by trying to answer the hypothetical question whether, if transaction costs
were zero, the affected parties would have agreed to the institution." See Posner, "The Ethical and Political Basis,"
p. 494.

33 John Rawls, "Justice as Fairness: Political not Metaphysical,"
Philosophy and Public Affairs 14(3)(1985): 223–51.

34 John Rawls, *A Theory of Justice* (Cambridge, Mass.: Harvard University Press, 1971).

35 John Rawls, "The Basic Structure as Subject," *American Philosophical Quarterly* 14(2)(1977): 159–65.

36 John Rawls, *A Theory of Justice*, p. 442.

37 Ronald Dworkin, "Liberalism," in Stuart Hampshire, ed., *Public and Private Morality* (Cambridge: Cambridge University Press, 1978), p. 127.

38 Ronald Dworkin, "Equality of Welfare," *Philosophy and Public Affairs* 10(3)(1982): 192.

39 Ibid.

40 A. O. Hirschman, *Shifting Involvements: Private Interest and Public Action* (Princeton, N.J.: Princeton University Press, 1982), p. 21 (italics removed). See also Carol Christian von Weizsacker, "Notes on Endogenous Change of Tastes," *Journal of Economic Theory* 3(1971): 345–72, and Scitovsky, *The Joyless Economy*.

41 Hannah Arendt, *On Revolution* (New York: Viking, 1965), p. 127.

42 Amartya Sen and Bernard Williams, "Introduction," in Sen and Williams, *Utilitarianism and Beyond*, p. 4.

43 Wilfrid Sellars, *Science and Metaphysics*, p. 217.

44 F. H. Bradley, *Ethical Studies*, 2d ed. (Oxford: Clarendon Press, 1927), pp. 204–5.

45 J.-J. Rousseau, "On Public Happiness," in *Oeuvres Completes* (Paris: NRF, Pleiade, 1964), vol. 3, p. 881.

6. NATURE AND THE NATIONAL IDEA

1 Perry Miller, *Errand into the Wilderness* (New York: Harper & Row, 1964), p. vii. Hereinafter cited as *Errand*.

2 Kenneth Lynn et al. "Perry Miller," *Harvard University Gazette* 60(17) (Jan. 16, 1965), n.p.

3 *Errand*, p. vii.

4 Ibid., p. viii.

5 Quoted in Perry Miller and Thomas H. Johnson, *The Puritans*, rev. ed. (New York: Harper & Row, 1963), p. 103.

6 Quoted in 12 *Proceedings Massachusetts Historical Society* 83(1871, 1873).

7 Thomas Huxley, "Wordsworth in the Tropics," *Yale Review* 18(1929): 672–73.

8 Karl Marx, *Grundrisse zur Kritik der Politischen Okonomie*, quoted in William Leiss, *The Domination of Nature* (New York: Braziller, 1972), p. 73.

9 *Errand*, p. 207.

10 Roderick Nash, *Wilderness and the American Mind* (New Haven, Conn.: Yale University Press, 1967), pp. 23–24.

11 Cotton Mather, *Magnalia Christi Americana* 1 (1855), p. 77.

12 This familiar description is the title of an election sermon preached by the Reverend Samuel Danforth in 1670. S. Danforth, "A Brief Recognition of New England's Errand into the Wilderness" (1670).

13 Miller and Johnson, *The Puritans*, pp. 198–99.

14 John Higginson, *The Cause of God and His People in New England* (Cambridge, Mass.: Samuel Green, 1663), pp. 10–11.

15 Ibid.

16 This was the synod of 1679–80, see Perry Miller, *Nature's Nation* (Cambridge, Mass.: Harvard University Press, 1967), p. 25; Williston Walker, *The Creeds and Platforms of Congregationalism* (New York: Scribner, 1893) pp. 409–40; cf. Perry Miller, *The New England Mind: From Colony to Province* (Cambridge, Mass.: Harvard University Press, 1967), p. 35.

17 Miller, *Errand*, p. 15.

18 Jonathan Edwards, *The Works of President Edwards* (New Haven, Conn.: 1879), pp. 217–18.

19 Cotton distinguishes between the study of nature for the sake of scientific and practical knowledge and the study of nature as a symbol of God. These are compatible, Cotton says, but those interested only in scientific or practical study are "very quick sighted in points of nature but very dull and heavy in matters of Religion and grace." The scientific study of nature is permissible if it does not lose sight of the symbolic; there is a "settled order" in the changes of the weather "as in the motions of the Heavens"; and we ought to understand it if we can. John Cotton, "A Brief Exposition with Practicall Observations upon the whole book of Ecclesiastes (London: A. Tuckney, 1654), pp. 64–65, quoted in Perry Miller, *The New England Mind: The Seventeenth Century* (1939; rev. ed., Cambridge, Mass.: Harvard University Press, 1954), p. 212. Miller writes "Young Elnathan Chauncy copied into his notebooks

from Samuel Purchase the truism, 'There is no creature but may teach a good soule one step toward his creator,' while Cotton . . . blessed the study of nature when nature was viewed as 'a mappe and shaddow of the spirituall state of the soules of men' " (p. 213).

20 Jonathan Edwards, *Images or Shadows of Divine Things*, Perry Miller, ed. (New Haven Conn.: Yale University Press, 1948).

21 Significantly, this is the motto of his essay "History." Ralph Waldo Emerson, "History," in *Essays & Essays*, 2d ser. (Columbus, Ohio: C. E. Merrill, 1969), vol. 1.

22 See Nelson Goodman, *Languages of Art* (Indianapolis, Ind.: Bobbs-Merrill, 1968), p. 68 ("metaphorical possession is not literal possession; but possession is actual whether literal or metaphorical").

23 Hector St. Jean de Crèvecoeur (Michel-Guillaume-Jean de Crèvecoeur), *Letters from an American Farmer* (1904; New York: Dutton, 1962), p. 54.

24 Thomas Jefferson, *Notes on The State of Virginia* (Chapel Hill: University of North Carolina Press, 1955), pp. 164–65. Published for the Institute of Early American History and Culture, Williamsburg, Va.

25 Leo Marx, *The Machine in the Garden* (New York: Oxford University Press, 1964), p. 73.

26 Alexis de Tocqueville, *Democracy in America* (New York: Random House, Vintage Books, 1946), p. 74.

27 *Errand*, p. 211.

28 Henry David Thoreau, *Walden* (Princeton, N.J.: Princeton University Press, 1971), p. 116.

29 Mark Twain, "Fenimore Cooper's Literary Offenses," in *How to Tell a Story and Other Essays* (New York: Harper Bros., 1904), p. 78.

30 George Bernard Shaw, "The Perfect Wagnerite," in *Selected Prose of Bernard Shaw* (New York: Dodd, Mead, 1952), pp. 218–33.

31 James Fenimore Cooper, *The Leatherstocking Saga* (New York: Pantheon, 1954), p. 681.

32 Roderick Nash, *Wilderness and the American Mind* (New Haven, Conn.: Yale University Press, 1967), p. 44.

33 Ralph Waldo Emerson, *Journal*, quoted in R. W. B. Lewis, *The American Adam* (Chicago: University of Chicago Press, 1955), p. vi.

34 Nathaniel Hawthorne, "The New Adam and Eve," in *Mosses from an Old Manse* (1900; Freeport N.Y.: Books for Libraries, 1970), p. 20.

35 Tocqueville, *Democracy in America*, p. 19.

36 *Errand*, p. 207.

37 F. Scott Fitzgerald, *The Great Gatsby* (New York: Scibner, 1953), p. 182.

38 Jonathan Edwards, *Works* (1843), pp. 261–304.

39 William Faulkner, *Big Woods* (New York: Random House, 1955), unpaginated, 6th page from end of text.

40 Quoted in Nash, *Wilderness and the American Mind*, p. 90.

41 Fitzgerald, *The Great Gatsby*, p. 99.

42 Faulkner, *Big Woods*, unpaginated, 3rd page from end of text.

43 Herbert Croly, *The Promise of American Life*, Arthur Schlesinger, Jr., ed. (Cambridge, Mass.: Harvard University Press, 1965), pp. 6–7.

44 See, e.g., Bernard Bailyn, *Education in the Forming of American Society* (New York: Random House, Vintage Books, 1960); B. Bailyn, *The Ideological Origins of the American Revolution* (Cambridge, Mass.: Harvard University Press, 1967); B. Bailyn, *The Origins of American Politics* (New York: Knopf, 1968); R. B. W. Lewis, *The American Adam: Innocence, Tragedy, and Tradition in the Nineteenth Century* (Chicago: University of Chicago Press, 1955); R. W. B. Lewis, *Trials of the Word: Essays in American Literature and the Humanistic Tradition* (New Haven, Conn.: Yale University Press, 1965); Henry Nash Smith, *Virgin Land: The American West as Symbol and Myth* (New York: Random House, Vintage Books, 1950).

45 J. Ortega Y Gasset, *The Revolt of the Masses* (1932; New York: Norton, 1957), p. 89.

46 Faulkner, *Big Woods*, unpaginated, last page.

7. CAN ENVIRONMENTALISTS BE LIBERALS?

1 Brian Barry, *Political Argument* (London: Routledge & Kegan Paul, 1965), p. 66.

2 Ibid., p. 74.

3 Allen Kneese and Blair Bower, *Environmental Quality and Residuals Management* (Baltimore: Johns Hopkins University Press, 1979), pp. 4–5.

4 Barry, *Political Argument*, p. 71.

5   Aldo Leopold, "The Land Ethic," in *A Sand County Almanac* (New York: Oxford University Press, 1966), p. 222.

6   NEPA sec. 2, 42 U.S.C. sec. 4321.

7   George S. Sessions, "Anthrocentrism and the Environmental Crisis," *Humboldt Journal of Social Relations* (Fall-Winter 1974): 80.

8   Gifford Pinchot, *The Fight for Conservation* (Seattle: University of Washington Press, 1910), p. 42.

9   Ibid., p. 43.

10 Aristotle *Nichomachean Ethics* 1115a–1157b.

11 Saint Augustine ascribes this view to Cicero. See Saint Augustine, *The City of God*, trans. Marcus Dods (New York: Random House, Modern Library, 1950), pp. 61–62.

12 Ibid., p. 706.

13 Andred Dobelstein, *Politics, Economics, and Public Welfare* (Englewood Cliffs, N.J.: Prentice-Hall, 1980), p. 109.

14 John Rawls summarizes: "Systems of ends are not ranked in value." *A Theory of Justice* (Cambridge, Mass.: Harvard University Press, 1971), p. 19.

15 Bruce Ackerman, *Social Justice in the Liberal State* (New Haven, Conn.: Yale University Press, 1980), p. 11.

16 Ronald Dworkin, "Liberalism," in Stuart Hampshire, ed., *Public and Private Morality* (Cambridge: Cambridge University Press, 1978), p. 127.

17 For a statement of these ideals, see, for example, John Muir, *The Wilderness World of John Muir* (Boston: Houghton Mifflin, 1976). Muir writes (p. 317), "Why should man value himself as more than a small part of the one great unit of creation? And what creature of all the Lord has taken the pains to make is not essential to the completeness of that unit – the cosmos? The universe would be incomplete without the smallest transmicroscopic creature that dwells beyond our conceitful eyes and knowledge."

For further development of similar themes, see Leopold, *A Sand County Almanac*; Marjorie Hope Nicolson, *Mountain Gloom and Mountain Glory: The Development of the Aesthetic of the Infinite* (New York: Norton, 1963); John Passmore, *Man's Responsibility for Nature: Ecological Problems and Western Traditions* (New York: Scribner, 1974); and Joseph Sax, *Mountains Without Handrails: Reflections on the National Parks* (Ann Arbor: University of Michigan Press, 1980).

18 See, for example Patrick Devlin, *The Enforcement of Morals* (New York: Oxford University Press, 1965). Devlin writes on pp. 13–14, "Society is justified in taking the same steps to preserve its moral code as it does to preserve its government and other essential institutions. The suppression of vice is as much the law's business as the suppression of subversive activities; it is no more possible to define a sphere of private morality than it is to define a sphere of private subversive activity. It is wrong to talk of private morality or of the law not being concerned with immorality as such or to try to set rigid bounds to the part which the law may play in the suppression of vice."

For a subtle defense of Devlin's general position, see Roger Scruton, *The Meaning of Conservatism* (Totowa, N.J.: Barnes & Noble, 1980), esp. pp. 71–93. For a liberal reply, see Ronald Dworkin, *Taking Rights Seriously* (Cambridge, Mass.: Harvard University Press, 1977), chap. 10, and H. L. A. Hart, *Law, Liberty, and Morality* (New York: Random House, Vintage Books, 1966).

19 Ronald Dworkin characterizes conservatism and various forms of socialism or Marxism as adopting the thesis "that the treatment government owes its citizens is at least partly determined by some conception of the good life." Marxism and conservatism differ, of course, in the conception of the good life they endorse. Dworkin, "Liberalism," in Stuart Hampshire, ed., *Public and Private Morality* (Cambridge: Cambridge University Press, 1978), pp. 113–43; quotation on p. 128.

20 The distinction between civil society and the state is defined by Hegel in T. M. Knox, ed., *Hegel's Philosophy of Right* (New York: Oxford University Press, 1952), esp. sec. 258, p. 156. For discussion of the distinction, see Shlomo Avineri, *Hegel's Theory of the Modern State* (Cambridge: Cambridge University Press, 1972), pp. 141–54.

21 John Rawls, *A Theory of Justice* (Cambridge, Mass.: Harvard University Press, 1971), p. 450.

22 Dworkin, "Liberalism," p. 136.

23 For discussion, see Dworkin, *Taking Rights Seriously*, pp. 94–100.

24 Rawls, *A Theory of Justice*, pp. 3–4.

25 Charles Fried, *Right and Wrong* (Cambridge, Mass.: Harvard University Press, 1978), pp. 8–9.

26 Ibid., p. 29. See also Ackerman, *Social Justice*, pp. 48–49, and Robert Nozick, *Anarchy, State, and Utopia* (New York: Basic, 1974), pp. 30–33.

27 Martin Krieger, "What's Wrong with Plastic Trees?" *Science* 179 (1973): 446–80; quotation on p. 446.

28 Aldo Leopold, "The Land Ethic," p. 240.

29 J. Baird Callicott, "Animal Liberation: A Triangular Affair," *Environmental Ethics* 2(1980): 320.

30 Ibid. See also Don Marietta, Jr., "The Interrelationship of Ecological Science and Environmental Ethics," *Environmental Ethics* 1(1979): 195–207. "The basic concept behind an ecological ethic is that morally acceptable treatment of the environment is that which does not upset the integrity of the ecosystem as it is seen in a diversity of life forms existing in a dynamic and complex but stable interdependency" (p. 197).

31 For a critical study of deontological liberalism and its relation to Kantian moral theory, see Michael J. Sandel, *Liberalism and the Limits of Justice* (Cambridge: Cambridge University Press, 1982), esp. pp. 1–14.

32 See Amartya Sen and Bernard Williams, "Introduction," in *Utilitarianism and Beyond* (Cambridge: Cambridge University Press, 1982), p. 4: "Essentially, utilitarianism sees persons as locations of their respective utilities – as the sites at which such activities as desiring and having pleasure and pain take place. . . . Utilitarianism is the combination . . . of welfarism, sum ranking and consequentialism, and each of these components contribute to this narrow view of a person."

33 For discussion, see H. L. A. Hart, "Between Utility and Rights," in A. Ryan, ed., *The Idea of Freedom* (New York: Oxford University Press, 1979), pp. 77–98.

34 Fried, *Right and Wrong*, pp. 7–17.

35 Nozick, *Anarchy, State, and Utopia*, pp. 71–84.

36 Arthur Okun, *Equality and Efficiency: The Big Tradeoff* (Washington, D.C.: Brookings Institution, 1975).

37 Ronald Dworkin, "Why Efficiency?," *Hofstra Law Review* 8(1980): 563–90.

38 Rawls, *A Theory of Justice*, p. 31.

39 Immanuel Kant, *Critique of Practical Reason*, trans. L. W. Beck (Indianapolis, Ind.: Bobbs-Merrill, 1956), esp. pp. 18–20.

40 Rawls, *A Theory of Justice*, p. 450.

41 See, for example, Bryan Norton, "Environmental Ethics and

the Rights of Future Generations," *Environmental Ethics* 4(1982): 319–37. For good anthologies collecting relevant essays, see Douglas MacLean and Peter Brown, eds., *Energy and the Future* (Totowa, N.J.: Rowman & Littlefield, 1983); Ernest Partridge, ed., *Responsibilities to Future Generations* (Buffalo, N.Y.: Prometheus Press, 1980); and Richard Sikora and Brian Barry, eds., *Obligations to Future Generations* (Philadelphia: Temple University Press, 1978). For an excellent review of the issues, see Annette Baier, "For the Sake of Future Generations," in Tom Regan, ed., *Earthbound: New Introductory Essays in Environmental Ethics* (New York: Random House, 1984).

42 For discussion of the social discount rate, see Talbot Page, "Intergenerational Justice as Opportunity," in MacLean and Brown, *Energy and the Future*, pp. 38–58, and sources cited therein.

43 See, for example, Christopher Stone, *Should Trees Have Standing? Toward Legal Rights for Natural Objects* (Los Altos, Calif.: Kaufmann, 1974), and Laurence Tribe, "Ways Not to Think About Plastic Trees: New Foundations for Environmental Law," *Yale Law Journal* 83(1974): 1315–48. I have commented on this literature most recently in Mark Sagoff, "Animal Liberation and Environmental Ethics: Bad Marriage, Quick Divorce," *Osgoode Hall Law Journal* 22(1984): 297–307.

44 Joel Feinberg, "The Rights of Animals and Unborn Generations," in William T. Blackstone, ed., *Philosophy and Environmental Crisis* (Athens: University of Georgia Press, 1974), pp. 55–56.

45 In reaching this conclusion, I have drawn upon a large literature, including Callicott, "Animal Liberation: A Triangular Affair"; Bryan Norton, "Environmental Ethics and Nonhuman Rights," *Environmental Ethics* 4(1982): 17–36; Eric Katz, "Is There a Place for Animals in the Moral Consideration of Nature?," *Ethics and Animals* 4(1983): 74–85. For arguments for an opposing conclusion, see Tom Regan, *The Case for Animal Rights* (Berkely: University of California Press, 1983), pp. 361–63; and Edward Johnson, "Treating the Dirt: Environmental Ethics and Moral Theory," in Regan, ed., *Earthbound*, pp. 336–65, esp. pp. 351–54.

46 Brian Barry, "Self-Government Revisited," in David Miller and Larry Siedentrop, eds., *The Nature of Political Theory* (New York:

Oxford University Press, 1983), pp. 121–54; quotation on p. 125.

47 Christopher Columbus Langdell, "Record of the Commemoration, November Fifth to Eighth, 1886, of the Two Hundred and Fiftieth Anniversary of the Founding of Harvard College (1887)," p. 96, excerpted in Arthur E. Sutherland, *The Law at Harvard* (Cambridge, Mass.: Harvard University Press, 1967), p. 175.

48 Bruce Ackerman, *Private Property and the Constitution*, (New Haven, Conn.: Yale University Press, 1977), p. 11 (footnote omitted).

49 Ibid.

50 Duncan Kennedy identifies and criticizes this kind of legal formalism in "Legal Formality," *Journal of Legal Studies* 2(1973): 351–98.

51 Ackerman, *Private Property*, p. 11.

52 Grant Gilmore, *The Ages of American Law* (New Haven, Conn.: Yale University Press, 1977), p. 95.

53 David Truman, *The Governmental Process* (New York: Knopf, 1951).

54 Arthur Bentley, *The Process of Government* (1908; Bloomington: Indiana University Press, 1949). For recent literature modeling the democratic processes by analogy with markets, see James Buchanan and Gordon Tullock, *The Calculus of Consent: Logical Foundations of Constitutional Democracy* (Ann Arbor: University of Michigan Press, 1962); and Anthony Downs, *An Economic Theory of Democracy* (New York: Harper, 1957).

55 "In the economic vision, it is only the prospect of overcoming the market's failure to capture gains from trade that can justify, from the individual's standpoint, the risks of exploitation inherent in majoritarian political institutions. Would it not, then, make economic sense to include in the constitution a direction to courts to nullify any majoritarian intervention which plainly cannot even make a pretense of being a solution to a market-failure problem?" In Frank Michelman, "Politics and Values or What's Really Wrong with Rationality Review," *Creighton Law Review* 13(1979): 487–507; the quoted passage, on pp. 498–99, does not necessarily reflect Michelman's own position.

56 Dworkin, *Taking Rights Seriously*, p. 147.

57 Ibid., p. 149.

58 Ibid., p. 147.

59 Ibid.

60 For an excellent analysis of the relation (or nonrelation) be-
    tween philosophy and law, see Charles Fried, "The Artificial
    Reason of the Law or: What Lawyers Know," *Texas Law Review*
    60(1981): 35–58. See also Michael Walzer, "Philosophy and
    Democracy," *Political Theory* 9(1981): 379–99. Walzer writes
    (ibid., p. 391): "So the philosopher asks judges to recapitulate
    in their chambers the argument he has already worked out in
    solitary retreat . . . by deciding cases in its terms. When nec-
    essary, the judges must preempt or overrule legislative deci-
    sions. This is the crucial point, for it is here that the tension
    between philosophy and democracy takes on material form."

61 Guido Calabresi, *A Common Law for the Age of Statutes* (Cam-
    bridge, Mass.: Harvard University Press, 1982).

62 Ibid., p. 15.

63 Ibid., p. 2.

64 Fried, "What Lawyers Know," p. 38 (describing Walzer's
    view).

65 John Rawls, "Justice as Fairness: Political, Not Metaphysical,"
    Philosophy and Public Affairs 14(1985): 225.

66 Michael J. Sandel, *Liberalism and the Limits of Justice* (Cambridge:
    Cambridge University Press, 1982), p. 168.

67 Ibid., p. 174. Sandel adds that "utilitarianism gave the good
    a bad name, and in adopting it uncritically, justice as fairness
    wins for deontology a false victory." Ibid.

68 Ronald Rotunda, *The Emergence of Liberalism in the United States*,
    B.A. thesis, Harvard University, 1967. See also Samuel Beer,
    "Liberalism and the National Idea," *The Public Interest* 5(1966):
    70–82.

69 Beer, "Liberalism and the National Idea," p. 71.

70 Stephen Fox, *John Muir and His Legacy* (Boston: Little, Brown,
    1981), p. 187.

71 Ibid., p. 217.

72 Ibid., p. 200; quoting Ickes in *Living Wilderness Magazine*, Sep-
    tember 1935.

73 Beer, "Liberalism and the National Idea," p. 76.

74 *Public Papers of the President of the United States: Jimmy Carter*,
    1980–81; Book 3, September 29, 1980 – January 20, 1981 (Wash-
    ington, D.C.: Government Printing Office, 1982), p. 2890.

75 T. S. Eliot, *Christianity and Culture* (New York: Harcourt Brace, 1949), p. 11.

8. PROPERTY AND THE VALUE OF LAND

1 Julian Simon, "The Farmer and the Mall: Are American Farmlands Disappearing?" *The American Spectator*, August 1982, p. 20.

2 *Second Treatise of Government*, V, 26, 1–12. In Peter Laslett, ed., *Locke's Two Treaties of Government* (Cambridge: Cambridge University Press, 1963), pp. 304–5. Page references to Locke will be to this edition.

3 Ibid., 42, 18–21 (p. 315).

4 Ibid., 42, 14–18 (p. 316).

5 Ibid., 32, 8–9 (p. 316).

6 Ibid., 31, 1–19 (p. 308).

7 Ibid., 33, 104 (p. 307).

8 Ibid., 51, 7–10 (p. 320).

9 Richard A. Posner, *The Economics of Justice* (Cambridge, Mass.: Harvard University Press, 1981), p. 98.

10 For a bibliography of this literature, see the appendix to D. Mitchell Polinsky, *An Introduction to Law and Economics* (Boston: Little, Brown, 1983), pp. 127–33.

11 Polinsky, *Introduction*, p. 18.

12 Robert D. Rowe and Lauraine G. Chestnut, *The Value of Visibility: Economic Theory and Applications for Air Pollution Control* (Cambridge, Mass.: Abt, 1982), p. 81.

13 Ibid.

14 Posner, *The Economics of Justice*, p. 70.

15 *Tenant v. Goldwin*, 1 Salk. 360, 91 Eng. Rep. 314 (K.B. 1705).

16 55 Misc.2d 1023, 287 N.Y.S.2d 112 (1967), *aff'd*, 30 A.D.2d 480, 294 N.Y.S.2d 452 (1968), *rev'd and remanded*, 26 N.Y.2d 219, 309 N.Y.S.2d 312, 257 N.E.2d 870 (1970) (granting an injunction against the nuisance until the trial court determined the proper amount of permanent damages for the plaintiffs in place of temporary damages previously awarded).

17 55 Misc.2d at 1024, 287 N.Y.S.2d at 113.

18 Ibid. at 1025, 287 N.Y.S.2d at 114.

19 E. F. Roberts, "The Right to a Decent Environment; $E = MC^2$:

Environment Equals Man Times the Courts Redoubling Their Efforts," *Cornell Law Review* 55(1970): 676.

20 Guido Calabresi and A. Douglas Melamed, "Property Rules, Liability Rules, and Inalienability: One View of the Cathedral," *Harvard Law Review* 85(1972): 1092.

21 Ibid.

22 William Prosser, *Handbook on the Law of Torts*, 4th ed. (St. Paul, Minn.: West Publishing Co., 1971), sec. 87, p. 576.

23 A plurality of respondents to a major Resources for the Future poll of the general population thought that environmental protection is too important to *consider* costs. U.S. Council on Environmental Quality, *Public opinion on National Environmental Issues* (1980), p. 3.

24 People are likely to demand much more to surrender than they would pay to acquire possessions. One reason for this is *hysteresis*, that is, the feeling that things we grow accustomed to and then lose are much more valuable than things we have never had. "Men generally fix their attentions more on what they are possess'd of, than on what they never enjoyed: For this reason, it would be greater cruelty to dispossess a man of any thing than not to give it him." David Hume, *A Treatise of Human Nature*, Book 3, pt. 2, sec. 1 (in L. A. Selby-Bigge, ed. [New York: Oxford University Press, 1978], p. 482). For a discussion of hysteresis, see R. Hardin, *Collective Action* (Chicago: University of Chicago Press, 1982), p. 82.

Although there is nothing surprising about the gulfs that separate prices people demand from prices they would pay to acquire the same rights, economists occasionally express surprise when their surveys reveal this disparity. See, e.g., Jack L. Knetsch and J. A. Sinden, "Willingness to Pay and Compensation Demanded: Experimental Evidence of an Unexpected Disparity in Measures of Value," *Quarterly Journal of Economics*, 99(1984): 508.

25 It is a commonplace criticism that the efficiency norm is meaningless because it is ambiguous between "bid" and "asked" prices. Another way of putting this criticism is that the efficiency approach depends necessarily on the Coasian view that when parties trade to an equilibrium, the same substantive allocation of resources will result, regardless of how property rights are distributed (or who is liable to whom) as long as there are no transaction costs. (R. H. Coase, "The Problem of

Social Cost," *Journal of Law and Economics* 3[October 1960]): 2–8. The theorem will not hold, however, unless individuals are willing to sell or willing to pay roughly the same amounts for the same resources. Because this is not the case – or anything like the case – notions of economic optimality or efficiency are meaningless, since they are ambiguous between prices bid and asked.

26 See John Hospers, "What Libertarianism Is," in Tibor Machan, ed., *The Libertarian Alternative: Essays in Social and Political Philosophy* (Chicago: Nelson Hall, 1974), quoting Rothbard, p. 15.

27 Rothbard suggests that this practical consequence does not excuse us from doing the morally right thing. He compares slaveholders who refused to accept emancipation because of its economic consequences, even though they agreed that slavery is morally wrong (ibid.). One might point, however, to another problem: Few would obey a law against all polluting activities (including driving, for example). How could these laws be enforced except in a police state?

28 *Village of Euclid v. Ambler Realty Co.*, 272 U.S. 365, 395 (1926).

29 *Berman v. Parker*, 348 U.S. 26 (1954).

30 Ibid. at 1024, 287 N.Y.S.2d at 113.

31 *Boomer*, 30 A.D.2d at 481, 294 N.Y.S.2d at 453.

32 Edward Lee Rodgers, *Hearings on S. 3229, S. 3466, Before the Subcomm. on Air and Water Pollution of the Senate Comm. on Public Works*, 91st Cong., 2d sess. 849 (1970).

33 Locke, *The Second Treatise of Government*, sec. 124.

34 Spinoza, *Tractatus Politicus*, in *The Chief Works of Benedict Spinoza*, trans. R. H. M. Elwes (New York: Dover, 1951), vol. 1, p. 294.

35 For a good review of these factors, see Willard Cochrane, "The Need to Rethink Agricultural Policy in General and to Perform Some Radical Surgery on Commodity Program in Particular," *American Journal of Agricultural Economics* 67(5)(December 1985): 1002–9.

9. WHERE ICKES WENT RIGHT

1 Harold L. Ickes, *The Secret Diary of Harold L. Ickes* (New York: Simon & Schuster, 1954), vol. 2, p. 38.

2 Letter from Ickes to Pinchot, dated April 20, 1933, quoted in Donald C. Swain, *Wilderness Defender: Horace M. Albright and*

Conservation (Chicago: University of Chicago Press, 1970), p. 220. These principles, as Pinchot formulated them, were market-oriented or what we might call "utilitarian." "The first great fact about conservation is that it stands for development," Pinchot wrote, soon after establishing the Forest Service in the Department of Agriculture. "Conservation demands the welfare of this generation first, and afterward the welfare of generations to follow." Gifford Pinchot, "The Fight for Conservation," quoted in Donald Worster, ed., *American Environmentalism: The Formative Period, 1860–1915* (New York: Wiley, 1973), pp. 84–95; quotation on p. 85.

3 Stephen Fox, *John Muir and His Legacy* (Boston: Little, Brown, 1981), p. 201. Pinchot liked to refer to forest conservation as "tree farming." See Donald Worster, *Nature's Economy: The Roots of Ecology* (San Francisco: Sierra Club, 1977), p. 167. Ickes argued against this view. See *The Secret Diary*, p. 314.

4 42 U.S.C. sec. 7409(b)(1) (Supp. 1977).

5 *Union Electric Co. v. EPA*, 427 U.S. 246, esp. pp. 246–60 (1976). See also 41 *Fed. Reg.* 55, 527 (1976). (The "Act does not allow economic growth to be accommodated at the expense of public health.") While statutes state these uncompromising goals, compromises must be struck by those who enforce them. On this, see David W. Barnes, "Back Door Cost-Benefit Analysis Under a Safety-First Clean Air Act," *Natural Resources Journal* 23(1983): 827–57.

6 Clean Water Act, sec. 101(a)(1), 33 U.S.C. 1251 (Supp. IV, 1980).

7 Resource Conservation and Recovery Act, sec. 3004, 42 U.S.C. 6924 (Supp. IV, 1980).

8 Occupational Safety and Health Act, 29 U.S.C. sec. 655(b)(5) (1976).

9 *Union Electric Company v. EPA*, 427 U.S. 246, 256 (1976).

10 "The shutdown of an urban area's electrical system," as Justice Powell warns, "could have an even more serious impact on the health of the public than that created by a decline in ambient air quality." *Union Electric Co. v. EPA*, 427 U.S. 246 (1976) at 272 (Powell, J., concurring).

11 For a sensible and informative study of these issues, see Lester Lave and Eugene Seskin, *Air Pollution and Human Health* (Baltimore: Johns Hopkins University Press, 1977).

12 See Baruch Fischhoff, Paul Slovic, Sara Lichtenstein, Stephen

Read, and Barbara Combs, "How Safe Is Safe Enough?: A
Psycho-metric Study of Attitudes Towards Technological Risks
and Benefits," *Policy Sciences* 9(1978): 127–52. See also sources
cited therein.

13 See Yair Aharoni, *The No-Risk Society* (Chatham, N.J.: Chatham
House, 1981). See also S. C. Black and F. Niehaus, "How Safe
is 'Too' Safe?," *International Atomic Energy Agency Bulletin* 22(1)
(1980): 40–50; S. S. Epstein, *The Politics of Cancer* (Garden City,
N.Y.: Doubleday, Anchor Books, 1979).

14 Clean Air Act, 42 U.S.C. sec. 7521(a)(3)(A)(ii)(I) (1982). For
discussion, see Arne E. Gubrud, "The Clean Air Act and Mobile-Source Pollution Control," *Ecology Law Quarterly* 4(1975):
526–28.

15 *Congressional Record* 116(1970): 32,080.

16 Ibid.

17 Quoted by James A. Henderson and Richard N. Pearson, "Implementing Federal Environmental Policies: The Limits of Aspirational Commands," *Columbia Law Review* 78(1978): 1459.

18 1970 Clean Air Act §111(a)(1) (42 U.S.C. §7411(a)(1)(C) (Supp.
IV, 1980).

19 Ibid. §202(a)(2) (42 U.S.C. §7521(a)(2)(Supp. IV, 1980).

20 Thomas Schoenbrod, "Goals Statutes or Rules Statutes: The
Case of the Clean Air Act," *UCLA Law Review* 30(1983): 759.

21 For discussion of ends and means in environmental law, see
Bruce Ackerman and William Hassler, *Clean Coal/Dirty Air*
(New Haven, Conn.: Yale University Press, 1981), esp. p. 121
("'ends-oriented' agency-forcing does not require Congress to
indulge in instrumental judgments beyond its capacity. Instead, it generates a process by which the ultimate aims of
environmental policy can be clarified over time").

22 The Clean Air Act only once mentions the protection of sensitive populations in relation to national ambient air quality
standards, at 42 U.S.C. §7408(f)(1)(C). The legislative history,
however contains an oft-cited commentary by the Senate Committee on Public Works, which states that primary air-quality
standards must be strict enough to protect more susceptible
groups. S. Rept. 91–1196, 91st Cong. 2d sess., 1970, 11, reprinted in Senate Committee on Public Works, *A Legislative
History of the Clean Air Amendments of 1970*, ser. no. 93–18, 93d
Cong., 2d sess., 1974, 411.

23 The costs of pollution control regulation seem to be relatively

small in any event, perhaps a modest 0.2 percent of the GNP. This sort of regulation, however, is labor intensive, and may increase employment by 0.3 percent. For an excellent review of the relevant surveys and studies, see George Eads and Michael Fix, *Relief or Reform: Reagan's Regulatory Dilemma* (Washington, D.C.: The Urban Institute, 1984), pp. 39–41.

24 Sheldon Novick, "In Defense of Irrational Laws," *The Environmental Forum* 3(1984): 15.

25 The 90 percent reduction requirements for automobile emissions under the Clean Air Act, for example, represent what Congress believed necessary to protect the public health, not what it thought was economically or technologically feasible. See Gubrud, "The Clean Air Act and Mobile-Source Pollution Control," pp. 526–28.

26 Energy Policy and Conservation Act, sec. 374(b)(2), 42 U.S.C. sec. 6344(b)(2)(1982).

27 As happened with respect to the Energy Policy and Conservation Act. For details, see William Rodgers, "Benefits, Costs, and Risks: Oversight of Health and Environmental Decisionmaking," *Harvard Environmental Law Review* 4(1980): 208–9.

28 Larry Wade observes that "politics is more than a struggle over the distribution of material values. It is also a social process through which symbolic values, representing needs for self-esteem, dignity, and personal rectitude are distributed and validated." Larry Wade, *The Elements of Public Policy* (Columbus, Ohio: Charles E. Merrill, 1972), p. 14.

29 Early in the 1970s, critics of pollution control legislation argued that the statutes should be more incremental and less revolutionary because, however revolutionary they may be, they can be implemented only incrementally. See, e.g., Paul R. Schulman, "Nonincremental Policy Making: Notes Toward an Alternative Paradigm," *American Political Science Review* 69(1975), pp. 1354–70; and Jeffrey L. Pressman and Aaron Wildavsky, *Implementation: How Great Expectations in Washington Are Dashed in Oakland* (Berkeley, Calif.: University of California Press, 1973).

30 Schoenbrod, "Goals Statutes or Rules Statutes," p. 766.

31 David P. Currie, Relaxation of Implementation Plans Under the 1977 Clean Air Act Amendments," *Michigan Law Review* 78(1979).

32 Richard Walker and Michael Storper, "Erosion of the Clean Air Act of 1970: A Study in the Failure of Government Regulation and Planning," *Environmental Affairs* 7(1978).

33 Barnes, "Back Door Cost-Benefit Analysis Under a Safety-First Clean Air Act," pp. 827–57.

34 The problem is not that an administration unsympathetic to environmental goals now enforces pollution control statutes. The same difficulties of enforcement plagued pro-environment administrations. Schoenbrod, in "Goals Statutes or Rules Statutes?," p. 762, notes: "Measures needed to achieve ambient air standards within the statutory time table included cutting gasoline use in the Los Angeles area by over 80%, eliminating 30–40% of the parking in the business areas of Manhattan, and prohibiting the construction of new plants whose emissions would cause or contribute to violations of the ambient air standards, even if the new plants would meet the New Source Performance Standards."

   The reason the law was not enforced in these and many other respects has little to do with the political persuasion of the president.

35 D. Costle, EPA administrator, remarks at the meeting of the Air Pollution Control Association in Montreal, Canada, June 23, 1980 (quoted by Schoenbrod in "Goals Statutes or Rules Statutes," p. 749.

36 George Eads, "The Confusion of Goals and Instruments: The Explicit Consideration of Cost in Setting National Ambient Air Quality Standards," in Mary Gibson, ed., *To Breathe Freely: Risk, Consent, and Air* (Totowa, N.J.: Rowman & Littlefield, 1985), p. 229.

37 William J. Baumol, "On the Taxation and the Control of Externalities," *American Economic Review* 62(1972): 307.

38 Susan Rose-Ackerman, "Effluent Charges: A Critique," *Canadian Journal of Economics* 6(1973): 512; Clifford Russell, "What Can We Get from Effluent Charges?" *Policy Analysis* 5(1979): 155.

39 For an excellent study of the issues involved in bubbles and other trading schemes, see T. H. Tietenberg, *Emissions Trading: An Exercise in Reforming Pollution Policy* (Washington, D.C.: Resources for the Future, 1985).

40 47 *Fed. Reg.* 15,076.

41 Tietenberg, *Emissions Trading*, p. 12.

42 Michael Levin, "Building a Better Bubble at EPA," *Regulation*, March–April 1985, p. 35.

43 Alan Gewirth, "Positive 'Ethics' and 'Normative' Science," *Philosophical Review* 69(1960): 311–13.

44 In 1977, Senator Muskie commented on the mood seven years earlier: "Our public health scientists and doctors have told us there is no threshold, that any air pollution is harmful. The Clean Air Act is based on the assumption, although we knew at the time it was inaccurate, that there is a threshold. When we set standards, we understood that below the standards that we set there would still be health effects." *Clean Air Act Amendments of 1977; Hearing Before the Subcomm. on Environmental Pollution of the Senate Comm. on Environment and Public Works*, 95th Cong., 1st sess., 1977, 8 (statement of Senator Muskie).

45 Environmentalists may remember that in 1981, during the impact of the Reagan landslide, Congress considered a Regulatory Reform Bill (97th Cong. 1st sess., S. 1080) that would have amended the Administrative Procedure Act to require that virtually all social regulation pass a cost-benefit test. This bill probably would have become law but for the press of business at the end of that year and a timely filibuster by Representative John Dingell in the Rules Committee.

46 For a useful discussion of these and related cases, see William F. Pederson, Jr., "What Judges Should Know About Risk," *Natural Resources and the Environment* 2(Fall 1986): 35–38, 69.

47 478 F.2d 615 (D.C. Cir. 1973).

48 Harold Leventhal, "Environmental Decisionmaking and the Role of the Courts," *University of Pennsylvania Law Review* 122(1974): 533.

49 *Portland Cement Ass'n v. Ruckelshaus*, 486 F.2d 375, 387 (D.C. Cir. 1973), *cert. denied*, 417 U.S. 921 (1974).

50 *Essex Chemical Corp. v. Ruckelshaus*, 486 F.2d 427, 433 (D.C. Cir. 1973), *cert. denied*, 416 U.S. 969 (1974).

51 Frank B. Cross, "Section 111(d) of the Clean Air Act: A New Approach to the Control of Airborne Carcinogens," *Boston College Environmental Affairs Law Review* 13(1986): 238.

52 *Industrial Union Dept., AFL-CIO v. American Petroleum Institute*, 448 U.S. 607 (1980).

53 *American Textile Manufacturers Institute v. Donovan*, 452 U.S. 490, 520 (1981).

54 *Natural Resources Defense Council v. EPA*, 804 F.2d 710 (D.C. Cir. 1986), *vacated, rehearing granted en banc*, 810 F.2d 270 (1987).

55 Ibid., p. 728.

56 Ibid., p. 738.

57 Ibid.

58 *Natural Resources Defense Council v. U.S. E.P.A.*, D.C. Cir. No. 85–1150, decided July 28, 1987. Slip opinion p. 42 (last page).

59 Ibid., p. 38–40.

60 Ibid., p. 41.

61 Pederson, "What Judges Should Know About Risk," pp. 37–38.

62 John Dewey, *Theory of Valuation* (Chicago: University of Chicago Press, 1937), p. 25.

63 Ibid., p. 29. Dewey's point is that learning from experience is a principal aspect of rationality. Moral reasoning, like other forms of reasoning, is experimental. Experiments with controlling pollution have made us aware of many facts, for example, that "safe" thresholds for many pollutants do not exist, that scientific uncertainty surrounds most attempts at risk assessment, that draconian measures are often unenforceable, that in reducing some risks, one increases others, and so on. Lessons such as these may – Dewey would say "must" – enter ethical deliberation over the ends of pollution control law.

64 The crucial distinction as Kant formulates it is this: "Ethical duties are of *wide* obligation, whereas juridical duties are of *narrow* obligation." The latter, being narrow or rigorous (e.g., Thou shalt not kill) is "perfect" because it "allows no exception in the interest of inclination." The former kind of duty, for example, to rescue, admits of exceptions (e.g., when one is an insecure swimmer) and is therefore "imperfect." Kant suggests the relation between this distinction and the concept of supererogation. "Imperfect duties, accordingly, are only *duties of virtue*. To fulfill them is *merit* (= +a); but to transgress them is not so much *guilt* (= −a) as rather mere *lack* of moral *worth* (=o), unless the agent makes it a principle not to submit to these duties." Immanuel Kant, *The Metaphysical Principles of Virtues*, part 2 of *The Metaphysic Of Morals*, trans., James Ellington (Indianapolis, Ind.: Bobbs-Merrill, 1964), p. 49.

65 For further discussion, see Roderick Chisholm, "The Ethics of Requirement," *American Philosophical Quarterly* 1(1964): 147.

66 Abe Fortas, the undersecretary of the interior, in a letter to Ickes dated September 24, 1942, discusses the problem of reconciling environmental protection to wartime production goals. See Edward Nixon, ed., *Franklin Roosevelt and Conservation: 1911–1945* (Washington, D.C.: Government Printing Office, 1957), pp. 559–60.

67 Harold Ickes, *The Autobiography of a Curmudgeon* (New York: Reynal & Hitchcock, 1943).

68 For this view, see John Dewey, *The Quest for Certainty* (1929; New York: Capricorn Books, 1960), esp. pp. 3–25; see also T. S. Kuhn, *The Structure of Scientific Revolutions* (Chicago: University of Chicago Press, 1962; 2d ed. 1969).

69 Richard Rorty, "Science as Solidarity," manuscript, November 1984, p. 8.

70 Examples include A. K. Dasgupta and D. W. Pearce, *Cost-Benefit Analysis* (New York: Harper & Row, 1972), and Edmund Crouch and Richard Wilson, *Risk Benefit Analysis* (Cambridge, Mass.: Ballinger, 1982).

71 John Barth, *The End of the Road* (New York: Avon, 1958), p. 89. I wish to thank Doug MacLean for pointing out this passage to me.

72 Ickes, *Secret Diary*, vol. 2, p. 176.

Index